Stevie Ray

Soul to Soul

Stevie Ray
Soul to Soul

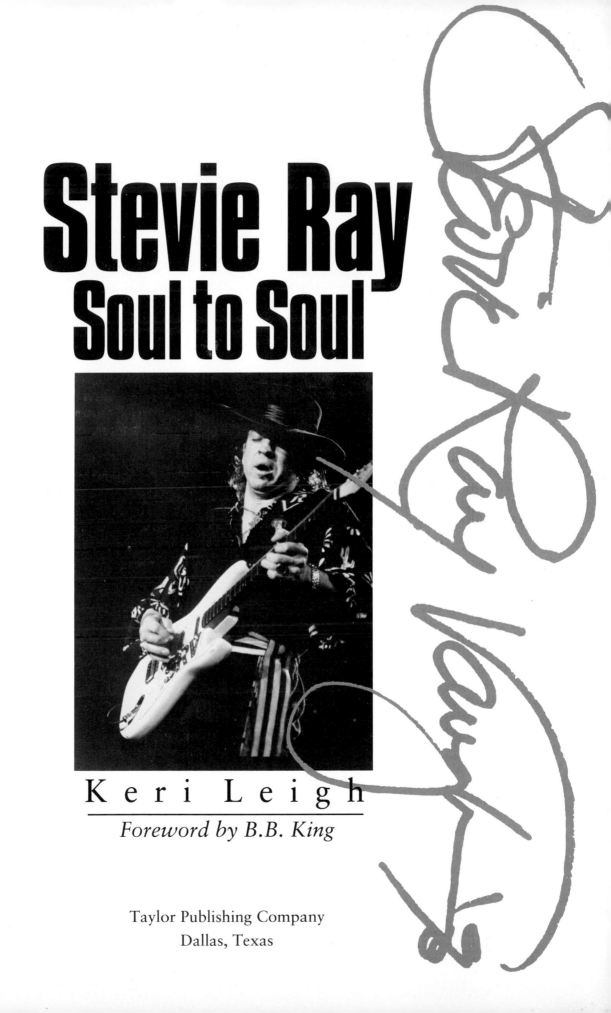

K e r i   L e i g h
Foreword by B.B. King

Taylor Publishing Company
Dallas, Texas

This book is for everyone who was ever touched
by Stevie Ray Vaughan's music
the way it should be—
Soul To Soul

Fly on, my friend...

Copyright ©1993 by Keri Leigh and Harold F. Eggers Jr.

Published by   Taylor Publishing Company
                      1550 West Mockingbird Lane
                      Dallas, Texas 75235

Designed by David Timmons
Photo on title page by and courtesy of W.A. Williams/The
Image Works.
The publisher extends special thanks to W.A. Williams,
Dale Allen, and Randy Jennings.

Library of Congress Cataloging-in-Publication Data
Leigh, Keri
    Stevie Ray : soul to soul / Keri Leigh.
        p.   cm.
    ISBN 0-87833-838-1 (paper)
    1. Vaughan, Stevie Ray. 2. Rock musicians—United
States—Biography. 3. Blues musicians—United States—
Biography.
    1. Title.
    ML419.V254L4   1993
787.87'166'092—dc20
[B]
                                        93-24011
                                             CIP
                                             MN

Printed in the United States of America

10   9

Acknowledgments

ASSEMBLING this book turned out to be a bigger job than I'd expected; unlike Hendrix, Joplin, or the Stones, who have been written about more times than God, Stevie's life had never before been documented on any large scale, so starting from scratch was the only way. The research process was exhausting—digging up every little newspaper and magazine article was time-consuming, acquiring photographs and rare old posters was quite an undertaking (many of these were over twenty years old and required extra special care), and tracking down sources (some had dropped out of sight altogether) to interview was no picnic, either. Most of this work I did myself, but I owe a great deal of thanks to those who assisted me. My greatest resource was the extensive Texas music collection at The Barker Texas History Center at The University of Texas at Austin. Sound Archivist John Wheat was supportive and informative as he led me on a magic carpet ride through Austin's music history, filling me in on all the years I'd missed. In fact, I was so impressed with the Barker collection that I agreed to donate my SRV research materials to the archives so that others may benefit from my research.

Wanting to involve Stevie's fans in this book, I sent out feelers to Vaughan's admirers around the world, and found myself flooded with return mail. Some wrote to donate posters, interviews, live performance tapes and photographs, others just wanted to write and share how much Stevie meant to them. They sent "care packages" containing hand-drawn portraits of SRV, poems, and their own music that Stevie Ray inspired. It was all very touching, and we grew into a family of "Stevie geeks," helping each other in every way. The list of contributors is long, but I feel the following must be recognized for their kind, unselfish deeds toward making this book possible: Christian Brooks and the Blues Suede Shoe family, Connie Trent, Mitch Mullins, David Brown, Rocky Athas, Lew Stokes, Margaret Moser at *The Austin Chronicle*, Susan Antone (who held me while I cried), Michael Ventura, Bruce Iglauer, W.A. "Bill" Williams, Randy Jennings, Lisa M. Hill, L.D. Agostino, Dale Allen, Natalie Zoe, Steve Wilson, Alan Paul, Brad Tolinski, Harold Steinblatt, and Robert Dye at *Guitar World*, Sidney Seidenberg for B.B. King, Scott Cameron for Buddy Guy, Barbara (B.B.) Becker for Dr. John, Tom Kreason at Rockabilia, Doug Green at Pepperland, Jane St. John at KWVS-FM in Corpus Christi, Don Ottensman at KNON-FM in Dallas, David Fusco at Music Unlimited, Ed Mayberry at KLBJ-FM in Austin, and Cary "The Red Rooster" Wolfson at *Blues Access* magazine.

Thanks also to: Julie Maxwell, Neal Black and The Healers, Craig Hopkins, Bill Mishoe, Kathy Siklosi, Mike Webster, Ralph Hulett, Sid Graves and the Delta Blues Museum, Delmark Goldfarb and the Memphis Blues Museum, Dennis Arnold, Tim Duckworth, Steve Moore, Greg Harris, Joan McQuillan, Dave Ranney of The Wichita Blues Society, John (J.C.) Christensen, Harold Dozier, Doug Castor, Craig Westfall, Steve Varga, Sherri Barber, Priscilla Gwilt, Mad Dog and Paula Mickelson, Mike Gardner, Ric Slagle, Christian Plicque, Rolf Stensletten, Mike Claspill at KTAB-TV, Bird Dawg Jones, The Kurt-man, Darrell Burnitt, The Walworth County Sheriff's Department, Coroner John T. Griebel, Jim Wincek, Connie Shutte at Alpine Valley, Peggy Meyer at Blue Note Promotions, John Maher at Fender Guitars, Liz Mann at the Dallas Hard Rock Cafe, Tom Marshall at Strike Force Management, and the publicity department of Epic Records.

Kudos to my transcribers and proofreaders: Joe Vitale, Deborah Block, Mike and GiGi Fair, Serena Verzhinsky, and Sandy Kay. Also thanks to Martha Vaughan for having such a wonderful kid, and to Jimmie Vaughan for helping to make his little brother's guitar fantasies real. Good thing you brought home all those records!

My biggest thanks, however, go to my wonderful husband Mark Lyon, who knew I was going to write this book long before I ever did, my mother Mary Jones, who encouraged me every step of the way, my literary manager Harold F. Eggers Jr. for never giving up, Mel Berger, Shelly Shultz and Rachel Pine at The William Morris Agency, my literary agent Tony Seidl, and especially to Amazing Records and my band, The Blue Devils, for having extraordinary patience while I finished this book. But most of all, thanks to Jim Donovan, Lorena Jones, and everyone at Taylor Publishing Company for making this dream come true. Your assistance, fairness, and relentless support have made this a most enjoyable experience—thank you for believing that Stevie Ray Vaughan's life was worth a proper tribute.

Contents

Foreword

*I*CAN'T HELP CHUCKLING to myself when folks tell me that I was one of Stevie's influences, one of the guys whose records he listened to over and over as a kid. It's funny to think of a talent like Stevie practicing to play the way I do. One of the things I remember the most about Stevie is that he was always quick to show gratitude to me and the other artists who've been around. But when it came to playing the blues, he earned plenty of respect himself.

I don't remember when I first came across Stevie, but I do remember being amazed by what I heard. In those years, he was just a shy, unsure, scrawny kid, but he sure did know the music. Once I got to know him, I saw that he studied, lived, and *felt* the blues like the musicians he wouldn't let people compare him to. How he came to this point is his story, but the fact is he affected the way blues will be played and heard forever.

I recall the excitement I felt when I finally hit the "crossover" point in my career with "The Thrill Is Gone" and went on tour with the Stones. It meant I'd have a chance to play more blues for more people. Like the rest of us, Stevie had a tough time getting more people to hear the music in the early years. But eventually, he did get to open up more souls and pour the blues in. When that point came, he never gave up his commitment to the music, insisting it was just his way—the only way he knew. Those of us who're still playing will always respect him for that.

Now that Stevie is gone, the blues world feels a little different. Like the rest of us Stevie believed there was something special about playing the blues, something worth spending a lifetime on. Stevie was a great talent who also understood what keeps the music alive through the years. I've said that playing the blues is "like having to be black twice." Stevie missed on both counts, but I never noticed.

B.B. KING

Preface

THIS BOOK was three long years in the making. Stevie and I had been friends and business associates for several years before the idea of a book was proposed in May of 1990. We spent the last three months of his life on the phone, discussing his vision of a biography and conducting interviews. I asked for his trust and he gave it to me. I asked for no money, funding everything out of my shallow pocket and giving Stevie Ray complete artistic control over what was said in the text (a rare privilege in this business). I wanted him to know that this was a labor of love, out of respect for his unbelievable talent and his life-saving message. The goal was to tell his story as he wanted it told—I wanted nothing more than to see him smile when he held the finished work in his hands and read it. Sadly, he never would. After his tragic death in the early morning hours of August 27, 1990, I put the book project away, too wrapped up in my sorrow to even think of carrying on without his guidance, patience, and inspiration. It took me several months before I could even bear to listen to his music. My interviews, research materials, photographs, and all reminders of Stevie were haphazardly thrown into boxes, where they sat for six months—waiting for me to gather enough strength to look at them again.

I began to hear rumblings of other Stevie biographies in the works around Austin; *Texas Monthly* senior editor Joe Nick Patoski and writer Bill Crawford were contracted to write an "unauthorized" version of his life, and former *Guitar Player* contributing editor Dan Forte was employed by the Vaughan family to pen the "authorized" story. My literary manager asked me why I wasn't finishing the project we had started together; after all, he said, I was perhaps the only writer who really knew what Stevie Ray wanted people to remember about his extraordinary life. Friends, acquaintances, and even total strangers began to approach me, encouraging me to pick it up again. After a lot of prodding, I finally dug out the cardboard boxes and tried to find a new perspective on what I had already done. It wasn't easy.

This was unlike anything I had done before; all of my previous subjects in newspaper and magazine articles were just that—subjects. But Stevie Ray was a friend. He was also dead. I did not wish to play the vulture, swooping down to gnaw on the bones. For the first year-and-a-half, I could hardly write a paragraph or read a magazine article about him without bursting out into tears. It hurt just to hear his voice, his sweet laugh over my tape recorder. I often felt cold chills when I would write certain portions, almost as if he were still here looking over my shoulder. Maybe it was deadline delirium, but there were nights when his voice rang clearly in my ears, assuring me that everything was going to be all right if I'd just "take it one day at a time."

As the project progressed, I grew past the grief and began to feel a certain kind of peace, even joy—I was holding up my end of the bargain, and somehow I felt that he was happy with it. Although some sources who were close to Stevie chose not to cooperate with any "unauthorized" book projects, numerous lesser-known but nonetheless crucial sources offered their time, stories, personal photographs, and souvenirs without a trace of greed or intentions of self-betterment. Most of all, these persons offered support and companionship to me; we laughed together over the good memories, we cried together over the bittersweet pain of loss. We all had something in common, although we were often thousands of miles apart—we had all lost a dear friend that we loved very much, and our mission was to insure that SRV's music and life be not only remembered, but celebrated.

As the author, my primary objectives were to document Stevie's life as accurately as possible, tell all the tales that matter (even deceased rock stars should have the right to keep some personal secrets forever), and most of all, to tell the truth. I hope that you will find this book to be a treasure, an intimate photo album to remember him by, an invaluable resource to assist you in your own research of Vaughan's life and music, and lastly, a fitting tribute to one of the greatest musicians (and humanitarians) of our time. This book is for you, written with all my heart, soul, and tears.

To Keri Leigh, with Love & Happiness!

Stevie Ray Vaughan

Introduction

Steve'd come and see me whenever I came to town—unless he was out of town himself. We'd run into each other a lot of places, too, not only in Texas. If he was free, he was where I was, if I was free, I was where he was. We got to know one another and became the best of friends.

One time that we got together really stands out in my mind. It was right after Stevie's first recording success in 1983, when John McEnroe brought us together in New York City. John really can play well... we all got together and played at this pier in a park in New York City—a lot of other tennis players were there playing too—and all the proceeds went to a charity for handicapped children. We hung around there for three days and then went to Chicago and played the blues festival together. Now that was a good time.

All the blues players were having a hard time back then making a living, even the late great Muddy Waters. Stevie talks about me, but it's just that blues has been handed down by Robert Johnson, Muddy, me, and Stevie himself. But Stevie did so much for the blues. I keep saying that he had a skeleton key and opened up the warehouse and let us all out, because our music was locked in the back room. It wasn't on the radio, it wasn't on the television. Stevie did open those doors when he came out and started playing his guitar like he did. He exploded and helped us all.

I remember Stevie saying his brother kept records locked up in his room when they were kids. Jimmie gave him all the Lightnin' Hopkins, and T-Bone, and whoever else's records, but he kept the door closed and played one record again and again. He wouldn't give up that one and Stevie wondered what it was. Turns out it was my album!

Stevie and I had another bond because he's a southerner and I am, too. Naturally, I know about the South, and although he wasn't as old as me, he knew too. And having a kid from Texas who was into black people's music and had love for all of us... well, you know I was thinking is this for real? Stevie coulda been my brother. We were so close. I remember I called him about a year before he passed and I had just opened a club in Chicago. I told him I needed him to stop by. He said, "It's just a matter of a plane ticket" and walked in the door that night.

Stevie was there at Legends every chance he got. Actually, on the night of his tragic accident he was goin' to New York, he was goin' to get married again or somethin'. He and Eric had talked me into fixin' the Louisiana gumbo and I was on my way out the door that mornin' to get the junk to make it. The phone rang... and I have never forgotten that moment and I know I never will—it will go with me to my grave.

BUDDY GUY

Prelude: And the Gods Made Love

IT WAS A HOT NIGHT in southern Wisconsin. Hundreds of sopping-wet bodies, miserable from the sticky air, crammed even closer together near the bug-swarmed stage to get a better look at the action. The date was August 26, 1990, and Stevie Ray Vaughan was claiming his place in history as he stood alongside Eric Clapton, Buddy Guy, Robert Cray, and his brother Jimmie Vaughan at the Alpine Valley Music Theater in East Troy. Despite the suffocating night and a very sore throat, Stevie Ray never felt better.

Thirty-five thousand souls sat there in the dark, eyes all focused on Stevie as he blasted into a guitar solo. His right hand fanned the frets of that old tattered Stratocaster so quickly, the rings on his fingers shone in the lights. His whole body was caught up in the throes of performance—a

blur to the crowd, he resembled a purple tornado against a dusty Texas sky. He stopped playing for a moment and barked at the crowd between some teeth-gnashing grace notes. Then he was back at it, totally in rapture. It was as if something otherworldly was playing his guitar that night, as if some force were bending the notes toward a melody it wanted to hear. But the melody was like nothing he had ever played before. It was unbelievable—it sounded like some manic metallic shit, bleeding, eating through the amplifier like a hungry monster. It surprised even Stevie, and all around him.

He performed that night as he always had, as if the song of the moment would be his last. During the blistering, all-star jam on Robert Johnson's "Sweet Home Chicago," it seemed as if the blues

2

had made a full circle. Johnson's troubled spirit was reincarnated in Stevie, who stood toe-to-toe with the white god of electric blues himself, next to the young savior of rhythm and blues, and shoulder-to-shoulder with Muddy's longest-lasting right-hand man. No moment this glorious could last very long, but the four musicians played on.

The song had stretched out for nearly twenty minutes, and everybody had taken a solo. They were just vamping and looking for a way to end it, not wanting to take it home yet. Then Stevie just erupted and took another solo. It was passionate, ingenious, and LOUD. When he finished, he looked over at Clapton. Eric knew he couldn't top it, shrugged his shoulders, forced a weak smile, and brought the tune to a close. They all joined hands, taking bows and hugging each other for the longest time before they left the stage. Stevie was the last one off, as usual. He took one final bow, tipped his hat to the crowd and exited stage left. It would be Stevie's last stand.

On the stage of Alpine Valley Music Theatre, Stevie Ray Vaughan had played an incredible set with his own band, Double Trouble, earlier in the evening. He was cleaner, sharper, and more energetic than ever. He played like his soul was on fire, ripping through "Texas Flood" with reckless abandon, bending and twisting his guitar in every configuration.

During "Pride And Joy," Stevie tipped his hat generously to his hero, Buddy Guy. Like several nights before, Buddy was standing on the wings of the stage, watching Stevie teach a new generation about songs like "Leave My Little Girl Alone," "Mary Had A Little Lamb," and "Let Me Love You, Baby," all once minor, obscure hits for him in the mid-sixties. But now, Vaughan's recorded versions had made them instant contemporary blues classics. For the first time in his 30-year career, Buddy Guy was receiving royalty checks and had Stevie to thank for it. "You tell 'em, kid!" Buddy thought to himself, breaking into a huge grin. He looked up to find Stevie staring right at him through the bright lights, as if he knew what Buddy was thinking. Stevie smiled and winked, then strutted away.

Robert Cray, still wiping the sweat from his forehead after his set, approached Buddy, tapped him on the shoulder, and said, "Stevie's kicking ass!" Buddy, laughing, told him, "It's damn sure the most incredible set I've ever heard him play. I've got goosebumps."

Goose bumps ran rampant during Stevie's tribute to his true mentor, Jimi Hendrix. For eight years, Stevie had ended his show every night with inspired guitar acrobatics—soloing behind his back and head; playing with his teeth or boot; and finally tossing the instrument to the floor, jumping on it, and shaking it for all it was worth. Stevie never grew tired of this routine, nor did his audience, although many of them had seen these gimmicks a zillion times before. It was the way he went after it, how he walked way out on the edge of music, with nothing but a thread connecting him to the notes, bars, and melody. But somehow, in the midst of losing himself altogether, he remained aware of the ground on which his feet were planted.

Tonight was special for another reason—Hendrix had also, coincidentally, given his last major performance on this very day twenty years before at the Isle of Wight Festival. Located below the British Isles, the Isle of Wight is literally one degree from the end of time—Greenwich, England.

Robert Knight, a photographer who had often worked with Hendrix, was on assignment to shoot a poster of the four superstars for Fender guitars. "I was right below him in front of the stage," he remembers. "I had never seen Stevie play so wild, so uncontrolled. I felt that tonight I had seen Hendrix again, only better. In fact, during the final number, 'Voodoo Chile,' I got gooseflesh so bad I left and went backstage."

As Stevie was nearing the end of his set, he introduced his epic "Riviera Paradise" with words that proved to be sadly ironic, dedicating the number to "anyone who's had pain in their life," and adding, "I wish and hope we all find the happiness we are looking for." His rendition that night was beautiful, imaginative, and personal; it was as if he were making a special apology to everyone he'd ever loved and hurt.

Jimmie joined him onstage for the last three songs, "Crossfire," "Couldn't Stand The Weather," and "Goin' Down," a most fitting close to his final show. The night ended the same way it all began—with the two brothers trading licks together. Stevie walked offstage satisfied. It had been one more night of playing the blues and spreading the news. He spied Robert Knight and stopped briefly to talk to him. "Hey! Why'd you leave during 'Voodoo Chile'?" he asked.

"Where were you the night Hendrix died?" Knight asked bluntly.

"Why?"

"Because tonight I saw Jimi Hendrix onstage. I've got gooseflesh all over me! Look at this shit!"

Stevie held up his arms proudly. "I know. Me too," he added, smiling. "Sometimes I don't know myself where the energy comes from."

He opened the door to his dressing room to find Jimmie sitting there. "Way to go, little bro'!" Jimmie yelled, slapping him on the back. "You hear that? Listen! They're going nuts! Stevie, I've never heard you play like that! You're great!"

Maybe it was the first time he heard Jimmie say it, maybe it was the first time he believed it, but Stevie's eyes watered up and he hugged Jimmie tight, saying, "Thanks, man. You know how much that means to me."

While Clapton was preparing to begin his own show, after having been thoroughly blown away by Stevie Ray and Double Trouble's performance, he turned to Buddy Guy with a worried expression and earnestly asked him, "How am I supposed to follow this guy?" "Well, Eric," Buddy replied, "You just do the best you can."

Later, all the musicians gathered around the wings of the stage to watch Clapton. During one passage, Clapton quoted "Strangers In The Night." Cray got Jimmie's attention and shouted, "Check him out!" "Aw," said Stevie, turning around, "he's been trying to do that all night and he finally got it right." Jimmie and Stevie had a good guffaw over that one. A few minutes later, around 11 P.M., the three of them were onstage grinding their axes with God himself.

One of the patches that was made for the musicians and crew at the Alpine Valley shows on August 25 and 26, 1990. Courtesy of Thomas Kreason/Rockabilia.

Shortly after the last note rang out at 11:20, the five exhilarated musicians left the stage through a rear exit, exchanging hugs and kind words. They posed for pictures together, signed autographs, compared callouses on their fingertips and chided each other, saying "Check this one out, man" and "No, look at this. Mine's bigger than yours!" It was all punctuated with uproarious laughter.

For well over an hour they talked about jamming together again soon and Clapton remarked, "Hell, this is so much fun we ought to take it on the road!" Clapton told Stevie plainly that he was the best he'd ever heard. Buddy stood behind, nodding and smiling. Cray grabbed Stevie's shoulder meaningfully, and, as always, Stevie pointed to Jimmie. It was a very human moment. Here were five of the most respected blues guitarists trading heartfelt compliments. A few minutes later, Peter Jackson, Clapton's tour manager, busted in and said, "Guys, I'm sorry, but the weather's getting really bad and we gotta move it out of here."

Four helicopters waited outside.

Brothers

STEVIE RAY'S STORY begins in Oak Cliff, Texas, a medium-sized suburb of Dallas filled with Baptist churches, schools, and small prefab houses that families of all colors called home. The city's designers surely had not planned for such an ethnic melting pot. Make no mistake, this was originally a neighborhood custom made for reasonably well-to-do white laborers from Dallas. But the "Utopia" the planners envisioned was hardly the Oak Cliff Jimmie and Stevie Ray knew.

The city within a city was established in 1888, the name derived form the massive oak trees that crown its rolling green cliffs. Oak Cliff proudly stands only 250 feet above and to the southwest of Dallas. Overlooking the city, its view, from the proper angle, can be breathtaking at sunset.

In 1890, The Dallas Land And Loan Company posted signs advertising the newly available properties. The ads told of a virtual wonderland, where the railroad was convenient for business, commuter cablecars ran to Dallas for five cents, the drinking water came straight from a clear spring, and the landscape was dotted with several rolling parks where children could run free. Residents were described as "live," "progressive," and "strictly moral." "Intoxicating liquors," the handbill declared, "cannot be found anywhere within her limits." "In keeping with this general policy," the statement continued, "no sort of questionable resorts are tolerated." Not much has changed in this respect—even today, Oak Cliff is dry and the residents remain deeply religious. But popular moral beliefs never stopped anyone from dancing or drinking in Oak Cliff.

It was this magical place that shaped not only Stevie and Jimmie Vaughan, but an incredible collection of lesser-known yet equally talented musicians who grew

The Vaughan family home in Oak Cliff.

up with them in the fifties. The longtime myth is that music runs pure through Texas water. But perhaps in this case, it was the cool southern breezes that blew through Oak Cliff, after rushing over hundreds of miles of unobstructed prairie, that brought the music. Regardless, one thing was certain: Up on the hill, Oak Cliff felt the winds of change long before Dallas ever did.

Big Jim Vaughan was from Rockwall, Texas, and was the son of a sharecropper. His father died when he was seven, leaving him and his twin sister Linnie Vee, his mother, and six other siblings to face the Great Depression. Jimmie Lee Sr. dropped out of school at sixteen to defend his country in World War II; he was proud to do it, and later would spin great yarns of his war experiences for anyone who would listen.

Martha Jean Cook was from Dallas and, after graduating from Sunset High School, took a job as a secretary at the Grove Lumber Company. She had already been married once, but only for a few months. She was independent, good-looking, and young when she first laid eyes on Big Jim Vaughan in 1949.

After the war, jobs were hard to find, even for ex-servicemen. Big Jim took a grunt job at a convenience store in Oak Cliff. The town was already beginning to slowly deteriorate from its original upscale status to a middle-class neighborhood that would soon become severed along racial lines. Jim was working the curb service. Customers parked, honked their horns, and everything they needed was delivered by a uniformed attendant. Nearly everyday, Martha would pull in after she got off work to have Big Jim fetch her an Eskimo Pie. They would flirt and talk, never bothering to exchange phone numbers, until Jim was called back to work by an impatient boss. He was soon transferred to another store near Sunset High School in Oak Cliff, and must have wondered if he would see Martha again. But she did

drive in one day, coming to get a loaf of bread for her mother. Figuring this might be his last chance, he worked up his nerve, walked out to the car with an Eskimo Pie, and asked her for a date.

Martha always said she fell in love with Big Jim because of his arms; "She said he had pretty arms," Jimmie remembers. Whatever the reasons, Big Jim and Martha had fallen in love with Oak Cliff and each other. They figured it was the perfect place to settle down and start a family, and took their vows on January 13, 1950.

Their first son was born on March 20, 1951 at Baylor Medical Center. His name would be Jimmie Lawrence ("Lee") Vaughan—just like his father.

Three-and-a-half years later, on October 3, 1954, another baby boy came along, and was christened Stephen Ray Vaughan; his name was chosen on the spot when it came time to fill out a birth certificate. He arrived two weeks late and was an incredibly tiny baby, weighing only 3 pounds, 9¼ ounces at birth. Doctors worried about his health, and kept him in the hospital for the next three weeks.

Although Stevie primarily grew up in Oak Cliff, many of his earliest years were spent traveling to follow his dad's work. Big Jim was an asbestos worker, which took the family to Louisiana, Texas, Alabama, Mississippi, and Arkansas. When the Vaughans finally settled in Oak Cliff, it was in a modest frame house at 2557 Glenfield, which would remain their address for the next thirty-seven years.

Big Jim and Martha Vaughan were devout pop music fans who loved to dance—they'd get out to a nightclub or ballroom anytime they could. Big Jim himself wasn't musically inclined, and didn't play an instrument. He liked to say he could barely play the radio. But "every time Daddy'd hear a great singer, he would get his hand goin' and he would start dancin' and every time he'd hear a bass, an upright bass or a walkin' bass of any kind, he'd get chill bumps all over," Stevie remembered.

For many years the big attraction in Dallas was the internationally renowned Big D Jamboree every Saturday night. The Big D was held at the Sportatorium down on Industrial Boulevard, and was the high-water mark of a certain kind of music in Dallas, namely the growth of rock and roll. Elvis played the Big D, and Hank Williams, Carl Perkins, and Johnny Cash were also regulars.

Many Dallas/Fort Worth heroes' careers—from Scotty McKay (who later joined Gene Vincent's Blue Caps) to Ray Campi, Johnny Carroll, Mac Curtis, Sid King, Billy Lee Riley, Gene and Bobby Rambo and The Flames, Groovy Joe Poovey, and rockabilly legend Ronnie "Rockin' Bones" Dawson—were launched on that stage.

While Jimmie and Steve were certainly more interested in going to see these hot young rockabilly cats, Mom and Dad had something a little more… *traditional* in mind for their musical upbringing. The top western swing bands in Dallas played the Manhattan club at Main and Exposition streets in Deep Ellum (the city's historic entertainment district), and the boys were often allowed to sit by the bandstand and watch while their folks "scooted a boot" on the sand-covered dance floor. Western swing was a passion for the elder Vaughans—even at home they kept a radio humming with the sounds of KRLD's "The Cornbread Matinee," listening to Dewey Groom, Al Dexter, and Bill Boyd. Big band jazz was also popular around the house in those years; Martha and Jim were particularly fond of Tommy Dorsey and Glenn Miller. Undoubtedly, the Vaughan brothers were surrounded by music of all persuasions from the moment they opened their eyes and ears.

Guys from Bob Wills' Texas Playboys band actually used to visit the Vaughan house for raucous, often drunken, games of 42, Nello, and Lowboy. Friends from Big Jim's local were often on hand for these parties, and some of them brought their Telecasters along. One of the guys had actually played with Chuck Berry and would show the boys how to play John Lee Hooker and Jimmy Reed. As Jimmie explained in later years, a lot of kids growing up in Texas are especially drawn to the guitar because they're surrounded by country music guitar players. The boys' uncles, Jerrel and Joe-Boy Cook, also played and Jimmie and Steve were influenced by

them as well. Later, Steve would say that their Uncle Joe gave them plenty of encouragement, and that there were other relatives, whose names and faces he'd forgotten, who had also urged them to play. "There were always family reunions we'd go to," Stevie said, "and the whole family'd be jammin'. Both sides.

"Far as I can remember," Stevie recalled, " I got my first guitar on my birthday in '61, so I was seven, I guess. It had catgut strings and it was a Masonite version of a Roy Rogers guitar. Maybe it was Gene Autry. I know it had a cowboy, and it had cows, and rope stencils on it, you know? It reminded me of a little blanket I had with the same designs on it. Anyway, it didn't work at all. The only way to tune it was to take three strings off and tune it like a bass. Didn't make any sense, but I tried it."

Little Stevie Ray and Jimmie Lee started playing guitar together before they even thought about it. "One of the things that really stuck with me from childhood is that there were always a lot of *characters* hanging around," Stevie once said. "I was a little beefheart. Every once in a while, there'd be, 'Hey Jim, Steve, come out here and show them what you can do.' We'd be little bitty midgets running around with guitars that were this big, trying to play." So it began with seven-year-old Stevie, on his Roy Rogers guitar, and ten-year-old Jimmie playing his Airline box acoustic, strumming duets.

Jimmie remembers their mom telling them to get their guitars and play, whenever someone dropped by. They'd happily comply, playing something like "In the Mood" (John Lee Hooker) or "Memphis" (Chuck Berry).

Jim and Martha quickly realized that the boys had some amount of talent, and made the rounds of the local talent shows as the proud, smiling parents of the amazing, guitar-pickin' Vaughan brothers.

Steve was a shy kid—

Jimmy Reed at the Vulcan Gas Company in Austin on March 14, 1969. Photo by and courtesy of Burton Wilson.

painfully so sometimes—which limited his ability to make friends early on. Perhaps his first true friend was Connie Trent, an adorable little red-headed second cousin that he kept bumping into at family functions. She was the only other kid his age in the family, and was also quite reserved. They developed a powerful bond, through helping each other out of their shells and always encouraging the other, that never diminished and lasted throughout Steve's life.

Connie's dad, her uncle Preston Vaughan, and Big Jim were asbestos workers who belonged to the same union local and hung out together. The Trents bought a house in Oak Cliff just a few blocks away from the Vaughans on Wilbur Street. Connie and Steve attended Lenoir Kirk Hall Elementary school together, until Connie moved across town after her mother passed away. Nine months later, her father committed suicide. Connie was only nine years old.

"I ended up moving back to Oak Cliff to live with my older sister Gloria," she remembers, "but ended up spending a lot of my time with Aunt Mae Mae and Uncle Preston, who were like my second folks. So, Stevie and I got to being buddies again. Stevie and I are not blood cousins; we are cousins by marriage. My Aunt Mae Mae is Florence Vaughan—she was my dad's sister. That's where the red hair comes from. When Stevie and I were kids, we were both redheads. We were both very shy, so there was a natural bond. He, knowing the circumstances that I came from, was naturally very protective of me. He knew the heartache and pain that I went through being this little girl that was always getting shuffled around. I always understood him too—the shyness, the little boy inside who was always trying to live up to his big brother, the guy who was always introduced as 'Jimmie Vaughan's little brother,' you know?

"When we were little kids we used to go over to my aunt and uncle's place and play checkers and listen to their old big band jazz 78's. My Uncle Preston was the guy who taught us both how to dance, as a matter of fact. We used to dance together a whole lot."

By 1960, rock and roll had a firm grip on Dallas' youth. Kids would flock to the Town East

Martha Vaughan and her brother Joe-Boy Cook (circa 1986). Photo by Harold Dozier.

shopping center in Mesquite and the Irving Youth Center to congregate, drink Coca-Cola, eat potato chips, and dance to the sound of Ray Sharpe and the Razor Blades.

Jimmie was smitten with rock and roll immediately, and searched for a like-minded friend he could share his fantasy with. He found one in Ronny Sterling, a stocky little kid who was practically Jimmie's mirror image. "I first met Jimmie at Hall Elementary School, probably in the fifth grade," Sterling recalls. "Jimmie used to come in with these long ducktails, tube of Brylcreem in his back pocket, black leather motorcycle jacket, and all of us would be standing there like, 'who is this little punk?'"

"I guess I was twelve when I got my first guitar," Jimmie recalls. "...Daddy bought us out of the Montgomery Ward's catalog this Airline record player, where the speaker'd come out with wires on either side, and we used to both stand in front of 'em with our guitars like this (stands up and looks cool), so it looked like we had amps. We were hooked."

Jimmie quickly became consumed with the guitar, immersing himself in the heavy sounds of Jimmy Reed, B.B. King, and Chuck Berry. At the tender age of thirteen, he was sneaking into clubs to hear T-Bone Walker and Freddie King. To Steve, his big brother had stumbled onto something that was happening, and he began sneaking into Jimmie's room whenever he could to check out these old blues records. "Jimmie was always bringing home all these different

Stevie's cousin Connie Trent, age six. Courtesy of Connie Trent.

records. It was like 'Here comes Jimmie with the record world!' Watching my brother, and seeing how much feeling he had with it, I picked up some big-time inspiration. I saw him get *excited* with something, and it excited me."

Steve heard these sounds coming through the bedroom door and wanted to know what the big deal was about this guitar, and why Jimmie always kept the door closed when he played it. One thing was for sure, though—Steve wanted to make music. At first Steve wanted to play drums. He made a makeshift drum set out of shoeboxes and pie pans, using clothes hangers for sticks. Next he wanted to play the saxophone, but couldn't manage more than a squeak or two. Steve then decided to follow his big brother's lead and try the guitar. His parents bought him a lap steel, but Steve wasn't sure what to do with the thing. He began sneaking into his big brother's room to play Jimmie's guitars, which were always lying around. They had long talks about Steve leaving Jimmie's records and guitar alone, but Steve would be messing with them the minute Jimmie left the house. In later years, he said he couldn't help but play Jimmie's guitar, so he "picked it up and tried to imitate him imitating Eric Clapton. I think the first one that really soaked in with me was 'Gotta Move,' " he added. Stevie said that this was the way it all started—that was when he discovered that playing the guitar felt right.

Martha Vaughan admits to being unaware of Stevie's six-string yearning. "Well, we were so busy watching Jim that little brother Stevie got pushed aside sometimes," she told Alan Govenar in *Meeting the Blues.* "We didn't pay much attention to him then all of a sudden he was playing, too. I can remember him practicing a lot in his bedroom. No one was home but me and I could hear him singing. He was working on it as often as he could."

"Oak Cliff was pretty racially mixed, so you'd hear blues and soul music around," Stevie said, "but for a white boy to pick up on Lightnin' Hopkins was still pretty radical.... In another part of Oak Cliff, across the tracks I suppose, was

Freddie King taking a breather backstage at Austin's Armadillo World Headquarters, October 1, 1970. Photo by and courtesy of Burton Wilson.

where T-Bone Walker was from, and Leadbelly. All those people were from there—Charlie Christian, Freddie King.

"When we started off," Stevie said, "the earliest things I learned were blues and surf tunes, like 'Pipeline' by Dick Dale and The Del-Tones.... I thought I knew how Jimmy Reed sounded, but I kept trying to play it differently. Jimmie would set me straight. A lot of it was watching him."

The first song Stevie ever learned to play on the guitar was an obscure but legendary record (*Wine, Wine Wine,* 1960) by a local Dallas rhythm and blues band, the Nitecaps. Back in 1961, the 'Caps released their debut album— their only album—*Wine, Wine, Wine,* on Tom Brown's fledgling Vandan Records label. It is a sorely overlooked masterpiece and a true cornerstone of Texas blues. The album produced two hot regional singles: "Wine, Wine Wine," which sold 10,000 copies in Dallas alone, and "Thunderbird," which hit number one that year on Houston and Dallas radio and became the rallying cry for a restless generation stuck on the prairie.

The band made a profound impact on Steve and Jimmie's impressionable minds; it was proof that white kids from Texas could play the blues after all. (This was still a few years before Janis Joplin, Johnny Winter, and Steve Miller came along and proved it.) In fact, the Fabulous Thunderbirds would take half of their name from that influential single fourteen years later. And "Thunderbird" would become the first song Stevie sang in public and a staple in his show for many years.

In a 1987 *Musician Magazine* interview, Jimmie and Stevie sat down together and remembered the early years.

Jimmie: ...rock and roll and blues...

Stevie: ...seemed all the same.

Jimmie: ...I mean, everybody says that British guys brought that back and that they turned

America on to it, but there was guys listenin' to that shit. Like Lonnie Mack: he was wilder than a giraffe pussy.

Stevie remembered that Mack would "flop around on the floor and do all that. The first record I ever bought was the 45 of Lonnie Mack's 'Wham!' b/w 'Suzie Q' in 1963," Stevie later said. "I was about ten or eleven, and I was tired of Jimmie always bringing home the records for me to hear. I figured it was time for me to turn him on. I'm glad it wasn't the Monkees or something. I went to the record store and asked the man to play me the wildest guitar record he had. He put on Lonnie Mack, and after about ten seconds it was like, 'Sold!' I must've played that record a hundred times that night. It's such a great record! I played it so many times, my dad broke it. I played it over and over and over and over, and when I didn't think it was loud enough anymore, I borrowed somebody's Shure PA Vocalmaster and put mikes up in front of the speakers and turned it up. It was LOUD in my room. After Dad broke it, I just went out and bought the album as soon as I saved up enough money; it was just incredible. He did all that wild-ass, fast-picking, whammy-bar stuff, then he would do a ballad, and it would sound like a cross between gospel and the blues—incredibly soulful and eerie. Lonnie Mack really taught me to play guitar from the heart, to really tap your insides."

Jimmie Lee had already been playing a year or so, and looked like a professional to Stevie, so as soon as Stevie got his hands on a guitar, the deep admiration for his brother that would last a lifetime began. "After he broke his collarbone playin' football," Stevie remembered, "someone gave him a guitar…. First day, he made up three songs. I saw how hard he worked at it, how much fun he was havin' doin' it, and how good he was. Within a couple-three years, if that long, he was the hottest guitar player around Dallas. Jimmie was hardly sixteen when he was backing up Freddie King! He got a lot of insight into rhythm playing that way, having to stand behind somebody else—he learned how to relax and hold back some."

In 1964, Steve turned ten and was tiring of acoustic guitar. Jimmie also grew weary of coming home and finding telltale signs that his little brother had been picking on his ultracool electric hollow-body Gibson Messenger. Steve had really taken a liking to that thing, and when Jimmie got a Gibson ES-330 for his thirteenth birthday, he passed the old, kid-size three-quarter scale Gibson Messenger ES-125T down to him. "That's kinda how it went with us from the start," Stevie said, "trading off guitars when one of us got tired of the one we had; when Jimmie got an electric guitar, I got his acoustic, and when he got a better electric guitar, I got his electric."

The Vaughan brothers would sit in their cramped bedroom for hours, with Jimmie working out the parts to blues and rock and roll records by ear, Steve watching his every move. They never really wanted to do anything else. They'd put records on—by everyone from T-Bone Walker, B.B. King, Buddy Guy, and Bo Diddley to the Stones and the Beatles—and play along. "We'd play hundreds of songs," Stevie later said, "but we'd only play halfway into the song, then quit and play another one. For the first few years, I didn't know any song beginning to end on the guitar—none!"

Steve struck up a friendship with David Brown, an American Indian kid who also had a passion for the guitar, and was known in the neighborhood as the cat who could eat anybody's lunch in a showdown. Although he was only eight years old, Steve looked up to him a lot, and David began to show him licks. "I first met Steve in 1958. I lived across the field from him over on Engle Street. We became friends as little boys, you know, four and five years old. We used to both play on Jimmie's guitar while he was gone. Boy, we'd see him coming up the sidewalk and get all scared, trying to put it away real quick so he wouldn't know we'd been messing with it. Jimmie scared us little kids, because he was a few years older and had his hair all slicked back, wore Stockard Junior High jackets—looked real tough.

Steve, in an early attempt to conform, tried out for the football team at L.K. Hall Elementary School with David Brown, and they both made it. (Vaughan home movies show the uniforms in the "Tick Tock" video.) Steve knew all along that he wasn't cut out for football; he was too small to be threatening, couldn't run very fast, and generally wasn't of much use to the coach. One day Steve went up and asked the coach why he didn't get a new uniform like everybody else, and the coach tactfully explained, "Well son, you don't start." Stevie tried to accept that, but eventually lost interest in the game altogether. He was dropped from the team after the coach finally called him into the game, only to find Steve daydreaming on the sidelines, staring into space with his helmet on crooked. The Coach yelled again: "Steve! Hey, Vaughan!" Steve's head snapped to attention.

"Huh?"

10

"You're in the game, kid," the coach bellowed. "Now, go play middle linebacker!"

Steve looked at him quizzically, and innocently said, "Yeah. Great! Where is that?"

One good thing that came out of Steve's brief encounter with school athletics was that he made a new friend in Rocky Athas, a good athlete and budding guitarist. Rocky was taller than most kids, with big, square football shoulders and a prankster sense of humor to match his stature. Athas is still a leading figure among Dallas guitar players, and remembers Steve Vaughan fondly.

"I was doing a talent show at L.K. Hall," Athas recalls. "Steve was sitting in the front row, just staring at me. We knew each other vaguely, but he came up to me afterwards and said 'I didn't know you played guitar!' He helped me carry my guitar home that day, called his mother from school, and I had a little red wagon that I carried my amp and guitar in—so here we go, dragging this thing down the alleyways home with people's dogs barking at us and shit. I was in the fifth grade, and he was in the sixth, so that would have been 1965.

"After that, we became best friends in school. Every Tuesday night, our folks would get together, and we'd all go down to Donnell's Cafeteria and eat dinner. Once we were wrasslin' at the table, and he was sitting on the end with me and my parents and ended up spilling the green beans. He started stuttering, you know 'Mrs. Athas, I...I...I'll pick those up....,' and Mom said 'Don't worry about it, Steve—just go sit with your own folks!' We had lunch together every day at school, traded sack lunches. His mom would always fix this goddamned olive loaf stuff—yuck!—and I'd have this super ham sandwich with lettuce, and after we'd trade and I'd see what he had, it was like 'Oh God, give me mine back!'

"...In music class, she had everybody bring in a record to study. And she told us not to bring in any rock and roll records, because they wouldn't count. Steve showed up with 'Magical Mystery Tour'; he wanted to play her 'Blue Jay Way,' just to throw her off. It starts off, *There's a fog upon L.A...,*' and she's sitting there turning green. I brought the single of 'I Am The Walrus,' and she really yelled at me. I pleaded, 'But it's got violins on it!' The whole class just fell out laughing. She got so mad, she banished me and Steve to sit on the floor behind the piano for the rest of class."

Rocky and Steve spent all of their time together after school, playing guitar while their mothers would chat in the living room. Their folks had a lot in common; the women were nice, humble ladies, soft-spoken and polite. The men in the families were just the opposite. The boys might yell conversations from across the house, while the women would speak in whisper-tones. Fathers played rough with their sons—sometimes too rough—especially when they drank. Several classmates recall Steve coming to school with scratches on his face, explaining that his dad had hit him the night before, a painful occurrence that prompted him to try drinking. He may have done it to kill the pain, or just because it was sitting there in the liquor cabinet calling to him. Or maybe he was attracted to alcohol because he saw all the grownups drinking it. Regardless of the reason, he tried it.

"He wore these long coats to school with pockets a mile deep," Athas remembers, "and it was like he kept a department store in there. First he'd pull out a guitar strap, then a pack of cigarettes, guitar picks, and everything else under the sun until he got to his little whiskey flask. He'd say 'Here, Athas, try this!' So, I'd watch him take a drink and then he'd start saying crazy shit for the next twenty minutes or until the buzz wore off."

David Brown agrees. "That's why he was such a smart-ass half the time," Brown says. "It was the alcohol filling him up with a bunch of bravery that he wouldn't have otherwise. Maybe it helped. He did things because of the alcohol that we would have been too scared to do."

It's hard to imagine David Brown being scared of doing anything. He was bigger, older, and already well ahead of Stevie on the guitar.

"He was like God to us, man," says Athas unequivocally. "There was Jimmie Vaughan and then there was David Brown.... David kicked ass. So, to all us little embryos who couldn't do it yet, he was a big influence." To hear David Brown play today, it is plain to see where Steve picked up so much of his style and finesse; Brown has the big, beefy Fender tones, amps that run clean, and a feather-light touch for emphasis. It's all there—one of the sources of Stevie's roots.

"We all learned through our own grapevine, through each other," Athas says. "Instead of learning songs, we thought of jamming around in certain patterns, like a blues or a shuffle pattern. We'd take lead rides for fifteen minutes until we each felt satisfied, then pass it on to the next guy. That's why when you listen to us, you can hear that we all play with the same vibratos, the same feel, the same approach. That's the 'Oak Cliff sound,' you know? When we grew up, we went in different directions musically, but the root was always there."

As Jimmie was getting a little older, his folks would occasionally let him out of the house to go play guitar at a nearby friend's house. Meanwhile, Steve stayed home with the record player and his new electric guitar.

"I don't necessarily look at myself as self-taught," Stevie insisted, "I would sit down and listen to something and if I couldn't find it on the neck yet, I would learn to find it singing the best I could. Trying to find the sound with my lips and my mouth, doing some bastardized version of scat singing. Then I would learn to make the sound with my fingers that I was making with my mouth."

It wasn't long before Jimmie had put together his first band, the Swinging Pendulums. The Pendulums were Jimmie on guitar, Phil Campbell on drums, and old friend Ronny Sterling on bass. "We played a lot of rock and roll," Sterling remembers, "tons of Chuck Berry. Jimmie was really into that kind of thing.... We would take any chance we could to play for people; if we could play the school auditorium, or the Senior Prom, or the cheerleader tryouts, we were in heaven. If they had a beauty contest and needed a backup band, there we were. We learned any songs they wanted us to play, no matter what kind of music. We definitely had the curtains shut on us a couple of times, because the teachers didn't like some of the lyrics we were singing, like 'Let's Spend The Night Together' [Rolling Stones], or 'Louie, Louie' [The Kingsmen].

"Steve was constantly hanging around, trying to hang out with us, but it didn't look very cool to have your little brother tagging along with you," Sterling says. "Of course, Jimmie and I took him with us a couple of times, and it was embarrassing. See, when Steve was a kid, he had a slight speech impediment; the bones in his nose had grown together, causing his sinus cavities to collapse, and he talked real nasal and funny. We used to tease him something awful, mimicking the way he talked, you know, like (he holds his nose) 'Hey Stevie, come over here!' and Stevie would get real upset and say 'Aw, you shut up, man, don't be talking to me like that!' (Steve later had a rhinoplasty operation to correct the condition.) Jimmie would always take up for Steve if somebody picked on him. Of course, he could beat up on him all he wanted to, but nobody else had better touch him!"

The Pendulums used to hold band practice in the front bedroom of Sterling's house, and all the neighborhood kids, including Steve and Rocky, wanted to come and watch these stars-in-the-making practicing their craft. The junior high-age kids were let right in, while the younger ones were made to watch from the outside, through the Venetian blinds; that is, until the band would tire of looking back at the many eager, bugged-out eyes staring at them, and pull down the shades.

Big Jim Vaughan and Al Sterling, Ronny's father, were good friends, and would take turns "managing" the Pendulums. "See, when some of the kids wanted to play the bars on Greenville Avenue," Al explains, "Big Jim and I would have to be chaperones, because they were too young to be in a beer joint."

"I remember one night we had to do a gig over in Fort Worth," Ronny adds, "and once I got there, I realized that I didn't have my bass. I had my amp, but I had left the bass at home in Dallas.... So we'd call one of the parents, Al or Big Jim, to get my bass and bring it to the gig. And they'd be there, like Johnny-on-the-Spot. Our parents did encourage us, more than we realized then."

Although the Vaughans were beginning to see some differences between themselves and other kids their age, in those days they were still fairly average kids with above-average musical talents and an appreciation for Lightnin' Hopkins, Jimmy Reed, Muddy Waters, and T-Bone Walker. While the other preteens were listening to "Johnny Angel" (Shelly Fabares), "Duke of Earl" (Gene Chandler), "Heat Wave" (Martha and The Vandellas) and "Wipeout" (The Surfaris), Stevie and Jimmie dug deeper into the blues, listening to KNOK and "Kats Karavan" on WRR, often checking out the latest hits on KBOX and KLIF, the two stations in Dallas that were constantly competing for the rock and roll market. They'd stay up late, digging Wolfman Jack's rhythm and blues show over border radio XERB, the swamp blues and rockabilly over WLAC in Nashville, and gritty urban blues on Chicago's WLS. What they didn't pick up over the airwaves, they gleaned from loitering around clubs on Hall Street and Greenville Avenue that they were too young to enter, listening through the exhaust fans out back. One place where underage R&B fans would converge was Lou Ann's, where the Nitecaps had a regular gig.

Steve would have to be in early on school nights, but would lie in bed, still wound up like a clock after watching the local bands play. Silently he'd wait for his mom and dad to go to sleep. Then he'd dig out his portable radio and hold the little white earplug up against the side of his head so it wouldn't fall out while he rocked himself to sleep.

While other kids spent their afternoons looking at baseball cards or playing intramural sports, the Vaughan brothers were practicing their guitars and talking about the three Kings: Freddie, Albert, and B.B.—the holy trilogy. Other kids in the neighborhood were checking out all the new British groups. The brothers listened to them too— but what they really lived for were the late nights spent trading the crystal radio back and forth and taking turns spinning the tuning knob on the gadget that glowed at them in the dark like a best friend.

During the days, Stevie still hung out with Connie Trent, hitchhiking over to her house in the far reaches of Oak Cliff to play games and listen to records. He developed his first serious crush on Connie's next-door neighbor Dana Kersey, a cute little girl with long blond hair. "He went absolutely ga-ga over her," Connie recalls. Steve, far from a Romeo in the sixth grade, finally worked up the courage to profess his undying love for the girl, and the two went steady for a while.

When the Beatles came to Dallas on their maiden 1964 U.S. tour, Connie Trent had tickets. "Steve was so jealous!" she laughs. "I mean, he wanted to go bad. He called me before I went to the concert, after I got back home, and just begged me to tell him all about it. He really did love the Beatles."

Connie was also fortunate enough to have a private phone line in her room and after Big Jim and Martha went to bed, Steve would creep into the dark hallway and call her. This is where their lifelong habit of nocturnal phone conversations began, the two yammering on for hours on end. "One night he had learned 'Classical Gas' [Mason Williams' acoustic guitar workout] all the way through, and he just had to play it to me over the phone! That," she adds with a smile, "was quite an accomplishment."

It wasn't long before Steve was playing in public, too. Again, wanting to follow in big brother's footsteps and wasting no time he put together a little band with some schoolmates. Although no one wants to admit to being in it, rumor has it that a later member of Double Trouble—a tall, gangly bass player named Tommy Smedley, who preferred to use the stage name of Tommy Shannon—participated for a brief time.

"My first real band was the Shantones," Stevie told *Musician Magazine*. "When I was ten, me and Tommy Shannon put together The Shantones. I remember the first talent show we were in. We played Jimmy Reed's 'Baby, What You Want Me To Do?' and in the middle of it, we just looked at each other and realized that we had never finished the song before. We went 'Fuck It!' because we discovered we didn't know the whole song. We were trying to play things like 'Sleepwalk' [Santo and Johnny's 1959 hit], although we didn't have a steel player. It ended kind of abruptly that night, and we weren't together for very long!"

Other people say that Stevie and Tommy didn't actually meet until 1969, when Shannon discovered Stevie playing at an after-hours club in the Deep Ellum area of Dallas. Tommy today denies the existence of the Shantones and that infamous talent show, but Stevie swore the story was true in several interviews.

The Pendulums finally stopped swinging in mid-1965, when Robert Patton, the guitarist for the Chessmen, a very popular local rock band, drowned in a tragic boating accident at White Rock Lake. Johnny Peoples, the Chessmen's other guitarist, extended an offer to Jimmie Vaughan to come on board. The Chessmen were about the hottest thing in Dallas at the time; they had a 45 out ("I Need You There") that was getting heavy airplay on KLIF, Dallas's biggest rock station. Jimmie was tempted by the money involved but wanted to be loyal to his own band too. "Jimmie was nice enough to come and tell us about it before he accepted the offer," remembers Ronny Sterling. "He wanted our blessing, and wanted us to still be friends after that. Which we were, friends for life. We said 'Hell, go for it!'"

The Chessmen were represented by the BizMark Agency of Denton, Texas. The agency was the brainchild of George Rickerge, a mild-mannered movie theater manager who found that these little rock bands could make him some serious money. The kids wanted to dance, and by God, he was gonna give 'em the best teen bands he could find. Also on his roster were the Jackals, Bricks, Beefeaters, and Velicity, a band which featured a young Don Henley on drums. When Jimmie left the Pendulums, Phil and Ronny joined the Jackals, who were also drawing big crowds in Dallas. "So me and Jimmie still crossed paths a lot," Ronny explains. We had the same agent, and we got booked together a lot."

The Jackals had a house gig at a joint called the Three Thieves at Lovers Lane and Inwood. The Chessmen would often drop in to sit in on nights off. Right down the street was another club that featured a band called the Playboys, an R&B

outfit whose lead crooner was a skinny kid named Paul Ray. "We'd go check each other out on breaks," Ronny remembers. "When we first saw Paul Ray, we thought 'Now this guy is a professional!' He just knocked us out!"

Speaking of professionals, Jimmie was absolutely mad over the drummer and singer for the Chessmen, Doyle Bramhall. Doyle was two years older than Jimmie, and the elder Vaughan knew that he could sing—Doyle reportedly sent the girls swooning at his soulful rendition of Ray Charles' "Georgia On My Mind." They struck up a friendship through the band, one that would last for decades. Ironically, Doyle didn't even know that Jimmie had a brother for months. What he remembers most about meeting Steve wasn't what he saw, but what he heard.

"I was over at their house one day; I'd come by to pick up Jimmie and he was running late," remembers Doyle. "And all of a sudden I hear this wonderful guitar playing coming from the bedroom. I knew it couldn't be Jimmie– I'd just passed him in the hall. So I crept over to the door, pushed it open, and there's this little kid inside. He must have been eleven or twelve, sitting on the bed, with these incredible sounds coming out of his guitar. I still remember the song; it was 'Jeff's Boogie.'"

Astonished by this mystery boy in Jimmie's bedroom, Doyle asked "Who are YOU?" Steve got up to introduce himself, setting down his guitar, and Doyle quickly stopped him, saying "No! No! Please, play some more...."

This moment became the start of a loyal, lifelong friendship based on mutual respect. Steve was flattered by Doyle's attention, because none of Jimmie's other friends even noticed him. But here was this cool drummer, five years his senior, who would not only talk to him but was not ashamed to be seen hanging out with him. Stevie watched Doyle closely, and hoped that someday he could follow in his footsteps.

Like Steve, Rocky Athas was also a big

Doyle Bramhall, the Chessmen's gravel-voiced lead vocalist. He would later work with Stevie in the Nightcrawlers and write several of SRV's best songs. Photo by and courtesy of Burton Wilson.

Chessmen fan. "That band was so cool," he says today. "They even had their own car—a black hearse that said The Chessmen in big white letters on the side. We thought that was a big organization."

Meanwhile, Rocky and Steve were still practicing their guitar skills over summer vacation, and trying desperately to grow up too fast: "...Remember the second Iron Butterfly album called *Ball*?" Athas asks. "Well, Steve got it before me, and asked me if I knew what the title meant. And I said, 'Sure,' and he said 'What, then?' And I went fumbling for words to explain something I didn't know either. We were always trying to stump each other, one-up each other. I'll never forget that. We tried to trick each other and it backfired on us!"

Steve began his freshman year at Justin F. Kimball High School in 1967, and already, he could tell that this teenage jail was not his kind of scene. "When I was in school, it was berserk," he said. "I had to get a note from the principal every day saying I looked all right to go to his school."

Although Steve usually struck out with the girls, he had begun to check out brother Jimmie's rap and was even picking up some girls of his own, although they were mostly Jimmie's seconds. At the same time, he was going through the painful process of making new friends because most of his old buddies, like David Brown and Connie Trent, were bused across town to other high schools.

To fill the time, Steve got a job, a paper route that he remembers as especially trying because his street divided the territories of rival gangs who often used it as a battleground. He was picked on unmercifully, and after he got his nose broken for being in the wrong place at the wrong time, his parents let him quit the job as long as he promised to get another one. But for the time being, he was busy putting together a new band: the Brooklyn Underground.

"That was a joke!" Stevie laughed. "We didn't think it was, but it was. I was listening to B.B. King, Ray Charles, and those guys, trying to figure out how to do it. Listening to those people—how they played so well and so relaxed—I'm still trying to learn to play that way. I probably will for the rest of my life. I was playing blues bass for Jimmie a little bit in the Chessmen, but the only gigs I could find were rock and roll."

"And then along came Albert King records," Stevie declared. "When I was twelve, I worked as a dishwasher to get money to buy records and guitar accessories; I was completely obsessed at that point. One day I had an accident at work, which turned out to be a pretty important point in my life. I was cleaning out the trash bin, and that involved standing on these big fifty-five gallon barrels with wooden lids on them, where they put all the hot grease. So here I am cleaning the bin, having a blast, and the top broke and I fell in. Just as I finally got out—I'd been up to about my chest in grease—they came with two fresh hot vats of boiling grease and I got out just in time. If I'd taken a break later I would have been a fried guy!… Well, the woman who owned the restaurant came over and started yelling at me for breaking the lid to the barrel. She didn't care if I was hurt; she just cared that I broke something, and she said I'd have to pay for it. I was so mad that I quit right then and went home with smoke coming out of my ears. I put on the meanest record I had, 'King Of The Blues Guitar' by Albert King, and right then and there, I made up my mind that I was going to be a guitar player like Albert King."

That after-school job pushing ice cream for seventy-five cents an hour at the local Dairy Mart was the last time Steve Vaughan ever worked a straight job. "I never was cut out for real work!" he joked in later years.

"He would sit in his room for hours on end, trying to pick out those Albert King records," Connie Trent recalls. "It was incredible. He would learn it note-for-note, then call me and show off what he had learned. Stevie wasn't a real social creature then; he was extremely shy. He could shine when he was onstage, even then. He wasn't making all those expressive faces like he did in later years, he just got up there and played, always holding his head down."

The Chessmen played on a local TV dance program called "Sumpin' Else" in 1967, and as they were packing their gear to leave, Jimmie noticed a promotional 45 of "Purple Haze" by some guy named Jimi Hendrix. Intrigued, he took it home.

"I went, 'Whoa! What is this?'" Steve later remembered. "I'll never forget that. He was IT for me. He had a sound that was old, like on 'Red House,' but it was brand-new at the same time. I was really into his music and a lot of stuff about his life for a long time. I used to dress up like Jimi on Halloween and took to wearing scarves around my legs and hats like he wore. I remember Mother and Daddy comin' to a lot of my shows: Here I'd be singing all these songs to them, singin' 'Sweet Thing,' and here were the two of 'em, dancin' and huggin'. It was great. And they would cry when I'd play Hendrix songs."

The Chessmen got a chance to open for Jimi Hendrix in Houston, and at Dallas' McFarlin Auditorium in 1967. Hendrix was reportedly interested enough in Jimmie's playing to tip him $40, along with his wah-wah pedal in exchange for Jimmie's brand new Vox one. "Jimmie managed to get his autograph for Stevie," Ronny recalls, "which I know Stevie carried in his wallet until it rotted away." Stevie also got a feather from Hendrix's hat, which he held dear.

That same night, Hendrix showed up at the Walrus, a local club, after his performance and autographed a 25-foot poster of himself for one ardent admirer named Christian Brooks. Besides an appreciation for Jimi Hendrix, Brooks had several things in common with Steve—they lived in the same neighborhood, hung out with the same kids, and, consequently, became friends.

"I always remember Steve being a sweet kid," says Christian Brooks, "real sensitive. It really bothered him when people were hurting. Even then, he'd always take the time out to ask 'Hey, what's goin' on?' I think that's the reason I always held him in my heart, especially when he made it. I was proud of him. You know, people used to ask me where I was from and I'd say 'Oak Cliff,' and they'd kinda go, 'Ohhhh.' I heard that for so long that I developed an attitude about it. Oak Cliff is like Dallas with soul, it's a cool place. So when he made it, Oak Cliff finally had someone to look up to."

Perhaps it was Steve's growing infatuation with Jimi Hendrix that led him to buy his first real guitar amp, a Marshall. "We'd go into the music store to look at guitars," says Rocky Athas. "He'd pick one up and turn the Marshall up to ten inside the store, and just start rockin'! I'd be like, 'Turn

Jimi Hendrix at the Matrix, San Francisco, 1967. Photo by and courtesy of Grant Jacobs.

one hundred dollar bills across the table to Yamini, who was flabbergasted. "Just wanted you to know I didn't forget, Bruce," Stevie said, smiling. Stevie was young, but that's the way he treated friends—then and always.

Mitch Mullins was fourteen when he met the Vaughan brothers through another set of musical brothers, Roy and Donnie Rogers. He had gone to elementary school with Connie Crouch, Jimmie's sweetheart, who would one day become Mrs. J.L. Vaughan. Mitch always admired her spunk from the day she brought a 45 single of Wilson Picket's "Land Of A Thousand Dances" to show-and-tell. He had seen Jimmie around lots of times, but he found himself gravitating toward Steve.

"Steve and I made a friendship based on quality," Mitch says. "We went to Kimball High together, but I was two years older than him. Stevie was searching for committed musicians but could not find them, so I tried to help by sneaking him into jam sessions where the older players were the pros. When they would refuse him the opportunity, I'd change their minds by telling them they had to

it down, Stevie! Damn!' But he'd sure enough have a little crowd standing there before too long, putting on a show for them. He wanted a Marshall so bad he could taste it."

Bruce Yamini, a close high school friend at Kimball, loaned Stevie the three hundred bucks it took to bring the amp home. Yamini believed in Steve, and didn't mind the fact that he would probably never see the money again—but still, three hundred dollars is a lot of money for any high school kid.

It wasn't until nearly 20 years later, in 1983, that he got the loan paid back. Yamini had taken a job working as a flight attendant for Southwest Airlines by day while playing in a rock band by night. Yamini's band, Boyfriend, was Stevie's opening act for the Dallas record release party for *Texas Flood* at Tango, a popular club. Yamini had forgotten all about the money, and just wanted to catch up on old times as he and Stevie settled down into a booth together. The waitress brought drinks, Stevie gladly paid for them, and then slipped three

listen to him. So they'd let him play a song, and he'd blow their minds. Established bands and guitarists like Steve Miller and his younger brother Jimmy, Boz Scaggs... they noticed him, all right."

Both brothers were duly blown away when Eric Clapton left the Yardbirds in 1966, declaring that he "really wanted to play the blues," and joined John Mayall's Bluesbreakers.

Remembering that Bluesbreakers' record, Jimmie told *Guitar for the Practicing Musician*, "He sounded really mad, he played like B.B. King and Buddy Guy and a lot of the great blues singers that I love. He played like a man. He obviously loved Freddie King, which was real close to my heart. Down here in Texas, bands back then had to play 'Hideaway' or 'Hold It.' Otherwise, you couldn't play a gig."

Stevie remembered having to learn "Jeff's Boogie" if they wanted to play in the Cellar. Later on he'd recall that no one—including himself—knew it was actually a Chuck Berry song or that the real title was "Guitar Boogie."

Meanwhile, Jimmie's grades had slipped to the point where he was told he had to repeat the ninth grade. At the time, he didn't seem to care much about it; it was just a drag that school had to interfere with his music, which was keeping him busy and taking him places. He was the lead guitarist in the hottest band in Dallas, which played numbers that ran the spectrum from Muddy to the Yardbirds, from the Ventures to Little Richard, B.B. King to the Beatles. He had all the girls he could handle, and all the alcohol and cheap speed he could consume to keep him going through school the next day.

Jimmie left home at fifteen, moving into an apartment with other band members. "Me and my dad sorta had a fallin' out, and that's the end of that story," he later told writer Ed Ward. "I didn't actually see Stevie for a couple of years, I wasn't comin' around a lot."

"I did basically the same thing, a little bit later," Stevie recalled. "I had already been playing around…in several bands, like the Epileptic Marshmallow," he laughed, adding, "it was just the *worst* name we could think of."

In 1966 Stevie finally got ahold of Jimmie's '51 Fender Broadcaster (actually an oddball Telecaster with only one pickup) when Jimmie got his first, and most prized, cream-colored Strat. "I just couldn't move out without leaving him something to play," Jimmie explained to writer Andy Aledort, "and I left him the Telecaster. Besides, I had two or three of them. You could get them for 50 bucks. They were cheap, nobody really wanted them…"

Even when Steve had guitars of his own to play, he never really broke the habit of sneaking in a few licks on Jimmie's growing array of cool guitars. Once Jimmie walked in unexpectedly, only to find little Stevie hiding in the closet, monkeying around on one of his favorite guitars. Jimmie boxed him but good, knocking his kid brother clean across the room, leaving Stevie broken-hearted, dazed, and crying on the floor. Jimmie hollered back to him as he walked out the door, "I told you, goddammit! Don't touch my guitar!" He affected a nasal, high-pitched child's voice as he mimicked his little brother's preferred new nickname, stolen from his favorite Motown soul singer, "*Steeeeev-ieeeeee!*"

D/FW

BIG JIM AND MARTHA were admittedly losing faith in their boys. Now it was Steve who was bringing home disappointing report cards. Those teenage years really put their parental powers to the test; it seemed like he was constantly in trouble for something, and, just like Jimmie, he usually arrived home from a gig as the sun was coming up with alcohol on his breath. As punishment, the folks often threatened to hide the guitars and cancel the gigs, but they always gave in at the last minute, allowing Steve to play but with a strict curfew—be home by 2 A.M., and in bed, or else!

Oh, but teenagers could have so much fun before two o'clock! Oak Cliff hosted a bevy of all-ages clubs that regularly showcased the toughest bands of that era: the Chessmen, Sammy Laurie and the Penetrations, Parsley Green, the Mint (with Jimmy Wallace), Southwest F.O.B. (Freight On Board), the Penthouse Five, and the Mystics played mostly adolescent haunts with names like the Funky Monkey, the Cellar, the Three Thieves, Soul City, the Studio Club, Strawberry Fields, Lou Ann's, the Fog, and Mother Blues. If the kids weren't dancing, they were cruising through Kiest Park. Or they'd be roller skating over at the Rocket Skating Rink in Cockrell Hill on a Saturday night, when local bands would play and teens from Sunset, Adamson, and Kimball high schools would congregate and mingle in numbers often reaching a hundred or more.

But the king bee of Oak Cliff's music venues

was Candy's Flare, located inside the old National Guard Armory on the south side of Red Bird Airport. It was way out in the sticks, a good place to smoke a joint and watch the planes roll in. Inside, it was just a big, black room with a psychedelic paint job on the walls. It had a concrete floor and cinderblock walls that housed an elaborate black lighting system, and also featured nightly psychedlic light shows courtesy of the White Trash Company. There were two stages, one at each end. Two bands would play, alternating sets between nine P.M. and 1 A.M. It was Dallas' equivalent to San Francisco's Fillmore, featuring bands that actually had hit records like the Strawberry Alarm Clock, the Nazz (with Todd Rundgren), the Five Americans, and Kenny and The Kasuals.

"Candy's Flare was the main place that scene really nurtured itself," says Christian Brooks. "It was everyone's favorite place in Oak Cliff to hear live bands, and a lot of younger musicians like myself got turned on to blues through that place. It was an incredible time to be exposed to this music through kids you knew from school up there on stage. If it wasn't for Candy's Flare, I don't think we would have seen as many hot players come out of Oak Cliff, because they may not have had another place to test their wings. Without that place, I think the history of Dallas blues would have been altered substantially... it was an amazing two-or three year period when it was all happening, from about 1967 to 1970."

Oak Cliff was generally regarded as a dangerous area of town. In addition to the obvious paranoia instilled by Lee Harvey Oswald's residence and subsequent arrest there, Jack Ruby was also from Oak Cliff and had a bad rap as a mobster who ran a chain of sleazy topless bars in Dallas. Minorities were often pushed to the city limits, adding to the already economically depressed township's troubles, and the racial combination wasn't always a peaceful one.

Oak Cliff rednecks didn't like blacks or homosexuals. Tough kids from local high schools took great pleasure in finding and roughing up gay men on Friday nights. Neither of the Vaughan boys condoned the racial or social attitudes. In fact they both accepted and admired blacks for their honest music and talent.

Steve's first black friend was a kid named Christian Plicque. Steve had first heard him sing at the Texas State Fair, and was in love with his roaring soulful voice. Although Plicque was privileged enough to have a day job at Neiman-Marcus

and wealthy parents who sent him to the best schools, Big Jim still wasn't impressed when Steve brought him home to meet the family. He told Christian in no uncertain terms that there was only one thing a nigger could do for him: shine his shoes.

Steve couldn't apologize enough to Christian, whose feelings were understandably hurt, but the friendship survived and Steve eventually convinced Plicque to join his band. There was only one problem, however—Steve didn't have one. He pulled together a little thing with friends Billy Knight and Steve Lowery, and they became the Southern Distributors for the first week, changed their name to Lincoln for the second week, and promptly split up.

Before Steve turned thirteen, he auditioned for his first almost-professional group. The band, called Liberation, had an opening for a bass player. Scott Phares, now thirty-eight, remembers the day quite clearly: "He played bass for maybe an hour of rehearsal. I was the guitarist. During the break he picked up my guitar and proceeded to eat my lunch. I told him we had this all wrong—that he was going to play guitar and I was going to play bass. He was just a kid, and he was almost as good as he is today. It was amazing. We'd play for school dances, and when Steve would cut loose on solos, they would stop dancing and gather around the stage, awestruck."

An eight-piece band, complete with saxophones and trumpets, Liberation appeared in after-hours clubs all over the metroplex. "That was the first club gig I ever had—Arthur's, on Commerce Street, downtown," Stevie remembered. "We worked several nights there and then after hours we'd go play a place called the Fog. We played for eight days in a row and made $650 for the week. Then we started playing the Funky Monkey. Played that gig from 10 P.M. to 6 A.M. with 10-minute breaks and a 20-minute break to eat on."

The band included Steve Vaughan—guitar, Mike Day—drums, Scott Phares—bass, Steve Lowrey—keyboards, Wes Johnson—sax, Scott Leftwich—trumpet, and Jim Trimmier on sax and several other assorted instruments. Eventually, Christian Plicque joined as lead vocalist. They played material along the lines of the then popular Chicago Transit Authority; Blood, Sweet and Tears; and the Allman Brothers, with a dash of Paul Butterfield's blues thrown in as well.

In 1968, Stevie bought his first guitar (from Jimmie, of course). It was a black 1954 Les Paul

TV Model. He started playing a long string of gigs at the Cellar (2125 Commerce Street), a fleabag underground club that fronted gambling, nude dancing, and anything else your pocketbook could fund. But a blues band could make decent money there, and the management didn't care if the musicians were eighteen or not. "It wasn't the kind of place you'd want to hang too long," Stevie said, grimacing.

Stevie started playing the Cellar (there were two—one in Dallas and one in Fort Worth) at age fourteen and continued until he was eighteen. Liberation would commonly play two sets at the Dallas club and then race over to the one in Fort Worth and play two more—all for $90 per musician. Stevie knew his parents didn't want him frequenting such clubs, but it was a gig that allowed him the freedom to play what he wanted—a rare opportunity. "I was trying to stay as close to this kind of music as I could," he later told *Guitar for the Practicing Musician*, "but at the same time I was going through a phase of playing through Marshalls—just turning up to 10 and being a teenager. I remember doing some Allman Brothers songs, which I liked at the time—but we were also doing Buddy Guy and B.B. King stuff."

"The music I really got into during that period," Stevie explained in another interview, "was stuff like 'Over, Under, Sideways, Down' by the Yardbirds. *Anything* by Hendrix. Clapton's stuff with John Mayall. I got my hands on a Rickenbacker bass and went crazy playing 'Lady Madonna.' I learned the bass part all the way through, thought I was hot shit because I got it right, and then I'd try to show off and screw it up! So I kept tryin'. I got into 'The Crawl' by Guitar Junior, and a bunch of T-Bone Walker. 'Stormy Monday' and 'Cold, Cold Feeling,' and all those songs. I don't even remember all the titles... but I just remember how they go, when I hear 'em."

"At the Cellar," he told the *Dallas Morning News*, "you just didn't go there if you were black. If you were black and tried to get in the door they'd ask for a reservation. If your name just happened to be on this fake list they had, they'd ask for $100 cover. And if you handed them $100, you'd damn sure get rolled before you got very far in the club.

"If there were three bands playing, we'd get two-hour breaks, so I'd go over to Hall Street to this club you didn't go to if you were white. But they fed me in the kitchen. I'd go over there and hang out, sit in whenever I could. Sometimes I'd even play the drums!"

Stevie fessed up to always having a passion for the drums. It wasn't so far out to imagine; the rhythm drove him crazy, and he might have found his true love there if he could have afforded a drum kit. "Jimmie plays the drums better than me, anyway," Stevie insisted. "He's one of those guys who—when he picks anything up, it just sounds right, you know? And it doesn't look like he's doing anything! He kept on playing guitar and picked up several instruments... everything from steel guitars to cornet, fiddle, '51 Chevys—and he's a *great* bass player as well. I played bass for a while in Jimmie's band. It was just a few months, but I learned a lot there, mainly steel guitar, more drums. I kept trying to fool around with the drums."

Freddie King (a.k.a. "The Texas Cannonball") was a native of Gilmer, Texas, and one of the greatest blues guitar players the Lone Star State ever produced. In the late '60s, Freddie was living in his "Palace of the King" right there in Dallas, and the Vaughan brothers knocked themselves out to see every show, eventually meeting the fiery guitar hero: "I got an autograph on that instrumental album he had (*Let's Hide Away and Dance Away With Freddie King*)," Stevie said. "Jimmie actually got to know him pretty well, but Freddie wouldn't talk to me in public for some reason. In private, but never in public. I guess I was a young white boy he didn't want to be seen with (laughs). I played with him once, sitting around a table when nobody else was around."

Buddy Guy—one of the Chicago bluesmen Stevie and Jimmie admired most. Photo by Don Ottensman/The Best of the Blues.

The short-lived Storm lineup, which featured both Jimmie and Steve, jamming at Lee Park (Dallas) in 1968. Photo by Jan Harris. Courtesy of Christian Brooks.

Jimmie had finally put together a great band in late 1968. He called it Texas. A couple of gigs proved that name too hokey, so he changed it to Texas Storm, and eventually it became just the Storm. The band was a motley crew of Texas hippies, destined to later become some of the most respected names in Texas blues. The Storm included Doyle Bramhall on vocals and drums (who went on to front the Nightcrawlers, the Millionaires, the Heartbeats, and the Juke Jumpers), Phil Campbell on drums, Sammy Piazza on second drums, Billy Etheridge on organ, and Jimmy Chilton on bass. Playing obscure blues, their habitats included such legendary nightlife dungeons as the notorious Cellar in Dallas and Fort Worth. When the Storm's bass player was thrown in jail, Jimmie asked his 14-year-old brother to fill in on bass for a few gigs, one of them being a road trip to Austin for the band's debut at the Vulcan Gas Company.

Steve was visibly excited about being in the same band with Jimmie, and tried a little too hard to keep up with the older guys. In fact he hardly remembered his first gig in Austin because he spent most of it upchucking his liquor outside the club. The rest of the band wasn't in much better shape; besides racing on speed, they were falling down drunk, too.

Robert "Cutter" Brandenburg saw Steve playing bass with the Storm that year, and was blown away by his skill, not even knowing the younger Vaughan played guitar. Cutter had been stricken with polio as a kid, but the sheer physical strength of this stocky, lumbering hippie impressed Steve enough to have him join the band as a roadie, a job he held for most of Stevie's career. Cutter was loyal; it didn't matter if the band was making three dollars a night or three hundred, he would dutifully haul the guitars, amps, speakers and drums around with nary a complaint because he simply loved helping Steve any way he could.

Steve Vaughan first met Vicki Virnelson when they were selling Cokes at a hot dog stand in the summer of 1969. He liked her style. She was intelligent, had long, flowing chestnut hair, soft eyes, and liked to rock and roll. He knew he'd found a soulmate. She would call a friend with wheels to drive them all the way to Irving, Texas, for band practice, and accompanied him to nearly every gig during that long, hot summer. They would spend nights stretched out on the lawn near Red Bird Pool, gazing at the stars and talking about the future.

One night at the Lamplighter club in Irving, Steve had just finished a set with "Jeff's Boogie," and walked over to his table to sit down with Vicki. A stranger walked up and said he was a guitar player, and wanted to know if Steve was such hot shit, why couldn't he play "Jeff's Boogie" in double-time? "Steve shot him a look like 'just you wait,'" Vicki recalls. "He got back up there and played that sucker in triple-time! But he really liked to play slow blues like "Sitting On Top Of The World" [Howlin' Wolf], that was one of his favorites. But they usually wouldn't let him. When

Stevie exuded pure attitude at fourteen, even on bass. Photo by Jan Harris. Courtesy of Christian Brooks.

you're in a cover band, you have to play the hits. But it was 1969; if you were playing the Top 40, at least it was pretty cool stuff like the Doors, and Hendrix. They were playing dances and sock hops, so they had to play songs people could dance to. You know, it's kinda hard to dance to 'Toad' [Cream's 1967 epic drum solo]."

In the summer of '69, Stevie again crossed paths with Tommy Shannon, who had graduated from the Shantones to the prestigious position of bass player in Johnny Winter's band during 1967 and 1968. After recording two albums and several tours, Shannon was let go by Winter, and happened onto a gig that Stevie, who was only about fifteen, was playing at a little after-hours place called the Fog in Dallas. "He claims that he walked in and saw this little midget playing guitar," Stevie laughed. "He was on his way to California with a band he'd just formed called Krackerjack... Tommy, for some reason, was the only one who would pay attention to me.... We played together off and on in bands ever since—and I even got to jam with Johnny Winter over at Tommy's house around that time."

Over at Tommy's house he met Lew Stokes, a full-time commercial graphic artist and part-time concert promoter. He was a friend of both Vaughan brothers in Dallas, and later became part of the great Oak Cliff migration to Austin in the early '70s. He designed crazy, psychedelic posters for concerts by Storm and Krackerjack, Shannon's new band which featured Uncle John Turner on drums; Mike Kindred on keyboards; Bruce Bowland on lead vocals; and John Stahely, Jack Morgan, and, later, Jesse Taylor on guitars. Later, he'd also do posters for Paul Ray and the Cobras, Triple Threat, and Jimmie Vaughan and The T-Birds at almost-legendary venues like Tolbert's Chili Parlor, Flight 505, Alexander's, and the Black Queen. He cut the bands a good bargain for posters and handbills; only ten bucks would get you a hundred flyers to post all over town. Not only that, but if you wanted some hooch, trip, or go-fast, Lew (now re-

Stevie and Vicki Virnelson (circa 1972). Courtesy of Vicki Virnelson/Connie Trent.

habilitated and a born-again Christian) could set you up with that too.

"Drugs really escalated quickly over here in Oak Cliff," Stokes recalls. "In the late sixties, the drugs of choice were pot and psychedelics. It all changed in 1969, radical change. Speed came in, and as soon as that happened, the heat turned up. I remember some FBI bust on a kid in the parking lot of Kimball High School that year. Once people started using the needle, you know, shooting up... the whole drug thing got out of hand immediately.

"There weren't any 'hippies' in Oak Cliff, you know. There were people with long hair, people that were 'hip,' but 'hippies?' We all thought that was a pretty strange deal. We were too cynical to be flower children. We were drinkers. All of our

One of Stevie's biggest heroes, Johnny Winter. Pictured here at the Vulcan Gas Company during his "Progressive Blues Experiment" days. Note Tommy Shannon on bass. Photo by and courtesy of Burton Wilson.

parents drank, and as a result, we kids drifted to alcohol. All my friends in school had little whiskey bottles that they carried with them, you know? Some of them carried a case of beer in the car and a pack of reefers, too."

Of course Stevie fell prey to the temptation of chemical highs, and, in fact, wanted to experiment with everything, as his heroes did, so that he could Make Music That Would Change People's Lives. "Stevie was just trying to *survive*," Stokes insists. "He was around people who used coke, people who used speed, and the big lie was that he wanted to take it for *'inspiration.'* He had done LSD a couple of times and didn't like it. It really weirded him out, he said it was just too strange. He did a lot of speed to get up, a lot of Seconal to mellow out... And drinking at that age was basically our way of building self-confidence that we didn't have, feeding our ego perhaps, making us something that we weren't, allowing us to spit on people instead of saying 'excuse me,' you know?

"Stevie was trying hard to get along, but it was all around him, and being what he did for a living, there's always people gonna offer you some, especially women. They always wanted to give him something. I, being the protective, fatherly promoter, always tried to intercept the drugs and take them on their behalf! (laughing) It's that lifestyle that nearly killed both of us. Wake up with a drink, do a snort of coke to get your heart started in the morning, and your day goes on into evening, and you get out of hand, you don't remember what you did, you wake up the next day with a drink and a snort to get over the guilt from the day before. It's a vicious circle.

"Real life with Steve was just kinda... nothing. Lots of music, watching TV and playing guitar. I'd sit around and listen to him playing guitar to 'The Rifleman' or something. There wasn't a whole lotta life there. You can laugh at it, but it's really kinda sad."

In October, Vicki bought Steve a pair of expensive brown leather dress shoes for his fifteenth birthday, something he desperately needed to look sharp on stage. She also gave him a silver pocketwatch on a chain, with custom engraving, that he carried with him faithfully for years. When Vicki would visit Steve at his house, they would sit and talk in his bedroom, adorned with black-light posters. Like most teenagers, he kept pretty sloppy quarters; clothes and records were strewn about, with guitars, strings, and a couple of amps stacked in the corner.

At the time, Vicki didn't even know he had a brother; he was never home. Jimmie was only eighteen, but was already weary from the pressure from his parents, from his school, from the society that didn't attempt to understand his greasy hair, shirts unbuttoned to the waist, and tight-fitting bell-bottom Levis. He dropped out of Oak Cliff Christian Academy, which was a joke anyway, married his girlfriend Donna, and before long they had a baby girl named Tina.

Jimmie's dissatisfaction was fed by lack of appreciation for the blues in Dallas, as longtime friend Mike "Cold Shot" Kindred told *Guitar World*: "In those days in Dallas, you either played the hits or you didn't play."

Vicki and Steve, still too young to drive, were forced to bum rides from friends everywhere they went; sometimes a date started and ended on the city bus. "I remember Steve and I went to the State Fair, and we got stranded after the buses stopped running. I had lost my glasses, and we had to look for them for hours. I ended up calling my mother at eleven o'clock at night to come pick us up. We did lots of stuff together, like going to see the Rolling Stones at SMU's Moody Coliseum, up in the nosebleed seats, I mean the very top row. Chuck Berry was the opening act, and we were both just in awe!" Neither of them suspected that Stevie Ray Vaughan would be the opening act some fifteen years later.

Vicki and Steve stayed friends after Steve developed a serious relationship with a schoolmate named Glenda Maples.

Jimmie split Dallas to head for the Hollywood dream in 1969. Photo by and courtesy of Burton Wilson.

Glenda was crazy about him, following him to gigs where she would dance like a dervish next to the stage all night long. She became his main squeeze, his first real girlfriend. Before Glenda, "love" usually amounted to an unrequited crush, a special friendship, or fooling around on the throw pillows at the Cellar.

By 1969, Storm had already seen its first complete personnel turnover; everybody left but Jimmie. He quickly recruited vocalist Paul Ray, who could shout the blues with the best of them although he was basically a slight little hippie with long hair. Doyle Bramhall came in on drums, and Jamie Bassett played bass. They decided to get out of Dallas and head for the Hollywood dream. Almost eighteen, Jimmie was ready to hit the road and did. Picking up his Strat, he slapped his initials on it, packed two bags and drove away dreaming of record deals and getting the band on stage at the legendary Whiskey-A-Go-Go. They played the gig, too—only they were fired after the first set and sent off with only the requiem "you guys are terrible!"

With Jimmie gone, Steve took to jamming all by himself. After school let out, Martha wouldn't see his face until dinnertime, when Big Jim would barge into his bedroom and bellow, "Take those goddamned nigger clothes off and get in here!"

"I was goin' through a deal where it was hard to get along with my father," Stevie later recalled. "I was tryin' to grow my hair out and stuff, all those things about growing up. Jimmie'd moved out, and I'm sure my parents thought they were going to lose their other son, too. So there was a lot of holdin' on, you know? Obviously I was gonna play music, too."

Then, while Steve was in the tenth grade, something happened that gave his parents some indication that maybe he would change his mind about playing "that damned guitar," as Big Jim always put it. He was accepted into an experimental arts program that held classes at Southern Methodist University.

"It was a night class, and it was just a few kids from around the city," he said. "It was completely wide open. We brought records and talked and worked. If you were working on a piece of sculpture and you decided to come in and smash it, you did it. If you wanted to look at it, you did that. The class was great. I learned a lot in it... but

it was on the nights when I was supposed to be rehearsing with the band."

Legend has it that Steve was playing the Adolphus Hotel in 1970 with Liberation, taking a rest between sets, when three young guys asked if they could play during the break. Their names were Billy Gibbons, Frank Beard, and Dusty Hill. Vaughan said sure, only knowing the characters vaguely, but after two songs he was begging to sit in with them. Swathed in the oversized sequin jacket (with ostrich feathers) that once belonged to Hendrix, young Steve jumped onstage and yelled out, "Let's do 'Thunderbird' by the Nitecaps!" He began to sing, perhaps for the first time ever onstage. The performance, by all accounts, was electrifying, and ZZ Top was so floored, they went on to record the song on their 1975 album, *Fandango*.

Storm returned to Dallas (on borrowed funds) in 1970, with its collective tail between its legs. The disgruntled musicians left one by one after the California debacle; Jimmie and Doyle were the only survivors. To support his new family, Jimmie took a day job at the City of Irving's sanitation department. "It was all I could get," he later explained.

Bramhall's work was nearly as demeaning; he got stuck digging ditches and laying pipe. Restless and eager to do something with their lives, Jimmie and Doyle took a weekend trip to Austin to check out the scene that was said to be

Stevie (seated) with Cast of Thousands, 1971. Mike McCullough is second from left. Courtesy of Robert Ware.

developing. It was even better than they had been told. They came back with renewed enthusiasm, and although Doyle wasn't quite ready to leave home, Jimmie couldn't make tracks fast enough. He came home and told Donna with wide eyes about this place where you could have long hair and not get beat up, play any kind of music you wanted, make money,

The 1971 Sunset High yearbook captured the night Stevie was kicked out of the Musicians' Guild jam. Here, he plays the Telecaster guitar. Jimmie's gold-top Les Paul guitar (borrowed for the evening) sits in the corner. Stevie autographed the photo in later years. Courtesy of David Brown.

then go spend it all on barbecue and beer. Donna wasn't crazy about the idea, so Jimmie went alone. They filed for divorce and Jimmie agreed to let her keep Tina. "I saved some money and moved to Austin," Jimmie explains, "because I knew that I could play the blues down there."

Liberation broke up around Christmas, and Stevie floated around until he put together a band with Kimball schoolmates called Cast Of Thousands. Mike McCullough was the group's second guitarist. "We hung out a lot together, because we had all the same friends," McCullough later said. "He used to come down to the music department and play guitar with me in the little practice rooms. I found out later he was really hiding out, cutting class, and that was about the only place where they'd never find him! Cast Of Thousands was really a fictitious band made up for that local record, *A New Hi*. It was really short-lived."

A New Hi was produced and compiled by a man named John Bothwell, who visited local high schools in 1971, looking to record young bands that he thought showed potential. He had an irritating habit of calling everyone "Tiger," while he coached them through their first studio experience at Tempo Two Recording. Steve, albeit shy and in need of a tone, played some smokin' stuff on the two cuts included from Cast Of Thousands. Bothwell made a deal with the Sunset High School Musicians' Guild to promote and sell the record, donating a dollar from each disc sold to the organization.

Robert Ware was the founder and president of the Sunset Musicians' Guild, and remembers the record selling "about twenty-eight copies" upon its initial release. In the back of the 1971 Sunset yearbook, all the Guild's members, real and fictitious, were listed, including names like

Eric Clapton, Jeff Beck, and Frank Zappa. "We just kinda made it up!" Ware admits with a laugh. Also on that page is a picture of a 17-year-old Steve Vaughan, burning it up on bass. The picture depicts the night of a Musicians' Guild jam at Sunset. Steve had phoned Rocky Athas and practically begged Rocky to take him along.

"But Steve, we go to Kimball," Rocky said.

"Come on," Steve pleaded. "They know us. Borrow your brother's car and come get me!"

"They're not gonna let us innnn...," Rocky warned. Steve still wouldn't give, and Rocky was over to pick him up in less than an hour.

When Rocky arrived at the Vaughan house, Steve was playing a very warped copy of the Beatles' *Rubber Soul* album on the turntable. He greeted Rocky holding a 1952 Les Paul gold top guitar that Rocky knew didn't belong to him. He noticed that Jimmie was home for a visit and figured it must be his.

"Ever seen one of these?" Steve asked.

"God, that's *really* ugly! Let me see it," Rocky said.

Steve literally tossed the guitar across the room to Rocky, but a large wooden bedpost intercepted it, and a loud crack followed.

"What was that noise, Steve?" Jimmie yelled from the kitchen.

"Uh, nothing, Jim," Steve stammered. The boys were in the room terrified, hands over their mouths, eyes bulging wide at their mistake. They immediately checked for damage to the instrument. It was indeed hurt. Rather than show it to Jimmie and get pounded, Steve opted to take the guitar with him to the jam without a case.

"We got to the door of the jam," Rocky remembers, "and Robert Ware is standing there saying 'You guys go to Kimball. Get out of here!' So we're standing outside, feeling all dejected, and Steve's eyes lit up. He said 'Let's see if we can just take this amp in.' It was this six-ten Silvertone amp. Old thing. So Robert went for it. He said that only one of us could come in, but Steve managed to push his way in, too. He could be very bold when he wanted to be, even then. So he's making his way through the crowd, running into people with this guitar—Jimmie's guitar—kept bumping into things and nicking the finish. Oh, God, it was hilarious."

Thinking back to that night, Robert Ware shakes his head. "I guess that's my claim to fame. I kicked Stevie Ray Vaughan out of a jam session," he chuckles.

"That was a real interesting night," Athas intercedes. "Once we finally got in, I was tuning my guitar by the side of the stage, and the announcer goes, 'Well, that's all the time we have for tonight, folks,' and I'm frustrated as hell. They let us in, but they wouldn't let us jam. Steve said 'To hell with that!' and he just jumped up onstage and played a number all by himself. He was burnin', too! Those guys are yelling for him to quit from the side of the stage, but the crowd was really digging it, so he just kept playing, and on, and on! He just looked at them as if to say 'No. I won't quit playing, and you can't stop me!' We recorded that night... I've been looking for that tape ever since."

After the boys had been kicked out the second time, a hippie approached Steve and Rocky and asked if they knew where he could get some grass. Steve, revealing his naivete, pointed at the ground and said "Right over there," with that goofy, gummy grin spread wide across his face.

"Naw, man," the hippie admonished. "The smoking kind."

"Oh." Stevie meekly replied. "In all honesty, I don't think he knew what grass was then," Rocky says now.

Not surprisingly, Steve used most of his gig earnings that semester to Jimmie to pay for the Les Paul he damaged that night.

❖

Steve Vaughan's old bandmates gathered together some twenty-three years later at the Hard Rock Cafe in Dallas to look back on those wonder years and swap stories.

Mike McCullough: "Steve wasn't in the music programs at Kimball, didn't take music, couldn't read music. I was the one with all the training. He did substitute for me in lab band for about a week after I quit. Since he couldn't sight-read, he didn't last long. I remember he used to borrow my guitar, and then tell me how shitty it was. It was a Trini Lopez, and like kids do, I'd say, 'Well, if you don't like it, why don't you go borrow somebody else's?' We saw each other every day in high school. I'd hang out at his house a lot; his room was real junky. You couldn't find anything in there. (laughter) Looking for something was like an archaeological dig, man; there was the junior high strata, and then the tenth grade layer. It was an obstacle course!"

David Brown: "In junior high, Steve wore these Beatle boots, and we all wondered where he got them. They were so cool, and we were envious. He had a bad crush on my sister Alice—they were in school together, and—she couldn't stand him. Because if you knew Steve then... (unanimous laughter) ...what would you call him?"

McCullough: "A dick!" (more laughter)

Athas: "Steve did have a real sharp mouth when he was young. I mean, if he didn't like what you were doing, he'd call bullshit."

McCullough: "Later on, I saw him play at Oak Cliff Country Club with some band. They had this big stage, with a riser and everything. So he's up there, playing away, standing on the riser, and then all of a sudden, he's gone. Just disappeared real fast. And then I noticed these two feet sticking up. He had fallen off, and continued to play the rest of the guitar solo on his back. I mean, you had to laugh. All people could see were his feet. He must have been embarrassed, but after the song, he jumped right back up and kept playing, looking around like nothing happened."

Brown: "When Steve used to play the Cellar, he always had to wear a hat to cover his face and make him look older. I think that's actually where the hat thing began. The Cellar. Man (deep sigh) ...that place. They had all these pillows on the floor...."

McCullough: "Yeah, dirty pillows! Then, you'd be playing along and this girl comes out and starts taking off her clothes, and of course, you're fourteen years old and losing it. Your guitar playing sure went to hell in a handbasket real quick! They had all these little dancing girls and messages on the wall in black light, like 'LIVE spelled backwards is EVIL.' They served near-alcohol and had this echoplex unit that would drive you crazy—even if you weren't on acid!"

Brown: "For a while there, me and Steve had a band called the Meat. I don't really want to explain the significance of Meat, but let's just say that Stevie made it up, if that tells you anything. This was late 1968. We played the Battle of the Bands at Eagle Lincoln-Mercury on Lemmon Avenue and we lost. (laughs) We were playing all this stuff off the first Zeppelin album, like 'I Can't Quit You, Babe' and 'Communication Breakdown.' One thing about playing with Steve was that if you got the lead ride, keep it as long as you could, because once he got his turn, he would just go on forever. There was no stopping him!

"Later on, guitar became a real competitive thing between all of us. Like, if you didn't know certain songs, you couldn't play. So we'd all get together and try and learn songs. Well, when Steve would learn a real good lick, he'd always turn to the wall and try not to show us what he was doing. Used to piss us off! And *I* was the one who showed *him* 'Jeff's Boogie'! All the other guitar players were like 'Naw, don't show him. Let him learn the hard way, man. He won't show us anything.' But, I taught him all I could."

❖❖❖

Steve could plainly see that his fabulous Oak Cliff scene was steadily dissolving. All the cool clubs, like Candy's Flare and the Cellar, were closing—blues and psychedelia were going out of style and would be replaced by hard rock and progressive country. The only other gigs left in Dallas were Top 40. Besides, most of his friends had graduated, married and had children. They had found some level of respectability, through a job, church, or other influence. In addition, the atmosphere in Oak Cliff was changing drastically; the burglary rate had skyrocketed, forcing many families to say goodbye to the old neighborhood and split up lifelong friendships.

In 1970, Steve bought his first Stratocaster, a '63 Maple Neck, and formed Blackbird, his first "real band"—as he called it—with Christian Plicque on vocals, David Frame on bass, Roddy Colonna on drums, and Noel Deis on keyboards. The band patterned itself after two of Stevie's favorite bands at the time: Hank Ballard and the Midnighters and Johnny G and The G-Men. "Blackbird went through so many different people, like one of those springboard deals," Stevie recalled. "We would play with someone until the energy was gone and before it was a really deadbeat thing, we would have sense enough to go ahead and change members so we could keep it fresh. It was a real neat growing experience."

Blackbird played loud and hard, and for once, Steve Vaughan was in a position to strut his stuff, peeling paint off the walls of clubs like the Zodiac with his two Marshalls cranked up to ten. He let Christian do most of the singing, but performed at least one song a night, usually Cream's version of "Crossroads." As the band's calendar started filling up with gigs, they hired John Hoff as a second drummer and Kim Davis on second guitar. Often the band would venture to Austin for gigs at Castle Creek and Mother Blues, or the Cheatham Street Warehouse in nearby San Marcos. The crowds seemed so free there, so totally uninhibited and into the music, hanging on every note they played. He liked this place, liked it a lot, as a matter of fact.

The shit was getting thick at Kimball High School. Steve had been going round and round with Principal W.P. Durrett since day one over the length of his hair. School rules decreed that boys' haircuts be off the collar and over the ears. Steve complied for as long as he could, but he soon got tired of letting someone else tell him how to look. He cut his hair very short in the back, leaving outrageously long bangs in front to cover his face, but the principal was still on his case. At the start of his twelfth-grade year, the last straw came in the ongoing war with Kimball administration, prompting Steve to drop out.

"The principal was announcing over the P.A. system that if I didn't pay my locker fees I couldn't get my diploma," Steve later recalled. "I only stayed seven more weeks. Besides, it was just too hard staying awake for classes that started at seven-fifteen A.M. after playing in the bars until six A.M. sometimes. See, I woulda graduated in '72, but I'd already been playing the Cellar for a year or two, and over at the Ali Baba and the Funky Monkey and the Fog, and I thought I was just too cool for school. I just began to realize that the schools I was going to cared more about how I looked and the way my hair grew. They weren't *teaching* me anything. I had already learned a lot on my own."

Jimmie had also quit his last year of school. Steve, just like Jimmie, had ditched so much school that he probably would have had to put in an extra year in order to graduate. The idea of staying in school even another day drove Steve nuts. In fact, he was absent so much of his junior year that several of his classmates at Justin F. Kimball High School contacted in later years didn't know who he was or remember anyone by that name. A few alumni have good memories of the shy, often outcast young Vaughan.

"That was a pretty confusing time," says

classmate Janie Paleschic, thirty-six, who was the editor of Kimball's 1972 yearbook. "Out of a senior class of seven hundred, only five hundred or so stuck around to graduate. I also went to Stockard Junior High with the brothers. We grew up arguing about who was better on guitar—Jimmie or Stevie." (Paleschic later became an editor at *The Dallas Morning News* and is now assistant business editor at *The Los Angeles Times*.)

By this time, people began to recognize him as "Stevie." He had wanted the nickname to stick years earlier, but his schoolmates, girlfriends and other musicians never quite got hip to it. He was starting to find his own identity with Blackbird, and now, without school to deal with, he could be whoever he wanted to be.

A few weeks later, he was paid a visit backstage by Christian Brooks, who by now was deeply into the Baptist church and wasn't coming around much anymore. Christian, who had always bordered on the straight-laced, was appalled at the behavior he witnessed that day. "Everybody was just trashed on drugs, all these people I knew from high school. I found myself being alienated from the group; I guess I wasn't cool enough to hang with them because I refused the drugs. I simply chose not to go that way, so I left the scene. I didn't see any future in it. Sure, I did my share of drugs in the sixties, but these guys scared me, this shooting up speed business when you're fourteen years old. I mean, that's crazy, you know? Needles? You *have* to shoot up before you play?" That was the last time he would see Stevie Vaughan until 1986.

Hillbillies from Outer Space

AUSTIN, TEXAS, has been called the Gay Place (dubbed such by novelist Billy Lee Brammer, another Oak Cliff boy) because of its unexplainable way of attracting politicians and poets; intellectuals, musicians, artists, and writers; and other assorted eccentrics since it was first designated as the state capital in 1839. Among the more distinguished (and often infamous) residents over the years are names like John and Alan Lomax (who recorded blues legends like Leadbelly, Muddy Waters, and Son House for The Library Of Congress), Water Prescott Webb, William Sidney Porter (or O. Henry, as he was better known), John Henry Faulk, Lavada Durst (a.k.a. "Dr. Hepcat," the piano-tinkling, jive-talking disc jockey who made his indelible

mark by being the first black deejay in the Southwest), and former U.S. President Lyndon Baines Johnson, perhaps the most widely recognized example of Austin's charisma and balls-to-the-wall politics.

The city has boasted a bevy of musical talent, from jazz greats Gene Ramey and Teddy Wilson, bluesmen Pee Wee Crayton and Robert Shaw, renegade country pickers like Willie Nelson, Jerry Jeff Walker, and Michael Martin Murphey to rockers Doug Sahm and The Sir Douglas Quintet, the 13th Floor Elevators, and Janis Joplin.

Austin's reputation has always been one of acceptance; embracing misfits, rebels and losers who just didn't fit anywhere else (except in poor Janis' case—she was dubbed "the ugliest man on

1970 poster promoting Storm's first Austin appearance. Art by and courtesy of Lew Stokes.

gressive Blues Experiment LP there. That's exactly what was going down at the Vulcan every night of the week: black and white Texas kids were coming together to revel in the fashion explosion, blues, and LSD.

The Vulcan was erected in five short weeks on a lot in seedy downtown Austin in 1967, and quickly gained a national reputation as a freaky free-for-all, scandalizing the Austin establishment. The acts that played there most often were those the management could afford: bands like the 13th Floor Elevators, Shiva's Headband, Conqueroo, black blues singers like Mance Lipscomb, Lightnin' Hopkins, Sonny Terry, Brownie McGhee, and Big Joe Williams. If a band had a slow night at the Vulcan, they were lucky to make gas money back home, which was the case more often than most bands might have liked to admit. Several top national acts like Janis Joplin, the Velvet Underground, and Moby Grape lent the Vulcan their support by performing in this smaller-than-usual venue, giving credibility to Austin's growing reputation as a musical mecca.

Back across the Colorado River, more bands were springing up from the deep "black bottom" of East Austin, but something was very different about this scene. Fresh-faced college kids ventured to these clubs to drink in the blues—and even wilder yet, white musicians were meshing onstage with hardened Texas bluesmen who had seen it all. That certainly attracted Bill Campbell, a slightly older guitar man from Dallas who was often spotted picking with Mance Lipscomb and Blues Boy Hubbard at Charley's Playhouse on East Eleventh. Down the

campus" by her University of Texas classmates). This freewheeling atmosphere encourages art, finding nothing too shocking or taboo—in fact, anything mainstream is vehemently spat upon.

Jimmie's best friend during his earliest days in Austin was Denny Freeman, who had been nicknamed "The Professor" for his vast knowledge of blues lore. "Even though I didn't know them (Jimmie and Doyle) that well in Dallas, right after we all got to town, they both came over and said, 'Let's play,'" Freeman recalls. "After I started playing with Jimmie, I realized, 'This kid is serious about a blues band.' He really turned my head around that somebody could be this serious about playing hard-core blues—not just an assortment of R&B songs."

Denny quickly hipped the newcomer to what was happening; white people were cool in Austin's east side blues clubs, long hair was outtasight and the barbecue was the best down at Sam's around 4 A.M. The IL club on East Eleventh Street was where they found Otis Lewis, behind a set of drums at a late-night jam session. The cat was slinky and they needed him. Otis jumped on board, bringing Lewis Cowdrey along for the ride. Storm arrived at a club called Flight 505 for the week of May 14–19, 1970, charging into Austin with all their might.

Storm moved on to another temporary home at the ultrahip Vulcan Gas Company, at 316 Congress Avenue, which Johnny Winter had just immortalized by recording his *Pro-*

Early Storm publicity photo. Jimmie is third from right. Photo by and courtesy of Burton Wilson.

block at the Victory Grill, James Polk and The Brothers were getting it together with a young white sister named Angela Strehli.

A few months later, Angela met W.C. Clark, a native of Austin who had just returned from a lengthy hiatus playing guitar with Joe Tex. He had a divine voice, a sweet soulful croon so reminiscent of Sam Cooke and Al Green. They took to each other immediately, and decided to "hook up a thang" with Denny Freeman. Denny recruited his rhythm section from the Hard Times Band. Andy Miller took the drum slot, Alex Napier held down the bass, and Southern Feeling was born.

Meanwhile, Storm was going through some heavy changes. Again, everybody but Jimmie and Lewis split for various reasons. Jimmie wanted to pursue the band with Lewis; he liked the way Lewis could sing like Slim Harpo (no small feat). Cowdrey was a lean, lanky, nutty frontman—the kind you couldn't help but notice. This shaggy blonde mop-topped, baby-faced kid was attached to a 6½-foot frame, blowing one loud blues harp and dancing about the stage like a man possessed. Jamie Bassett was replaced by Danny Galindo on bass, the great Otis Lewis was soon bumped for Freddie "Pharaoh" Walden on drums, and Storm rolled on.

Shirley Beeman, Jimmie's friend since the Chessmen days, soon moved from Dallas to Austin, following in the footsteps of him and friends Denny Freeman, Paul Ray, Doyle Bramhall. She rented a house out on Manchaca Road, but most of her time was spent hanging out with Jimmie at his South Congress home. She religiously attended Storm's Monday night gig at the One Knite, an unconventional new club that opened up a few blocks away from the Vulcan, and also offered blues as the main course.

In the months that followed, a flurry of sidemen rotated through Storm. Among them was Mike Kindred on keyboards and Keith Ferguson on bass, who went on to become a founding Thunderbird. They primarily played Austin's most notorious nitespots like the One Knite ("The dive where all your dreams come true" its T-shirt proclaimed), Rolling Hills, and the Hungry Horse. It was a long, hard climb, but the Storm, especially Jimmie and Lewis, began to receive some hard-earned respect.

In the summer of 1970, the Armadillo World Headquarters opened its doors in Austin at 501 Barton Springs Road. Next door was the old Austin Sportscenter, a skating rink/basketball arena that housed the birth of rock and roll in town on an August night in 1955 when Horace Logan stepped up to the "Louisiana Hayride" radio microphone and announced to the world: "Ladies and gentlemen, Elvis Presley!" There was no better spot for the Armadillo to again change the face of music in Texas.

The gargantuan warehouse was not as visually exciting as the Vulcan, save for a mural on the wall that depicted Freddie King in agonizing guitar play while an Armadillo burst from his chest, splattering blood. (Freddie King also recorded the 1975 album *Bigger Than Life* here.) That first year the South Austin enterprise appeared particularly ill-fated, but it survived due to the tenacity of its founders, who were obsessed with the dream of maintaining a community center for artistic expression.

The Armadillo World Headquarters grew in acceptance, if not profitability, and became known as the only place to see the unique blends of music it offered, which included everyone from Tom T. Hall to Frank Zappa and The Mothers of Invention. The 'Dillo was soon flooded with calls from international booking agents whose artists had heard about the wild audiences and wanted to play there. Soon Austin was swarming with visiting rock stars, their groupies and henchmen, mixing and mingling with the locals. Through the interest of a curious national press and word-of-mouth communication between touring musicians, Austin gained acclaim almost overnight as one of the most exciting centers of musical activity in the country.

Although the Armadillo catered mostly to cosmic cowboys like Willie Nelson, Michael Martin Murphey, Kinky Friedman, Jerry Jeff Walker, and Leon Russell, the occasional blues band found its way to the 'Dillo's stage. By the time Storm had a gig there, they had again done a thorough housecleaning. Lewis, Keith, and Jimmie were still around, but Paul Ray returned to the band on bass, singing less than he used to, taking a back seat to the sweeter vocals of Doyle Bramhall, who was now back on the drummer's throne.

The Christmas of 1971 brought Jimmie home to Dallas for the holidays, and Stevie picked his brain nonstop about the bustling music town down south that Stevie felt was calling his name. While Jimmie was in Dallas, he visited a local club and fixed his eyes upon a beautiful young redhead standing across the room. A little drunk, he stumbled up to her and gave her a big hug and kiss, thinking she sure looked a lot like his cousin Connie Trent. The girl, horrified at first, turned to

"THE YEAR WAS 1972. I WAS A HIGH SCHOOL DROP-OUT DETERMINED TO MAKE MUSIC MY LIFE."

"MY BROTHER JIMMIE WAS PLAYING SOME *DANGEROUS* BLUES GUITAR IN AUSTIN."

AUSTIN 100 miles

"I FIGURED IT WAS TIME TO JOIN HIM."

Frame from a cartoon strip titled "The Rise of Stevie Ray Vaughan," which appeared in *Guitar World*'s Fall 1992 SRV tribute issue. Written by Brad Tolinski, art by Stanley Shaw, lettering by Richard Howell, and edited by Harold Steinblatt. Courtesy of *Guitar World*.

31

slap Jimmie when she realized who it was. He recognized her, too; it was his old teenage sweetheart Connie Crouch. Now that he was available, Connie wasted no time in following him back to Austin.

Stevie was itching to get the hell out of Dallas. The cops made him paranoid, the rednecks wanted to beat him up, and the music scene was going nowhere. One night after a Blackbird gig at the Player's Lounge, Stevie and Mitch Mullins were listening to the club's manager rave on about how he thought the band really had star potential, and how he was going to send them to Las Vegas dressed in matching polyester jumpsuits. Stevie had heard enough; he flew out of his seat and exclaimed, "Mitch, get me out of here!"

"So I said, without any hesitation, 'Let's go!'," Mullins recalls. "I told him that if he really wanted to see what was happening in Austin, if he wanted to go for a while, that I'd drive. I wanted to open that door for him, because honestly, Dallas was making us both miserable. He saw his destiny in Jimmie when he would come home to Dallas and tell Stevie all about this cool place where he was living."

Stevie made arrangements for Blackbird to play a gig at the Rolling Hills Club, and decided that he was going to stay in Austin before he even arrived on that New Years' Eve of 1971. Blackbird spent the night sleeping on top of the pool tables, which became their beds for the next few weeks.

"It was great," Stevie later remembered in an interview with *Guitar World*. "A friend of mine owned the place. I slept on the pool table, the stage, the floor, whatever the weather permitted. And to tell you the truth, those were some of my favorite times. I didn't have a dime, but who cares? I was doing what I wanted and around good people and there was *always* good music.

Mitch Mullins had stayed with him through the move, and his collection of cool cars made him very popular with the band. They would cruise around town, showing off in his cream-puff '64 Cutlass, and for nights at Rolling Hills, they earned their keep by delivering kegs of beer in Mitch's '57 Chevy truck. Mitch was appointed official band chauffeur and valet, so Stevie could look out the windows as they drove around the hilly, winding roads of Austin. His eyes grew wide as he witnessed real-life hippies, dressed in long caftans adorned with bangles and beads, walking the streets of Austin barefoot. Dallas was never like this. "I was trying to figure out 'Hey, what's happening here? How are these people getting away with all this? This is the capital. Where are the police?'" Stevie later said. He could go out to Hippie Hollow on Lake Travis and watch the thin, nude girls swimming and tanning, and maybe even follow suit. For a boy who hadn't seen much outside of the Oak Cliff city limits, Austin looked like heaven on earth.

Soon after moving to Austin, Stevie was sitting in with Storm at the IL Club on East Eleventh Street. That was the night Denny Freeman, a friend of the brothers since the sixties, noticed that little Stevie was really kicking ass on guitar. "I was *impressed*," Denny later remembered. "Here was this little white kid that I never paid much attention to, playing the blues the way it ought to be played. I was thinking, '*This is not your ordinary guitar player*. We'll be hearing more of this guy.'"

Jimmie Vaughan was with Denny at the IL Club that night and was shocked and amazed at how good little brother had become on his guitar. "I hadn't heard him play in a couple of years. He just walked onstage and started playing like he'd been doing it forever. Last time I saw him, it's like—he was still struggling with it, you know? But he stood up there and smoked that first night in Austin," Jimmie later raved to *Guitar Player*. "At that moment, I knew he was gonna be famous."

With no real friends to speak of in Austin, Stevie had nothing better to do than follow his big brother around to every gig, which was a nuisance to Jimmie. Stevie would get drunk and go apeshit watching Jimmie play; he'd stand on his chair and yell encouragement at the top of his lungs. Stevie pestered his big brother to come see him in Blackbird, and sometimes Jimmie would begrudgingly oblige, only to tell Stevie he sucked and that he shouldn't try so hard to play the guitar—"Don't fight with it, Stevie, it should roll out naturally," Jimmie coached. Stevie remembered Jimmie telling him to relax and say what was in his soul, not to be so damned overanxious, to turn down a little, to leave that rock and roll shit out, and to play the blues. These were words he'd heard before.

The winter of 1972 was one of the coldest in Austin's history, but it didn't seem to matter much to Stevie, hardly eighteen, who likened it all to a camping trip. He moved from couch to floor, occasionally bunking up for the night with a female admirer, although his affections were still with Glenda. Knowing his roving, lusty Libra ways, Glenda wisely followed Stevie to Austin to keep her eyes on him. Glenda, Stevie, and the rest of Blackbird got a house together in South Austin for $30 each. "That didn't last too long," Stevie laughed. "Couple of months, anyway; God, every month there was someone new in the band."

"Stevie didn't care about making money then," says Mitch Mullins. "Neither of us did. So what if we were just playing small clubs? If we made the bar tab and maybe a little change, we were doing good. If we earned a few dollars to eat tonight, we were happy. We didn't worry about what we were gonna do next weekend, or the next gig, for that matter."

Tensions rose within the band. The pressure of being new in town, unknown, broke and hungry was just too much for most of Blackbird, and they headed back to Dallas. Stevie stayed behind, and soon found himself desperate for a paying gig. He needed to eat, didn't have a band and the thought of a day job made him wince. Connie Trent and Vicki Virnelson came to his rescue one night, bringing with them a carload of groceries, and took him out on the town. Connie was his angel, Stevie would say as the years passed. She was always there for him when he really needed someone—a family member who understood the screwed-up relationships kids have with their parents—and yet, she loved him for who and what he was, expecting no more than what he wanted to give. Seeing Connie and spending a few hours with her was great therapy for him, especially when he was troubled.

One night he stopped into a jam at a funky little bar (the Lamplite) on East Sixth Street to meet Jimmie, who promised to introduce him to some musicians. He met Natalie Zoe, a saucy brunette who could sing like an angel and play the guitar to boot. "I remember we all played together, Jimmie, Stevie, and me," Zoe says, "and we did some old Jimmy Reed tunes. I was in love with Jimmie's playing—even then, he had the touch, you know?—but back then, I didn't think Stevie was anything remarkable. Neither one of them would sing, so it was all up to me. We played all night long to a grand total of four people!"

Stevie, Mitch, and Cutter had been hanging out at the Krackerjack house a lot lately, a big two-story place on Sixteenth Street where the entire band lived and practiced. Stevie was finally getting to know Tommy Shannon, who he considered a sanctified minister of the blues/rock gospel. Hell, Shannon had played Woodstock, and had seen the world with Johnny Winter, who Stevie was convinced was the Lord God Almighty. It didn't matter that Winter fired Tommy because of drug busts and skirmishes with the cops, or that Winter had nicknamed Tommy "The Slut"—Stevie was honored to have Shannon's friendship. Rumors were flying that guitarist Jesse Taylor was going to leave Krackerjack, and Stevie was ripe, joining the band with Roddy Colonna, who replaced Uncle John Turner on drums. The Krackerjack gig wasn't built to last; they were moving in the direction of glam rock, complete with makeup and platform boots, a notion that Stevie found absolutely hideous. Shannon had to leave the band after he got popped for possession of LSD, because the judge insisted that he stop playing music for two years.

Stevie wasn't squeaky clean by any stretch of the imagination; he certainly didn't dabble when it came to drugs—he plunged right in. Speed, in any form, was a particular favorite. He could take it and play guitar for hours, never getting tired, his overworked brain producing ideas as fast as his fingers could work them out in an endless stream of furious licks. The guitar would speak for him: it could cuss for him when he was angry, tell ghost stories of Hendrix and Robert Johnson, and might actually arouse his heart's yearnings, speaking sweet words and emitting primal, amorous sounds when they were alone together. Hendrix called it "Praying through the guitar." Stevie took it one step further—the guitar was no longer just a communication line to heaven above—the guitar *was* heaven, delivering urgent messages through Stevie's channel. Stevie treated the guitar as if it were alive, talking to it, stroking it like a lover, and even sleeping with it.

Marc Benno arrived in Austin in late 1972 to make his fourth record for A&M. A principal songwriter for the Dixie Flyers, Rita Coolidge, and Leon Russell, Benno had a dream of making a blues record and wanted to do it deep in the heart of Texas. Sadly, his lead guitarist Charlie Freeman died of a heroin overdose while in Austin in January 1973. Benno called Jimmie Vaughan and asked him to join his group, the Nightcrawlers. Jimmie politely declined, preferring to play "real" blues with Storm, but strongly suggested that Benno go and hear his little brother. He took the recommendation and ventured over to Mother Earth, where Little Stevie was reportedly bringing the roof down. Before the night was over, Stevie had a gig—a damn good one. A&M's major bucks promised to set him up good on the rent for a while, and he even got an all-expenses-paid trip to Hollywood to make a bonafide album.

First the record company bought them all new backline equipment, put them on a salary plus per diems, and secured some lucrative high-exposure gigs opening for the J. Geils Band and Humble Pie. The band then consisted of Stevie, Doyle Bramhall, Billy Etheridge on keyboards and Bruce "B.C." Miller on bass, all Texas hippies getting their first real taste of the really big time. In April 1973, A&M flew them to Los Angeles to record at Sunset Sound, settling them in a posh hotel right down the boulevard. It was during these sessions that Stevie and Doyle wrote and recorded their first song together, "Dirty Pool" (which later appeared on *Texas Flood*). The rest of Stevie's contribution to the album is fairly unremarkable, probably because Benno asked him to clean up his tone, play sweeter licks, and basically sound like any other L.A. session cat. Unfortunately (or fortunately, depending on how you look at it), A&M hated the record, and promptly fired the Nightcrawlers. Marc Benno remained in Los Angeles, starting all over again. Stevie's heart was broken; he'd blown it.

The Nightcrawlers miraculously stayed together through the ordeal, having only to replace the bass player with Keith Ferguson (who defected from Storm—a move that surely made Jimmie's skin crawl) and adding Drew Pennington on lead vocals and harmonica. The band took up residency at the One Knite, a grey stone building located at Eighth and Red River with a coffin for a front door that warned Abandon Hope All Ye Who Enter Here.

Danny Thorpe had been trying to talk Stevie into getting a new guitar. He had known Stevie since 1971, when Stevie stopped into Ray Hennig's Heart of Texas Music store in Waco to shop around. They struck up a quick friendship. "There used to be a pretty hip club there called the Abraxas," he remembers. "I first heard him play there with Blackbird, and Stevie was playing this ugly Firebird guitar out of a Marshall stack! He was young, probably seventeen or eighteen, and… well, he was just different. You could tell that he was going to be great, even then. He just had that spark. But I *did* try to sell him another guitar!"

Stevie finally took him up on the invitation in the summer of 1973, driving back from a Nightcrawlers gig in Dallas, and stopped at the music store. Today would be the day he met his number-one Stratocaster. "I saw this '59 Strat hanging in the window," Stevie told *Guitar World*. "I didn't even have to play it—I just knew by the way it looked that it would sound great. I was carrying my '63 Strat, and asked if he wanted to trade. Thank God he did, and it's been my main axe ever since. The guitar was officially put out in 1962, but the neck has a '59 stamp on it. There was also a sticker under the bass pickup that read 'L.F., '59'. I think Leo Fender put it together with spare parts and issued it in '62. But to me it doesn't really matter; all I know is I've never found another one like it. The neck is shaped differently from the others. It's a D-neck, but it's oddly shaped—it's real, real big, and fits my hand like a glove."

Margaret Moser (now a senior editor at *The Austin Chronicle*) was around the scene quite a bit then, having landed her first newspaper job as an office cleaner and occasional listings compiler at the *Austin Sun*, the city's only alternative paper in the spring of 1973. "I must have been about nineteen or twenty, and Stevie would have been the same age," Moser recalls. "It was a good time to be young and in love with the blues… For me, fun was hitting the One Knite as often as possible. There were other good clubs around Austin at the time—the Black Queen, Alexander's, La Cucaracha, Flight 505, and of course, the Arma-

Albert King— Stevie's "spiritual godfather." Photo by Lisa M. Hill.

dillo... I lived for nights at the One Knite. I especially lived for seeing Stevie Vaughan in the Nightcrawlers."

The Nightcrawlers—what better name for this motley crew with long, greasy locks and beer-soiled shirts? They had about every Tuesday booked at the One Knite in '73 and '74, sandwiched in between Storm on Mondays, Paul Ray and The Cobras on Wednesdays, and Otis Lewis and the Cotton Kings on Thursdays.

"He was Little Stevie Vaughan then," says Moser. "The Look, however, was already there. Hunched over that Strat that was beat-up looking even then, eyes screwed closed and fingers doing the fast slide from Texas blues to rock and roll, the Nightcrawlers covered the ground the way a good bar band should. I don't think I thought of him in terms of 'that boy's gonna be a star,' but I was absolutely galvanized by his performance on that tiny stage.

"Stevie always had to try harder on everything. He wasn't as tough as Jimmie and he wasn't as old as Jimmie. You know, there was always that rivalry there, and... well, there was no love for each other back then. You can see it in the Sixth Street photo shoot we did later; it was nearly impossible to get them to pose together, because they were not getting along at all. Jimmie had the rep in this town, and Stevie was kind of the scrapper, you know. Jimmie had the rich girlfriend; Stevie was sleeping on everybody else's couch. Jimmie was king of Austin, and Stevie was the pretender to the crown, or so it was perceived. Jimmie was a really economical player, and Stevie was all over the neck of the guitar... whichever one was, the other wasn't."

During a particularly dead gig at the One Knite, Stevie heard that Albert King was playing the Armadillo. King was to play in place of Bobby Bland, who was in the hospital. When Stevie heard

Albert was due to play that night, he packed up his gear and announced his intent to spend the rest of the evening soaking in the master's music, telling the crowd "if you've got any brains, you will too!"

"There were only about 75 people there when Albert played," Stevie recalled in an interview with *Guitar World*, "but every single person was there for Albert King, so the vibe was really happening. During the show, I went behind a PA stack and stood on this table right beside the stage. I just stared at him, you know? Part way through the show, he takes his mike stand and walks over to the side of the stage, plants his mike stand and just stood there singing and playing to me the rest of the night. He didn't know me from Adam. I mean, here was this little kid, all of eighteen. I guess I yelled right or something, 'cause he really took a liking to me. After he finished playing, he walked over to me, handed me his guitar, and shook my hand. I was like, stunned. I'll never forget that evening. There wasn't very many of us there, but he gave us everything he had."

Stevie was a wild beast in the Nightcrawlers, often going off on Hendrix medleys and stumping his bandmates, who were doing everything they could to play songs they didn't know. He certainly pissed off as many people as he impressed with his fiery licks and coke-fiend nervous manner. Eddie Stout, a local Austin musician, once aptly summed up the difference between the Vaughan brothers' approaches: "Jimmie makes love to you the way he plays, but Stevie just throws you down and rapes you."

Kathy Murray was an aspiring blues singer herself when she first heard the Vaughan brothers play. "That was the first time I had ever seen live music in my life...fall, 1972," Murray warmly recalls. "The Nightcrawlers at the Armadillo... Storm was on the bill too, with Lewis Cowdrey and Jimmie, along with the early Cobras: Paul Ray, Alex Napier, Rodney Craig, and Denny Freeman. The place was far from full, even with all three bands, but they were getting a great response. I remember Paul Ray getting on the mike and shouting, '*Don't tell me they don't like the blues in Austin, Texas!*' That cosmic cowboy thing was really riding high then, but that night changed my life, my younger brother David's, too.... We thought the Nightcrawlers wrote all those blues songs, you know?"

Kathy's brother David Murray was still learning the guitar, and immediately attached himself to Stevie's side, trying to pick up every trick he could from the guitar virtuosos who David had a hard time believing was his same age. After all, Stevie played with all the knowledge, skill, and feel of an old bluesman. Stevie couldn't help but feel flattered by his new friend's unceasing barrage of technical questions. The two spent days on end together, Stevie teaching him B.B. and Albert King signature licks. It was the first time Stevie had been asked to instruct someone else, and it felt good. To Stevie, David was like the little brother he never had.

Shirley Beeman was always Jimmie's friend, but grew closer to Stevie. Jimmie brought Shirley to Alexander's (inside an old Arco gas station on Brodie Lane) to see the Nightcrawlers in 1974. "I think we may have dropped some acid that night," she laughs, "and *that* was our first encounter! Unfortunately, none of us remember it very well!"

About this time, the Soap Creek Saloon opened up out west of town (on Bee Caves Road) in the hill country. Known as an ungoverned, neutral spot in the boonies where you could do anything you favored and not get hassled by Austin's Finest, it became the place to see the Storm every Monday night with its revved-up new crew consisting of Jimmie Vaughan, Lewis Cowdrey, Keith Ferguson, and a new sax section of Jeff Barnes and Ed Vizzard, Mike Kindred on keyboards, with Freddie Walden again replacing Doyle, who was off in the Nightcrawlers.

Paul Ray had already left the blues band to indulge his dream of a honkin' R&B/soul group, taking Denny Freeman with him to form the Cobras. Alex Napier joined in on bass, and Rodney Craig took the drum stool. In October 1974, the Cobras became established in Austin after a well-received gig opening for Doug Sahm at the

grand-opening of the Ritz Theater. After that, the band was able to draw good crowds nearly anywhere they played in Austin.

After a Nightcrawlers gig in Corpus Christi, Stevie woke up convinced that he had to have a tattoo. In fact, he wanted to get so many tattoos that he'd look cooler than Johnny "The Illustrated Man" Winter. He envisioned a phoenix rising from the ashes, spreading its tremendous wings all the way across his chest. Keith Ferguson, who also had a fetish for tattoos, took Stevie to a Corpus Christi artist known as Old Man Shaw. Once Stevie was suitably drunk and laying in the chair, he was informed that no anesthesia would be given. The pain drove Stevie crazy. He gritted his teeth and took shots of tequila to kill it, but was in visible agony. Old Man Shaw couldn't very well draw with Stevie squirming around in the chair, so the grand phoenix began to look more like a baby peacock on a miniature swing. Stevie was sore for weeks, and swore that he'd never even think of getting another tattoo.

Back in Austin, the band took gigs anywhere they could. They could be found in south side country bars like the South Door on Riverside, and the Cricket Club, which was just a couple of blocks away in what was known as Apartment City, an area inhabited by college students. The Cricket was located in the clubhouse of the mammoth English Aire apartment complex, and regularly hosted cosmic cowboys like Rusty Weir and Willis Alan Ramsey. Occasionally Southern Feeling could get away with some blues there, but the Nightcrawlers didn't fare very well with the ten-gallon-hat crowd, and were never rebooked. However, one of English Aire's new residents could always be found at the Cricket's blues nights, hanging out with the musicians. His name was Clifford Antone.

Coming from a well-to-do Port Arthur, Texas, family that ran an imported foods busi-

Nightcrawler Stevie with his new favorite guitar (notice fresher paint job), a '59 Fender Strat he dubbed "Number One" (Austin 1973). Photo by Kathy Murray.

36

ness, Clifford had come to Austin with intentions of opening a family store, but was distracted by the burgeoning underground blues community begging for exposure to a larger audience. Antone struck up friendships with hotshot guitarist Bill Campbell, Jimmie and Stevie Vaughan, Doyle Bramhall, Angela Strehli (a vocal powerhouse and now twenty-one years old), and Denny Freeman, and made a silent promise to himself that someday, somehow, he was gonna do something good for them—and the blues.

The blues were anything but fashionable in the age of the cosmic cowboy; Austin's musical royalty were crowned with straw cowboy hats and held acoustic guitars. Musicians who played anything but renegade country were not only geeks, they simply didn't exist. Still, Antone found kindred spirits on Austin's east side, where white kids played the blues for the love of it, free red beans and rice, and pocket change. Clifford played bass himself at some miraculous after-hours jams in the back of his import store. Along with his new blues buddies, he began to learn more about the Chicago and Delta blues masters who influenced Cream and Fleetwood Mac, his favorite bands at the time. Soon, he too was preaching about Muddy Waters, Eddie Taylor, and B.B. King with the fervor of a Baptist minister.

The Nightcrawlers did appear to be cursed with an unusually large helping of bad luck and trouble. Another wacky near-offer and road test came down the pike from ZZ Top's manager, Bill Ham. He sent them on a bungled southern tour with some of Billy Gibbons' practice amps that were constantly breaking down or frying. Sometimes the band would pull up to a gig, only to hear "Who are you guys?" from the puzzled clubowner.

One day they ended up stranded in Jackson, Mississippi, without a gig or money to get back home. When they finally did (several days later), Ham was furious with them and wanted his money back. Stevie walked out pissed and crying, slammed the door, and never gave Bill Ham one lousy dime. After all, it was Ham who blew the tour, not them. There weren't any contracts on the gigs they played, making it too easy for clubowners to cancel or just not pay the band. Bitter and mad at himself for even attempting to make a career in this crooked business, Stevie made a silent promise to give it a rest and try something new. He broke up the band in late 1974 without much fanfare, and Stevie Vaughan, all of twenty, felt he had given the music biz his best shot. Maybe he just didn't have it, he told himself. Maybe he

wasn't going to be a STAR—*to hell with it.*

Stevie didn't stay discouraged for long. As soon as Paul Ray heard he was available, an offer was extended to join the Cobras. His job, however, wasn't going to be a cake walk; he had the duty of keeping up with Denny Freeman every night as the newly appointed second lead guitarist for the band. He played his first show with them on New Years' Eve, 1974.

Shirley Beeman was on the bill that night with the Fabulous Ritzettes, a vocal and dance troupe that ran around in flapper dresses and entertained rowdy crowds between sets. Ringing in the new year with the Cobras were headliners Willie Nelson and Doug Sahm. "It was Stevie's first night in the band, and he was pretty nervous," Shirley recalls. "The Ritzettes had already rehearsed 'The Locomotion' with the band. But Stevie didn't know the song yet, and started complaining. Denny said: 'Just play the damn song, and watch me, kid.' That's how the Cobras treated him, from day one. He was the youngest in the band, and they pushed him around a lot, yelled at him when he was wrong. But Stevie never let it get to him, even though he was the underdog. He let Denny have his space, but…Stevie made his own space quite forcefully sometimes—and he showed all of them that he wasn't gonna be manipulated."

In addition to being a well-paid stripper, Shirley was also a graduate of comedy theater and dance companies like the Swinging Swamboli Sisters before forming the Fabulous Ritzettes. Jimmie Vaughan thought the Ritzettes were great fun—in fact, he liked them so much that he borrowed the "Fabulous" concept for a new blues band he was forming in his mind—and the girls were more than flattered.

Paul Ray had little to say about Stevie's years in the Cobras, but told *Guitar World*, "When Stevie came to town, it didn't take long before everybody was talking about this skinny little guitar player. I was glad to get him in my band and lucky that he stayed for two years. What can you say? He was great."

The Soap Creek was sacred ground for Stevie; it was the first place he slept in Austin (on the pool table) back when it was still called Rolling Hills. The Cobras moved right into a regular slot at Soap Creek, playing once or twice a week for the next two years. Onstage Denny and Stevie made a great pair and a fascinating contrast; on stage left, Freeman's understated licks would set the pace for Stevie, on the right, to blast off and steal the song.

When Stevie would get real gone, Freeman would put down the guitar and bang out some boogie on the piano, letting Stevie have center stage. Word hit the streets about the new, improved "X-rated" band quick; the Cobras now came forward as the new kings of Tuesday nights, and Soap Creek was the place to be.

After walking in the door and paying a 50-cent cover charge and grabbing a 25-cent draft from the bar, patrons could get a seat in front and dig the Cobras whipping up Little Junior Parker's "Driving Wheel." There would be Stevie and that look: eyes sealed shut, head thrown back, peeling off one emotional, soul-packed lick after another, until it got exhausting just watching him. Sometimes he might even brave the mike himself to sing a song like Larry Davis' "Texas Flood" or the Nitecaps' "Thunderbird." He sounded hoarse and unconfident, but patrons would cease conversation and listen anyway. Despite all its flaws and limited range, there was undeniably something about that *voice*…

Kathy Murray thought Stevie had a splendid voice, and always wanted him to sing more: "First, all he sang was 'Thunderbird.' That was his one token song for the night. He didn't have any belief in his voice then, I guess. Then came 'Texas Flood.' I remember he played that song *so much* that some people would just roll their eyes like 'Oh, boy, here he goes again.' 'Texas Flood' was everybody's cue to go to the bathroom. He also sang 'I Believe' by Ray Charles, really did it great. But he was still more comfortable leading the band through an instrumental, like 'Hideaway.'

"That Tuesday night Cobra Club thing—now, that was a real happenin' scene…. This is back when it [Soap Creek Saloon] was still way out on Bee Caves Road, you had to drive down this horrible, deeply rutted dirt road to get there. So, by the time you arrived, you were in a different mindset. All these people from the city would sneak away together. It was like our own exclusive little club, and nobody could bother us there."

The Cobras had a hard time putting a record out in their day, but a couple of 45 singles still exist, albeit rare. The local hit "Texas Clover" featured Denny Freeman on lead guitar, while the flip side, "Other Days," highlighted Stevie's lightning Strat work. It's the earliest known recording that captured the Stevie Ray Vaughan "Gotmortone"—as he liked to call it. Although he was only 21, it was obvious that Stevie already had a pretty good inkling of what he wanted in the studio. His tone and technique on "Other Days" were lovely precursors to what would later become a trademark.

Although the band was popular, times were lean. In a band as large as the Cobras (ranging six to eight pieces, given the show), a good paying gig usually meant twenty bucks each. Multiply that by five nights a week, and he had 100 bucks to live on. Stevie collected and sold Coke bottles, passed the hat, and sneaked off to Ernie's Chicken Shack to hear the east-side cats play the blues and eat free barbecue. He had no problems scoring the cocaine that his system was already beginning to crave; it was usually complimentary at the obligatory after-gig parties that would roar on til the break of day. That's how he earned the nickname Stevie Rave On.

He met a new girl that he was crazy about, too. Sure, the guitar was his one love, but he craved a woman's charms at night. Since Glenda left him, he'd been sleeping wherever (and with whomever) he could. Then came Lindi Bethel, Denny Freeman's down-the-street neighbor. Jimmie made it clear that he had plans for Lindi, but she only had eyes for Stevie. She was sharing a house with best friend Mary Beth Greenwood at 3403 Hampton Road when Stevie came to stay. Mary Beth was a photographer who was dating guitarist Eric Johnson, and once Stevie moved in, the place turned into an all-hours frolic. They were all frustrated young artists, desperately needing to make some kind of impact with their crafts—they staged wild photo shoots, painted, wrote poetry—and naturally, Stevie provided the soundtrack, playing his git-fiddle as loud as the neighbors would allow.

The Cobras' famous logo. Courtesy of The Center for American History, The University of Texas at Austin.

38

Mary Beth would run Stevie around in Lindi's run-down Volkswagen Bug. On rainy days, they had to use their hands for windshield wipers, occasionally stopping to pull a crazy prank in the middle of traffic. These were carefree days, and they were the three musketeers. They needed each other to communicate. "Stevie and Lindi had a hard time relating to each other without me as an interpreter," Mary Beth claims, "they were both artistic, kind of hard-headed people, and couldn't always see eye-to-eye."

Lindi was an excellent seamstress who would toil for days making stage outfits for Stevie, and the three of them became obsessed with fashion. "Lindi would wake up in the morning telling us what we were going to wear," Mary Beth recalls. "It was all she thought about. She was the household person, too. I remember one time she was sick and me and Stevie were in the living room trying to iron clothes and we burned up some stuff. She got really mad at us because we were so hopeless on the household stuff. We'd write each other little notes when we left the house each day. Lindi'd write me a note, Stevie'd write a note—we all loved to write.

"Stevie was insanely jealous over Lindi, and was always telling her not to undress in front of the windows. Like every time he left the house, he'd say, 'Be good.' He was very active sexually; Lindi used to tell me, 'Girl, he's wearing me out!' He liked to be with us all the time, but Lindi and I were best friends before they even got together, and now it was like, 'Can't we get rid of him sometime?'" Mary Beth laughs and winks. "But he just kind of grew on me...."

There were three serious young guns competing for the title of Austin's guitar god in those days: Eric Johnson, Little David Murray, and Little Stevie Vaughan. Stevie had heard all about Eric Johnson's wild jazz/rock style through Mary Beth, and finally let her drag him—"like a mule" Mary Beth avows—down to the Armadillo one night to watch Eric in his band, the Electromagnets. "He just went nuts," she recalls. "He ran up and down the aisles, jumped up on the chair and started screaming 'Fuck so-and-so,' and starts listing off every great guitarist that ever lived at the top of his lungs. Me and Lindi were like, 'Sit down, Stevie! Jesus, this is embarrassing.'

"He was wild over Albert King, and his brother. He would drill us for hours about how great Jimmie was, we became so shy we could hardly talk to Jimmie—we'd turn all red and stuff 'cause he was so fabulous in our minds. He dug everyone from Stevie Wonder to Wes Montgomery, Horace Silver, Little Johnny Taylor, and Marvin Gaye. He was like a disc jockey around the house, putting on one album after another. He was bombarding us with so much music, I didn't retain who they all were. But he gave me a George Benson album for my birthday, which I thought was real cool.

"I truly believe that Stevie wanted to be black more than anything on this earth. He was always trying to imitate that culture, the way he talked, you know 'Ya' got meh flippin' lak a flag on a po''; I could hardly understand a word he was saying half the time. He was always writing shit like that down. Like the night Lindi found him naked [but for his hat] in the living room in the middle of the night, writing lyrics...that turned out to be 'Pride and Joy.'

"Me and Lindi liked to dance, so Stevie'd keep an eye on us during the gig. If anybody was rude to us, he'd stop the show. He could give a look that would blow people away. He just sent out this strong aura of 'let that girl dance.' I don't know how he did it; he just gave them 'The Look.' He had a lot of charisma, was very, very intelligent. He was into a lot of new-age things like acupressure, reflexology, the afterlife.... He read the book of Urantia, carried that book everywhere. Best I could tell, it was a warped kind of Christianity. But he would read us passages about the archangels and the masters and what happens after you die. He was really into it," Mary Beth emphasizes, "Big time."

Stevie and Lindi moved into a house on Thornton Road, where a long line of ratty crackerbox homes ran parallel to the railroad tracks. Since most respectable home buyers wouldn't touch them with a ten-foot pole, the area began to draw low-income artists and musicians interested in building their own community. Everybody on the block was free and easy, and Stevie fit right in. He could sit on the front porch and play electric guitar if he wanted to, and not only would his neighbors not yell at him, they'd come over and applaud. Nobody in the neighborhood was paying more than 100 bucks a month for a house. This left money to party with, and party they did; it was a 24-hour parade from house to house, sometimes seven different gatherings were happening on the same street. He shared his block with band members from groups like the Berzerko Brothers and Bubble Puppy, and even a few bonafide Banditos (Tex-Mex motorcycle gang types). They kept their Harleys parked in the yard and cranked them up at three in the morning (loud enough to wake the dead—as if anybody were sleeping), and threw big, friendly barbecues, inviting all the neighbors to come and mingle. The tiny houses were poorly insulated and had no air conditioning, so occupants usually spent the long, hot Austin summers on the front porch, waiting for the next breeze.

It was here that Stevie saw Natalie Zoe, who now lived at 2209 Thornton, again. He found her on her front porch picking guitar one afternoon, and they became immediate best friends. When he would come over to visit, they sat out on the porch for hours, because Natalie didn't allow smoke in her house. "I didn't smoke, didn't drink, never did drugs," she announces proudly. "Stevie used to give me shit. *All the time.* All the years I knew him, he never called me Natalie. He'd make up all these little names like 'Z,' 'Little Miss Zoe,' 'Little Miss Goody Two-Shoes,' 'Granny Zoe'; in fact, he used to come over to my house, saying 'Well, I miss my grandma, so I thought I'd just come see you.' He was *bad*. It didn't seem to me that the drug use was that out of hand then; they mostly just smoked pot and drank a lot of beer.

"Most of my contact with Stevie was playing guitars together in the daytime, listening to records, and just being neighbors. One of the reasons we got so close was because I had a ton of blues records."

Zoe began to introduce Stevie to female blues artists like Memphis Minnie, Ida Cox, Koko Taylor, Big Mama Thornton, Billie Holiday, and a singer/slide player that Natalie had been hanging out with lately—Bonnie Raitt. "I also turned him on to Charlie Christian's music, which he really flipped for," she recalls. "He was one of the few people I would loan my records to, because he would actually bring 'em back. We would put these records on, turn them up real loud, and sit on the front porch, playing along. Typical guitar player—he was always fidgeting with every single one of my guitars—couldn't keep his hands off them. I kept a bunch lying around in different tunings, like open G, and he hadn't used alternative tunings much, but he could pick up any guitar and make it sound good, even if he didn't know what he was doing. He just had *the gift*. David Bromberg taught me, and I passed it on to Stevie. But Stevie was as good an acoustic guitar player as anybody—he was *incredibly* good."

Another passion that Stevie and Natalie shared was an infatuation with Jimi Hendrix. "Oh, we were totally bonkers over Hendrix," Zoe

Natalie Zoe and friend at her Thorton Road "home." Stevie lived just down the road. Courtesy of Natalie Zoe.

says. "We thought Jimi invented the wheel." Natalie was also the only one on the block with wheels that actually ran; her Ford Courier truck was often Stevie's taxi to and from gigs, and Stevie was always willing to help Natalie tote her heavy equipment around. Natalie chalks up his chivalry to the machismo that was expected of little boys growing up in the fifties. "Stevie was a MAN," Zoe insists. "He was a little short guy who was physically very strong. Hell, he used to come over and fix my car; didn't give a shit about tearing up his hands. But he was always such a gentleman."

Kim Wilson was living in Minneapolis when he got a call from Shirley Beeman, raving on and on about a blues band called Storm and its dynamic lead guitarist. "I got a round-trip ticket to Austin and met Jimmie," Wilson said in *Meeting the Blues*. "I met him in a place called Alexander's. It was a rib joint, a Sunday matinee. Jimmie was playing with Storm, and Stevie asked if I could sit in and they said 'No.' So Stevie, Doyle and I got up during the break and played and the crowd went crazy over it." Jimmie was obviously excited by Wilson's wicked, Little Walter-style blues harp, and joined them onstage for a couple of songs. In the middle of Slim Harpo's "Scratch My Back," a humiliated Lewis Cowdrey walked out. Jimmie, oblivious to this, looked over his right shoulder at Wilson and gave him a devilish grin that said, "Man, you're killin' me, but I like it!"

Needless to say, Lewis quit that night, and never looked back. Meanwhile, Jimmie Vaughan didn't know what to do. Without a singer, Storm was sunk. He kicked around the Soap Creek for a month, watching Stevie smoke his ass with the Cobras every Tuesday night. To his amazement, his annoying kid brother had become a much better guitar player than he was. He went home one night, drank a beer, and thought it over. He was twenty-four years old, jaded and tired, and something had to give. He was ready for a change. He finished the beer, dug through his wallet for Kim Wilson's number, and set it beside the phone.

When Kim picked up the receiver the next day, he was surprised to hear Jimmie Vaughan on the other end and, even more astounded, that he wanted to come to Minneapolis. Jimmie did as promised, and spent the next three weeks playing guitar for Kim's band. He developed a bad case of homesickness, missing his friends and especially Connie. He had made up his mind to marry her. He came home alone, without Kim and still without a band. As he sat in the airport bar, the radio played "London Homesick Blues," the unofficial national anthem of Austin in the seventies. Jimmie may have despised the whole idiotic "comic cowboy" movement (as some bitter musicians called it), but he found himself singing along quietly—under his breath, of course, so as not to blow his cool.

It wasn't long before Jimmie was back on the phone to Kim, asking him to move to Austin for good. Jimmie promised to make it worth Kim's while, saying something big was bound to hap-

Lou Ann Barton, a.k.a. "The Thunderbroad," in 1975. Photo by Kathy Murray.

pen. A few nights later, Kim and Jimmie were hanging out at the Soap Creek, drinking and making plans for constructing the meanest blues band on the planet. The conversation ceased when a long-legged brunette stepped onto the stage and started singing a blue streak. At first they thought it was just another drunk that might have staggered onstage to lift her dress for the crowd, but when she busted into "Shake a Hand," a powerful sound came pouring out. Jimmie vaguely knew her from the Fort Worth blues crowd as Lou Ann Barton, and raised his eyebrows at how good she really was. Kim and Jimmie visually followed her as she pranced through the bar, accepting compliments and shots of tequila from knocked-out barflies. She was clearly able to take care of herself; Lou Ann could cuss as loud as any man in the joint and put away more whiskey than the whole band put together in one sitting. Both Wilson and Vaughan admired her fire. Besides, she was a stone cold fox; long and lean, her legs made up most of her frame, along with long silky arms and big sensuous lips. She had a smile that would melt hard candy, and a voice as sweet. Jimmie asked her to join a new band he was forming with Keith Ferguson on bass, Freddie "Pharaoh" Walden on drums, and Kim Wilson. The name, he said, would be the Fabulous Thunderbirds.

In the Open

SRV

AT THE BEGINNING of 1975, Clifford Antone had a crazy idea: If he opened his own blues club, he could provide a lasting service to the music he loved and to those who played it. By the spring, he had managed to get out of the family food business and scrape together enough bread to secure a lease on a large two-story building (formerly Levine's Department Store) at East Sixth Street and Brazos. These were the days when Sixth Street was nothing more than a broken-down district of abandoned historical properties with bums sleeping in the doorways. Nowadays, this strip is Austin's own Bourbon Street. Antone's next-door neighbors were a record store, a Cajun café, a porno bookstore, and a shoe shine parlor. What better place for the blues?

On July 15, 1975, the big daddy of all Austin blues clubs opened its doors with a much-touted performance by Clifton Chenier and his Red Hot Louisiana Band. The grand opening was well attended, with fans lining up around the corner to get in. Clifford was ecstatic, but some people thought he had lost his mind—the building was an expensive albatross, a sure-fire money-losing proposition. Why on earth would somebody want to open a blues showbar in the seventies, anyway? "I did it because there was hardly ever any music in town that catered to someone who happened to like rhythm and blues instead of hard rock or progressive county," Antone later recalled. "Another reason is because I'm a blues collector and I wanted to meet the men who made the blues before they aren't here anymore. Money was the last thing that motivated me."

"Clifford got the idea to start the club," Stevie recollected, "and *everybody* wanted to be the house band there. Everyone was claiming to be the house band that week, but we were all friends." Antone thought of his friends first, hiring Angela Strehli to run the club. He was blown away by her earth-mother good looks, her business savvy, her undying faith in the blues, and—she was the only person he knew who didn't consider running the house P.A. system a royal pain in the ass. For a while, the Houserockers (featuring Bill Campbell) were the house band, but Jimmie and Kim kept pestering Clifford to give the Thunderbirds a break, a reason to exist—a gig, in other words.

"The Thunderbirds got their *start* at Antone's," Clifford declares. "Those clubowners wouldn't have pissed on the T-Birds if they'd been on fire. They were like the plague. Back then, the Cobras and the T-Birds together didn't make $100 between them." Antone gave them a stage to play on every Monday night, and deemed the T-Birds the official house band at his self-declared "Home of the Blues,"

Clifford Antone, owner of Austin's most respected blues club and record label. Photo © 1986 by Cindy Light.

The early Fabulous Thunderbirds. *Left to right:* Jimmie, Mike Buck, Keith Ferguson, and Kim Wilson. Photo by Kathy Murray.

providing them the opportunity to play backup to musical heroes like Sunnyland Slim, Buddy Guy, Junior Wells, Otis Rush, and James Cotton.

Suddenly, in the sugar-coated disco years that originally put them out of work, the blues masters were back on the road—to Texas. "They come for me anywhere," Antone told writer Brad Buchholz. "They'd play outside if I asked them to. You see, I'm known all over this country by all the bluesmen and all I need is a telephone call, and they'll be here, any of them…the big and the small." Antone's gave these musicians the credit and reverence they had been unfairly denied for most of their lives.

When the Fabulous Thunderbirds' name began popping up in local Austin papers, curious listeners started filtering into Antone's to check out the band with the coolest name in town. The handle fit like a glove; it suggested a mingling of the glamorous and the utterly tacky. Jimmie described his original concept for the band as "Bo Diddley on acid."

It didn't take long before the playing for tips routine at the One Knite and mere pennies at Antone's grew weary. With only the occasional opening slot for Freddie King or somebody at the Armadillo for seventy-five bucks, this new band had everything; the formula, the chops, the charisma, and even the following. But, they missed one crucial link—a record and a regular circuit on the road. Getting paid for it would be nice, too. Hell, that was still a pipe dream.

Wilson and Vaughan enjoyed good fortune by finding each other when they both seemed to be drifting in their respective careers, and they were lucky to find like-minded musicians in drummer Mike Buck and bassist Keith Ferguson. Buck was from Fort Worth, and had put in time with the legendary Robert Ealey as part of the Careless Lovers, the house band at Ealey's funky Bluebird Cafe. Ferguson had Johnny Winter on his résumé, and had survived both Storm and the Nightcrawlers, proving that he could handle any-thing tough times could dish out. With the added bonus of Lou Ann Barton (now dubbed "The Thunderbroad") as a dual frontperson, the T-birds were cruising in style, or, *almost*.

Arguably the King T-Bird, Kim Wilson didn't dig sharing the spotlight with Lou Ann Barton. First of all, she was a girl, second, she might just steal the show right out from under-neath him. The two lead singers were so strong individually that they nearly canceled each other out onstage. Her voice was thin but sassy, and Lord knows she could bring men to their knees. His singing was smooth and hearty, making him the perfect vehicle for party hollers and sexual innuendo. Lou Ann didn't care to be his target for such shenanigans, either.

She was fired from the band the day before they were due to begin their first tour of the East Coast. The whole band knew that Keith and Lou Ann had been carrying on together, so they gave Keith the dirty deed of telling her. She was irate, and engaged Kim Wilson in a screaming match that left him without his voice for the first five days of the tour. Keith would watch him drinking hot tea, moping in the van, waiting for his voice to return, and chided him constantly: "Hey Kim, we sure could use old Lou Ann now, huh?" Keith may have been joking, but somewhere inside he must have resented Kim for making him fire his own girlfriend. After all, he really loved her. They would later even get married. But for now, she was moving in with Denny Freeman while Keith was away on the road.

One of Clifford Antone's greatest memories was the cold winter's night in 1975 when he managed to get Jimmie Vaughan onstage next to Muddy Waters himself, after the Thunderbirds had opened the show. Jimmie even got to trade slide licks with his hero, who was pleasantly

Bonnie Raitt (circa 1975). Stevie and Bonnie's friendship began in the mid-seventies and lasted to the end. Photo by and courtesy of Natalie Zoe.

surprised at this 24-year-old white boy playing his trademark delta blues licks so brilliantly. Waters was especially taken with Kim Wilson's blues harp; his tone and phrasing reminded Muddy so much of his old partner, Little Walter Jacobs. He told Kim af-ter the show that he could have a job in Wa-ters' band anytime he wanted it.

Clifford's next great deed was to get "Little Stevie" Vaughan onstage with Albert King. "Oh, now that was something!" Clifford says. On that summer's night in 1975, Antone says he "must have gotten fifteen phone calls that day from Stevie asking when I was gonna introduce him to Albert King... 'When is Albert coming, can I play with Albert, *please?*'" He thought of Stevie as a scruffy, serious kid, barely twenty-one, who still needed a few miles on him before anyone could take him seriously as a bluesman. Albert King sure as hell had never heard of Stevie Vaughan, but Clifford promised he'd try to get Stevie onstage that night with his idol. When Clifford approached Albert about letting little Stevie jam a song with him, he was met by Albert's usual gruff indifference.

"Who is he?" said Mr. King skeptically.

"Trust me," Antone implored. "I wouldn't put him up there with you if he couldn't play. And believe me, he can play."

So the skinny kid with the hip-hugger bell-bottom jeans, beret, and downcast eyes blew old Albert King away that night by all accounts. Little Stevie Vaughan may even have scared him with his unbelievable grasp of King's style and tone. At one point, Albert stepped away from Stevie and hid his guitar behind the stage curtains as if to say, "this kid is scaring my guitar!"

Buddy Guy met Stevie the same night he first shared a stage with Jimmie Vaughan at Antone's in the late seventies. "He's unbeatable when it comes

44

Promotional poster for a Paul Ray and The Cobras gig at Antone's. Courtesy of Keri Leigh.

to blues," Guy maintains regarding Jimmie. But Buddy was as impressed with Stevie as he was with Jimmie. However, Stevie cut out of Buddy's show early and was later spotted across the street, sitting on a car hood, playing guitar with a red-headed girl that nobody recognized. A small crowd gathered around them, and as they were packing up their guitars, Stevie introduced the pretty young woman: "Miss Bonnie Raitt, ladies and gentlemen. Ain't she somethin'?"

Antone's was a great idea, and a vital shot in the arm to the Austin blues community, but not every show was as successful as Clifton Chenier's red-hot opening night gala. In fact, blues masters like Albert Collins, Bobby "Blue" Bland, and John Lee Hooker played to audiences of less than fifty people, a reality that broke Antone's generous heart. "People don't want good music anymore," Clifford once remarked. "They want stages blowing up and shit. The blues has always been neglected. Most of the good bluesmen had to quit or glected. Most of the good bluesmen had to quit or change their music when the Beatles and the Rolling Stones came along. I'm building a little appreciation here, but you know, you just can't teach people to have a soul."

The Thunderbirds and the Cobras split a bill one winter night at the 'Dillo; it was the only way they could get a much-coveted Friday night show. Sure enough, the place filled up, and both bands gave it hell. The T-Birds opened, putting the crowd in motion with "The Crawl" and packing the dance floor with Jerry McCain's "She's Tuff."

By the time the Cobras hit the stage, the crowd was well-oiled and ready to get crazy. Stevie ate it up that night, playing to a crowded, rowdy rathskellar. That's when the music really happened for him. He could see their eyes, and they could read his soul. Dressed in his favorite suit— a brown velvet vest and pant combo offset by a pink polyester shirt—Stevie resembled one of Bill Cosby's Atlanta pimps in *Uptown Saturday Night*. Nobody really gave a damn how he looked anyway; it was how he made the guitar scream that kept a good portion of the crowd gathered near his side of the stage, just standing there gawking. The T-birds joined them onstage for an encore of Muddy Waters' "Got My Mojo Working," which turned into a drunken sing-a-long, judging by how many emptied free beers the musicians had sitting atop their amps and speakers.

After the show, everybody got sloppy drunk

Cobras jamming with the Thunderbirds (on "Got My Mojo Working") at the Armadillo in December, 1976. *Left to right:* Kim Wilson, Jimmie, Alex Napier, Paul Ray, and Stevie. Photo by Kathy Murray.

and backstage guests witnessed a memorable exchange between the Vaughan brothers. A toasted Jimmie clung to Stevie's leg and, looking up at him, mumbled, "You surrrpssssd meh, Lil' bro'...." Stevie didn't understand. "What did you say? I *suppress* you?" Stevie asked.

Jimmie looked forlorn and ready to pass out. He managed to get the message out, though, loud and clear: "You *surpassed* me."

Shirley Beeman was constantly settling arguments over who was the better guitarist. "Stevie really hated it when people would compare him to his brother, which was always happening," she says. "He'd ask, 'Why are they saying that I'm better than Jimmie, or that Jimmie's better than me? We're just doin' our own thing.' It would just drive him *nuts*." But they *were* playing in rival bands, and the Vaughan one-upmanship became a major point of gossip around Austin, especially when the two would jam together, which was *rare*.

Stevie ran into his old buddy Rocky Athas at the first annual Texas Guitar Show that year. The two childhood pals hugged each other tightly, then picked up guitars and began playing together, just like they had done as little tykes. "We were sitting in Charley Wirz's booth," Rocky remembers, "and we played 'Little Wing' together, and it sounded really beautiful. Charley [Wirz, founder of the Guitar Show, and owner of Charley's Guitars] even recorded it.

"You know, I did notice a change in him after he moved to Austin. He used to be a real rude kid, and Austin humbled him somehow. I think it was just through watching the veteran players; you know, the guys who were great but didn't have to say they were." Indeed, Stevie Vaughan had changed; maybe his big mouth had gotten him in trouble one too many times, and he had learned to let his guitar do the talking.

In the April 12, 1976 edition of the *Daily Texan* (the UT campus newspaper), reporter Chico Coleman managed to get all of the future Texas legends together in one room to discuss the state of the blues. Coleman got them to share some fascinating stories and strong opinions:

"People tend to lump all blues bands together," Paul Ray noted, "but like the Thunderbirds are playing that alley music, low-down and blue. We play city music and spread it out a little bit so we can make some money."

"Contemporary music is stagnant," Jimmie Vaughan said sharply. "I really don't pay attention to it."

But when the story appeared in print, Coleman focused his compliments on the Cobras: "To be sure, the Cobras are the least esoteric of the bunch. With Paul Ray's David Clayton-Thomas-like vocals and the guitars of Stevie Vaughan and Denny Freeman, this R&B band is definitely for dancing fools. Vaughan is a power guitarist; Freeman, an intricate stylist who peppers his work with jazz riffs. Together, the two are a joy, as they play rhythmic patterns that offset one another, then weave those patterns into a whole.

"The Cobra repertoire includes around seven original songs and a smorgasbord of blues and R&B standards like 'St. James Infirmary,' 'Song For My Father,' a blasting version of Otis Redding's 'I Can't Turn You Loose,' and Jimmy McCracklin's 'The Walk.' Outstanding among their originals are 'Texas Clover' and 'I Ain't Gonna Be Your Cryin' Towel.'"

That same year the *Austin Sun*'s readers ranked Jimmie Vaughan and the T Birds last, behind Paul Ray and The Cobras (at #2), in the Best Blues/Soul Band category. Paul Ray placed third as Best Male Vocalist, behind Willie Nelson and Willis Allan Ramsey, respectively, and the Cobras placed fourth for Band of the Year behind Asleep at the Wheel, Doug Sahm's Texas Tornadoes, and Too Smooth.

Stevie began to sing more and more, out of sheer necessity. Paul Ray was having trouble with his vocal stamina

Little Stevie Vaughan burns it up with the Cobras, 1976. Photo by Kathy Murray.

The Soap Creek was one of Stevie's favorite hangouts and where Paul Ray hosted "Cobra Club Tuesdays" for several years. Poster by Kerry Awn. Courtesy of Keri Leigh.

blown his voice after the first set each night. It was eventually discovered that he had developed nodes on his vocal cords and was instructed by his doctor to stop using his voice—or else. When Paul had to leave the Cobras in early 1977, the singing chores fell in the laps of drummer Rodney Craig and Stevie Vaughan. Totally unprepared for the task and without enough material, they asked Angela Strehli to join the band while Paul waited for his delicate voice to heal.

While things were getting better for the T-Birds, Stevie was watching closely and plotting his next move. Several East Coast tours had yielded them interest from legendary producer Doc Pomus (recommended by Roomful of Blues), the man behind "Teenager in Love," "Lonely Avenue," "There Is Always One More Time," "Save The Last Dance For Me," and over twenty hits written for Elvis Presley, including "Little Sister" and "Viva Las Vegas." He brought the Thunderbirds to New York City and put them up in the Mayflower Hotel on Central Park West for a demo session that took only two days, as Doc was only working with

Stevie at Soap Creek, spring 1977. Photo by Ken Hoge.

lately, and needed help from a relief singer. Stevie never really wanted to be a vocalist, but remembered the advice Jimmie gave so many years ago: "Trust me kid, you've got to sing. If you sing, nobody else can tell you what songs to play. If you sing, you're the boss."

Joe Sublett was a fantastic tenor sax player and a friend to the Cobras. When he finally got the opportunity to join the group in late 1976, he jumped at the chance, bringing the Cobras that fat, honkin' horn sound they dreamed of. Joe and Stevie became tight buddies fast. They were nearly the same age, and Stevie loved the way he made that sax wail, prompting each solo with "Blow, Joe, blow!"

In the meantime, the voice problems got worse for Paul Ray, to the point where he had them on speculation. "I do the blues as a labor of love because there's no money in it," Pomus told the *Dallas Times Herald*. "If we break even, we're happy. I don't know if Texas will buy 10,000 Thunderbirds albums. But I know one thing—it's a good album." Pomus did greatly believe in the band, and vowed to help them find a record deal, using the tapes as bait.

Meanwhile, more changes were happening in the ever-evolving blues circles; although the Cobras had just been voted Band of the Year, and Best Blues Band in the 1977 *Austin Sun* Readers' Poll, Stevie had tired of life with the Cobras and yearned to do something more experimental, more dangerous. In fact, his true aim was to get close to Lou Ann Barton—he wanted her as a singer for his new band, and for some personal reasons, too.

To Stevie's surprise, she accepted his offer to form a band. Indeed, she had her big almond eyes on him as well. She went out of her way to seduce him one night, tricking him away from Lindi and into her motel room. Lindi eventually found out about the affair and promptly left Stevie and Lou Ann to find whatever it was they were looking for. Stevie left the Cobras in July 1977, and moved out of the Thornton Road place to be closer to Lou Ann.

Mary Beth hated to watch Stevie and Lindi break up. "For the longest time, they were inseparable," she says. "I think as the pills and alcohol increased, so did the promiscuity. And he would piss her off and she would piss him off, and they were terribly in love—it was really funny watching it. When Stevie would get emotional about one of their fights and he'd beat on our window, I wouldn't understand. Lindi and I had this kind of 'go away, Stevie' attitude. She was

At the *Austin Sun* Music Awards, March 20, 1977. The Cobras were voted "Best Blues/R&B Band." Photo by Ken Hoge.

more in control than Stevie, emotionally. She knew that he was seeing Lou Ann, and then she'd have to hang out with Lou Ann at the gigs. It was really hard on her."

"He *loved* women," Natalie Zoe stresses. "But I do think he was easily fooled, and he'd give in to them. He just couldn't say no. He was a moody guy though, and that led to some really volatile relationships with women. I overheard a lot of loud fights. He never even made a pass at me, because he knew that I would say no. Besides, I wasn't his type; he liked pretty little blond girls." Zoe was most likely the only woman Stevie had a platonic relationship with, and she had a decided influence on his opinion of women.

That summer, Stevie and Lou Ann had managed to put together a whopping good band,

Soap Creek calendar that featured Triple Threat: Stevie, Lou Ann Barton, Mike "Cold Shot" Kindred, and W.C. Clark. Art by Kerry Awn. Courtesy of Kerry Awn/ The Center for American History, The University of Texas at Austin.

adding Freddie "Pharaoh" Walden on drums, Mike Kindred on keyboards, and the powerhouse W.C. Clark on vocals and bass (Stevie had tracked him down and found him repairing cars at McMorris Ford). With three strong leaders (and three equally strong egos), the band came to be aptly called the Triple Threat Revue, and played their debut gig on August 8, 1977, at the Soap Creek Saloon. It was one extraordinary sound: W.C.'s Joe Tex and Al Green soul numbers mixed with Lou Ann's Irma Thomas and Janis Joplin covers and Stevie's Hendrix-like guitar pyrotechnics made them a very hot combination.

Playing slide with a wino glass—Triple Threat at the After Hours Club on September 25, 1977. Photo by Ken Hoge.

Triple Threat played their inaugural gigs at South Austin joints like After Hours, the Continental Club and the Austex Lounge on Congress Avenue, and became regulars at both Antone's and the Soap Creek Saloon. The group was billed as Stevie Vaughan and Triple Threat, which bugged W.C. and Lou Ann—weren't they supposed to be leaders, too? After all, this was the Triple Threat Revue!

The band demanded that Stevie sing more—not because they particularly liked his voice, but because Lou Ann wouldn't sing for more than thirty minutes at a time before retreating to the bar, and somebody had to carry the show while she was gone. W.C. obliged with a few numbers, then turned the mike over to a bashful Stevie Vaughan, who was so shy about his voice he wouldn't take his eyes off the guitar, keeping his head down while he sang a favorite B.B. King number: "*Oh baby! You done lost your good thing now...*"

Natalie Zoe was always lecturing Stevie about his singing. "He would come to my house just to hear me sing," says Zoe, who has an angelic soprano, "and he'd say, 'Damn, girl, you sing like a bird. I sure wish I could sing like you. Come on, Little Miss Z, let me hear those pipes.' And I'd tell him, 'Stevie you have a beautiful voice! If you'd

just stop smoking those damn cigarettes and try, you could sing too.' He told someone several years later that I was the person who taught him how to sing. We sang together a lot, and I helped him to get over his shyness, and stop looking at the floor." Steve did idolize Natalie; here was a girl who had played with everyone from Bonnie Raitt to Muddy Waters, made a good living on the road, and actually had the balls to do it by herself without a band. She was the hottest thing in Austin, winning readers' and critics' polls hands down as Austin's best female vocalist and songwriter.

In the April 28, 1978, edition of the *Austin Sun*, Bill Bentley gave the Vaughan brothers their first-ever cover story. Called "Young Giants of the Blues," it provided a fascinating glimpse at two young musicians who had their acts together. They had developed that distinctive look, an attitude, and had refined their sounds into personal statements. In fact, to hear them play in 1978 sounded little different than 1988. Bentley wrote that "Jimmy [sic] and Stevie Vaughan are blues boys in the first degree. Both are guitarists capable of catching afire. Taking a long range look at the music business—seeing it as a lifetime—the two will someday walk tall."

Bentley interviewed the brothers separately, starting with Jimmie. Stevie then took the hot seat, revealing his perspective for the first time in print:
SUN: To you, what's the reward?
SRV: There's a lot of them, but one stands out. When you're playing and all of a sudden you realize your toes are...just...tightened up, and you get a chill all the way up your back because of what you just gave somebody and they gave it back. That's probably the biggest thrill. Or, you're playing someplace and you hit a note and people start screaming—that's it. You gave them a thrill,

or you soothed them. That's what the blues do to me. If people tell me they don't want to hear a blues band because it brings them down, they're not paying attention at all. I like a lot of different kinds of music, but if it doesn't have any soul I can't relate to it.

SUN: Jimmy told me that music is all he can do.

SRV: Yeah, if I couldn't play or hear music for even a week, I'd probably just check out. It's a life. I figure it's something that's going to take me past this, because it doesn't stop here. There's no reason for anyone to believe it does.

SUN: Have you always sung and played?

SRV: Not really. Ever since I was sneaking around playing Jimmie's guitar I'd try to sing some, but I didn't really work hard at it all along. But it's like there has always been a constant flow of reasons to play. It's bound to be something real serious going on in the air. The music that's come out of Texas has always seemed deeper—to me, anyway.

That same year, a new music venue opened up at Twenty-ninth and Rio Grande that would also make a profound impact on Austin music for years to come: the Rome Inn. The first floor was for the dancers, covered with tattered, checkered black-and-white linoleum, the white squares stained grey from years of dancing feet. A rickety staircase led to the tiny balcony, stocked with tables for the sitting patrons. By the stage was a round porthole where somebody had installed a huge stained-glass window that depicted a rising star. It was a low-key, no-frills joint where the music was hot, the beers were cold, and the barbecue sauce was drippin' all over the dance floor. The succulent grub came courtesy of the bar's new manager, L.C. "C-Boy"

Parks, an older black man with a knack for ribs, chicken, blues, beans, and beer—all the essentials for a blue night out.

C-Boy immediately became a focal member of the Austin blues family with his nonstop jokes and upbeat attitude, creating a down-home atmosphere that made his employees and customers feel right at home. This wasn't an uptown joint where you paid ten dollars a ticket to see a band in matching leopard suits—this was the hole in the wall where you paid two bucks to boogie with some low-down, funky blues band. There were no fancy tablecloths (just wax paper to catch the bones), no valet parking (lock your car), or elaborate advertising. Just word of mouth kept the Rome Inn alive and well for the next two years.

The Rome Inn became one of the few places in Austin in the seventies where an established blues band could find immediate acceptance and a new group could begin building an audience. "C-Boy always wanted to make you feel welcome," says Paul Ray. "If you want to know what was really great about the Rome Inn, it was him." Before long, tales of the intimate dive and the man who ran it began to spread, and the Rome Inn drew admirers from everywhere—musicians like Doug Sahm and Johnny Winter would drop in to jam with the T-birds; the Allman Brothers would always stop by when in town, and Billy Gibbons used to bring busloads of people from Houston just to hear the music, dig the atmosphere, and of course, pig out on C-Boy's famous barbecue.

ZZ Top even immortalized the joint in the song "Lowdown In The Streets" on their *Deguello* album,

The Vaughan brothers, shooting their first magazine cover together in 1978—an experience *Austin Sun* staffer Margaret Moser described as "hellish" because the brothers weren't getting along at the time. Photo by Ken Hoge.

Lou Ann and Stevie share a laugh at a Triple Threat gig, June 1978. Photo by Ken Hoge.

band, so they decided to avoid the local politics and start playing out of town, loading up the van for short road trips to Faces in Dallas, Fitzgerald's in Houston, Cheatham Street Warehouse in San Marcos, and Fat Dawg's in Lubbock.

Lubbock was the legitimate birthplace of Texas rock and roll. Buddy Holly and The Crickets had started the ball rolling there in the fifties, and the following years produced revered talents like Joe Ely, Jimmie Dale Gilmore, Terry Allen, Butch Hancock, and the Supernatural Family Band. Stevie felt the town harbored a special energy, and it must have liked him, too, because Triple Threat became immensely popular in the college-area bars, packing Fat Dawg's so full that people would wait in a mile-long line just to get a seat if somebody else left the filled-over-capacity bar.

Stevie used to venture over to Stubb's Barbecue on East Broadway for the Sunday night jam sessions and of course, C.B. Stubblefield's unequaled grub and homemade Love and Happiness Sauce were an enticement, too. Stubbs really took to Stevie, making sure that he always had a good meal in him, a place to play, and free reign over the jukebox that Stubbs kept stuffed with blues and soul 45's. Legend has it that it was Stubb's Barbecue where Stevie first heard "Tin Pan Alley," done by Jimmy Wilson and the All-Stars. He was so knocked out by the number that he taped it on his portable cassette deck, and proceeded to learn it that very same day.

where in the chorus they encourage everyone to "*Rome on Inn, it ain't no sin.*" (Gibbons' lyrics also mention several familiar faces, including Jimmie Vaughan, Kim Wilson, Keith Ferguson, Mary Beth Greenwood ("M.B.") and his girlfriend, Gretchen Barber ("Little G.B.").

The Thunderbirds moved their regular Blue Monday party from Antone's to the Rome Inn in 1978, bringing with them the sizable crowd that they had managed to build up over the last three years of hard gigging. Kim Wilson recalls, "We played some of the best music of our careers at the Rome Inn.... Most musicians in this town would do more for C-Boy than they would for their managers and agents, because he didn't want anything from you—he wasn't gonna rip you off. There were no games, no bullshit. He was someone you could put your absolute trust in, and he would stick with you through anything. He just believed in people overall, loved 'em."

Triple Threat held down Sunday nights at the Rome Inn, and most of the time, nobody bothered to come see them. They might knock off early, and walk down to Conan's Pizza, where they knew a free pizza would always be waiting for them. Austin obviously had no use for the

Stevie picks up a few tricks from Hubert Sumlin at the Soap Creek. Photo by Ken Hoge.

Shirley went to see Triple Threat play at Soap Creek, but she had no idea she'd come home that evening with a new roommate. "Stevie told me he needed a place to stay, because he couldn't make his rent," Shirley recalls. "I had a house over at 4803 Sinclair Street (off of Forty-fifth and Burnet Road) where all the poor little rock and roll boys went in and out of, like a rooming house. At the time, I was living there alone, and I had split up with my husband, so I said, 'Yeah, you can come live with me if you want to,' and he accepted."

The house had two rooms; one was the "Fillmore West Dressing Room," as Doug Sahm christened it; a trashy psychedelic freak-out chamber with red and blue lights, red velvet curtains, and pictures of old movie stars on the walls. Of course, this was the room Stevie took for his own. "I remember when he moved in," she laughs, "he drove up in a pickup truck that had one little suitcase and this huge antique wardrobe closet. I didn't know he was going to bring furniture! He had one pair of boots and a guitar."

Shirley drove a bad-to-the-bone cherry red 1977 Monte Carlo with white leather seats and a white top. She enjoyed tooling around town with Stevie; driving him to the music store, to gigs at Soap Creek, and especially, over to Jimmie's house. "Jimmie had a Cadillac that was similar to it," Shirley says. "So for a while, Stevie thought he was just as cool as Jimmie!

"Once I was driving him to a sound check at Soap Creek; and he had a change of clothes with him for the gig. Somehow or other, he forgot to take his boots off the top of the car. So we're driving along, fixing to jump on the MoPac freeway, and we hear these boots go flying away. He *screamed*, just went *totally crazy*, and made me stop and drive *backwards* down MoPac to find his el-cheapo brown-and-white cowboy boots in the tall grass. Once we found them and got back in the car, he pulled out a tape of this song called 'Tin Pan Alley.' I had never heard it before, and he wouldn't let me speak a word through the entire song while we listened—and he would say, 'listen to this part' or 'man, isn't that cool?'—and I'd be trying not to laugh."

"He was real cool to my parents. Stevie might be sitting there in the middle of the living room floor, changing strings, making a big mess—and he'd get up and answer the door, shake my father's hand, and talk to him for a long time. He was a total gentleman. Very polite, well-mannered. He only lived with me for three months, and never had enough money to help on the rent, but I'd cook for him, and give him dope, and be his little girlfriend, and it was a real sweet, respectful relationship. And whenever he'd get a little money from a gig, he'd take me out for dinner once a week at La Fiesta. I thought he was terrific. And he had a lot of dignity.

"While he was living with me, I heard a lot of other people talkin' about how much he was drinkin' and that he was shooting up speed. But I didn't let him do that around me. It's kinda funny because I decided that 'I was gonna save him....' Me! Shirley The Angel, who drank and snorted like crazy, too," she laughs. "But he did not shoot up while he was living here—he'd just snort it with the best of us!

"I had done a lot of road travel with Billy Joel and Martin Mull, and had seen a lot of the 'glamorous life.' Cocaine was a big part of that, and *Newsweek* ran that big cover story proclaiming 'Cocaine Is Not Addictive.' So, I thought I was doing Stevie a favor. He really got into the ritual of pulling out a mirror, chopping the stuff up with a razor blade, drawing these really long, clean lines of white powder, and sniffing it through a straw. Everything centered around drugs and music," Shirley sadly stresses. "Sex, drugs, and rock and roll."

Let Me Love You, Baby

I T'S HARD TO IMAGINE Stevie Vaughan as much of a ladykiller. His thin hair, big protruding ears, flat nose, and skinny runtlike physique were not the stuff dreams are made of. But he had a bizarre power over women (often very beautiful women), some who just fell under his spell, gave up their happy homes and became his faithful keeper for a while. Stevie was blessed (or cursed, if you asked him) with a mug that simply refused to age; at twenty-five, he still looked fifteen. His boyish face, playful ways and most important, the way he moved with that guitar spelled pure sex appeal to some girls—to others, he was just another ugly guitar player who didn't believe in showers, combs, or toothpaste.

"You couldn't help but love him," says Shirley Beeman. "He was so ugly, he was cute." Through music (rock and roll, namely), Stevie incorporated animal magnetism into his own unrestrained come-on—and he was serious. He learned a lot from Jimi Hendrix about how to gyrate and make faces that the girls would understand. And they did. Stevie's little black book was brimming with women's phone numbers who had offered themselves freely to him. He took them up on their generosity more often than not, and loved the feeling of being the studly guitar man, surrounded by his harem of adoring women. He chose no favorites, and took no prisoners.

While Stevie liked to brag that he was balling Lou Ann Barton (and everybody else), he developed eyes for another girl. Her name was Lenny

Bailey. He had met her one late night at a club and although she was attached to another man, Lenny, apparently smitten by his soft laugh and soul-brother jive, handed him her phone number. Stevie recognized the number as belonging to Diamond Joe Siddons. He wasn't necessarily friends with Diamond Joe, but they hung with the same crowd, and because they were both guitarists they were always in competition with each other locally. Diamond Joe often kidded Stevie that if he kept practicing, Stevie might one day match his own skill. Stevie also knew that Diamond Joe dealt coke, and it was apparently profitable enough to satisfy his craving for Cadillacs and Afghan fur coats. He added it up and concluded that Lenny was Diamond Joe's girl—and that was trouble. Now the competition had reached another level, and a love-struck Stevie had his work cut out for him.

It was obvious to everyone around that Stevie was in hot pursuit of Lenny from that day forward. She was different from the other girls; she was tough, wild, and independent. Her blonde hair, deep brown eyes, and smooth olive complexion drove him crazy. He considered her a beauty queen, and she had actually taken home the blue ribbon in a small-time pageant once. He called, sent flowers when he could afford them, and would sneak away to see her anytime he could. He'd wait for any opportunity in a crowded bar or a small party of friends to pry Lenny away from Diamond Joe and get her alone for just a few minutes.

The attraction between them grew, and one day Lenny called up to inform Stevie that Joe had gone out of town on a gig and wouldn't return for a couple of days. His mama didn't raise no fool—Stevie high-tailed it over to her house and romanced Lenny the entire weekend, sweeping her off her feet. Before the weekend was all over, the two admitted they were in love. The next day, Stevie emerged triumphant from the bedroom wearing a pair of Joe's pants (twice his size, of course), announcing that he had slept with Lenny, and—even crazier yet—that he loved her.

The secret love affair didn't remain a secret for long. Stevie and Lenny couldn't hide their attraction from a blind man. The long, hot nights spent together were getting harder and harder to explain, and they found themselves becoming detached from their current lovers. Lenny and Diamond Joe finally split up around July 4, and she met Stevie at a Mexican restaurant to talk it over. According to Lenny, it was on this day that

Stevie wrote "Love Struck Baby," a tune he crafted for her.

He moved out of Shirley's house after he met Lenny. "He really fell for her, which was okay with me, because our relationship was basically nothing serious, just friends," Shirley says with a smile. "And friends slept together back then." Stevie was ready to have a real girlfriend again; he missed being in love; he knew it wasn't love with Shirley or Lou Ann. Hell, both of those girls would just as soon be out carousing with the guys than waiting at home for anybody. Stevie always wanted to try a little harder for Lou Ann, actually thinking he was in love with her for a while, but the relationship was plagued by myriad problems.

Triple Threat was steamy but unstable; stories about Stevie and Lou Ann's inner bickering floated down to the community like falling leaves. The yelling bouts after gigs, or even during gigs, were just plain humiliating for anyone who was privy to it. Stevie's jealous streak would often spark when Lou Ann would pay more than ample attention to all the young, sexually motivated men buying her drinks at the bar while he observed the whole thing from his vantage point onstage. Sometimes she accepted offers, leaving Stevie to grab a last-minute date out of spite, and they would parade their carnal stories about the night before in front of the rest of the band all the way home from a gig. And there were the arguments about who had artistic control of the group; Lou Ann wanted to play strictly R&B and soul music, and was constantly nagging Stevie about his wild rock and roll tone. She scolded him, saying he needed to relax and play like Jimmie, that he should "just play the blues, and leave that Jimi Hendrix shit at home."

Of course, Lou Ann hated it when Stevie would steal the spotlight by playing the guitar behind his back or with his teeth onstage. And he disliked her lack of professionalism when it came to dealing with clubowners, booking agents, and the press. Lou Ann was hardly known for her diplomacy; in fact, she'd just as soon tell a manager "fuck off" as say "thank you," especially once she'd had a few drinks, which was now all the time.

The conflict didn't prevent Stevie from including Lou Ann in the original lineup of Double Trouble (named after his favorite Otis Rush song), which he formed in May of 1978, after they had both grown dissatisfied (or at least that's what they said) with the direction of Triple Threat. What really happened was that the other band members couldn't put up with the knock-down drag-out arguments between Stevie and Lou Ann anymore. The band thought the two seemed to be drifting further into outer space, riding a rocket fueled by speed and cheap wine. They played their first gig as Double Trouble at Soap Creek on May 15, 1978.

For the new band, Stevie and Lou Ann recruited Jackie Newhouse on bass, Johnny Reno on saxophone, and a young drummer named Chris Layton. "The first time I heard him play was on a Tuesday night at the Soap Creek Saloon in late 1976 or early 1977," Layton told *Guitar for the Practicing Musician*. "When I walked in, they were already playing. Immediately, Stevie caught my ear, 'cause of his energy and this feeling from his playing. He was with the Cobras, and they were doing Bobby Bland stuff, a couple of James Brown things, and a song by Ronnie Laws called 'Always There.'"

Stevie barely knew Chris at first. "I went to his apartment," Stevie recalled in an interview with *Musician Magazine*, "and he was set up in the kitchen with drums and headphones; seems he was playin' along with 'Conversations' by Max Roach. I stood there and watched him for ten minutes…you know how we get—oblivious to everything. He turns 'round and sees me and gets red as a beet, and all I can say is, '*Hey man, you wanna start a band?*'" And so this, the original incarnation of Double Trouble, sharpened its teeth around town in the summer of 1978, to an average of twenty patrons—and that was a good night!—moving back into the Sunday night slots at the Rome Inn, doing Wednesdays at Soap Creek, Thursdays at Antone's. Stevie would take any gig he could scrounge, regardless of pay or whether he had a band to play it.

In Double Trouble, Stevie sang half of the material. He had finally learned to tolerate, almost enjoy, the sound of his voice. He and the band would open sets with tunes like Otis Rush's "All Your Love (I Miss Loving)," Howlin' Wolf's

Stevie Ray with Double Trouble at the Rome Inn, 1979. He later gave this Rickenbacker guitar to Hubert Sumlin. Photo by Kathy Murray.

immortal "Howlin' For My Darlin'," and Albert King's "Crosscut Saw." These years were lightly referred to as his Guitar Slim phase, because he did four numbers by the Louisiana guitar legend (whose real name was Eddie Jones): "Letter To My Girlfriend," "They Call Me Guitar Hurricane" (Jones recorded it as "They Call Me Guitar Slim"), "Hug You, Squeeze You," and "The Things That I Used To Do." He still did the o b l i g a t o r y instrumentals, favorites like Albert Collins' "Frosty," "The Rhinogator" (a brief craze in which dancers would make grunting noises and flop around on the dance floor with their jaws wide open), and Freddie King's "In The Open" (a song he would play live throughout his entire career), before even calling Miss Lou Ann Barton to the stage.

Danny Thorpe, who had sold Stevie his favorite Strat six years before, moved back to Austin and went to check on Double Trouble at the Rome Inn. "I attended many of the band's first gigs, and I'll tell you—it scared me to death!" Thorpe says, his eyes bulging. "Stevie had really gotten *that* good. I'd swear to God, some spirit came into the room and overwhelmed everybody when he played. It was amazing; and Stevie's approach was incredible…so much fire!"

Kathy Murray recalls seeing Double Trouble at the Rome Inn in 1978. "Stevie was standing by the speaker stacks," she says, "trying to hear himself better, I guess. He was dressed in a kimono, looking like Jimi Hendrix, and I thought it was strange that he couldn't hear because his guitar sure was LOUD! I Mean, Stevie was really, really loud. I had never heard him turn it up that much before. He was no freaking violet before, but now he was louder and meaner than ever."

Margaret Moser gave Double Trouble its first media exposure in town, writing a story for the *Austin Sun* (which ran on July 27, 1978) and proclaimed "Stevie rules his audience with an iron hand and his scepter is his guitar...."

"I thought Lou Ann was great," Moser raves, "'cause she was real young and sassy and wore those big old taffeta dresses that came down to her knees, and stuff like that. Man, I'd never seen that kind of stuff. And I got it in spades from her.... And even with all those strong personalities, Stevie rose above it all. He played an extra two feet off the ground."

After a Double Trouble gig at Antone's, Stevie grabbed Margaret and took her out back to smoke a joint. As they were sitting in a pickup truck, three-to-a-seat, smoking some great pot, Stevie turned to Margaret with a serious expression and remarked, "You know, my nose isn't really like this. I don't have any cartilage in my nose because my brother broke it."

Margaret looked at him crazy and said, "Stevie, what the fuck are you talking about?" Stevie demonstrated, pressing his nose flat as a pancake against his face.

"See?"

Margaret was mortified, and her face showed it. "Yeah, my brother used to beat up on me all the time when we were kids and he broke my nose a couple of times and that's how come it looks like it does," he said. Moser got over her horror soon enough—she loved him anyway, "tomato nose" and all.

Stevie's eyes nearly popped out when he picked up the August 1978 issue of *Buddy* magazine, and saw that Jimmie Vaughan was ranked high among Texas' finest guitarists—listed alongside Billy Gibbons, Bugs Henderson, John Nitzinger, and Rocky Athas—in the annual Texas Tornadoes Awards.

A good break happened for Double Trouble in the spring of 1979, when Joe Gracey walked in on a Rome Inn gig. He was the most popular deejay in Austin, doing mornings on KOKE, the town's aptly named progressive country station. Gracey had a little studio he called "Electric Graceyland," and invited the band to come over and cut anytime they wanted, giving them free reign over the studio and even their own key. It took Double Trouble six months to finish their first demo, recorded on a cheap quarter-inch tape. The session, which still circulates in the bootleg market, is the precursor to the sound that Stevie was working hard to ultimately perfect. Several familiar cuts are here: the first recorded versions of "Love Struck Baby," "Rude Mood" (influ-

enced by Gracey's label, which was Rude Records), "Empty Arms," and "Pride and Joy." Surprisingly, when Stevie took "Pride and Joy" home to Lenny she threw a fit, convinced that the song was about Lindi and not her. Wounded, Stevie returned to the studio alone late that night, wrote some new words and retitled it, "I'm Cryin'."

Stevie and Lenny had moved into a house together on Rabb Road in the fall of 1978, and Lenny realized that she couldn't play housewife like she had with Joe; while Siddons was always in the money, Stevie was down on his luck. He'd just started a new band, and the gigs weren't rolling in like he'd hoped. He could barely scrape together enough change to buy a pack of cigarettes, much less pay rent. So Lenny got a job as a computer programmer by day, took Stevie out at night to get loaded, then the two would make love until daybreak. With Stevie's insatiable sexual appetite, Lenny would be lucky to catch an hour of sleep before reporting to work at 7:55 A.M. sharp. It's no wonder Lenny developed a monstrous coke habit. Their very survival depended upon her making it to work each and every day—how else was she to stay awake?

Lenny solved the problem by fueling it; she soon discovered that cocaine made more money for them than her day job ever would. She let the job go, which allowed her to spend more time at home with Stevie and The Habit, their ever-present roommate and best friend.

Life was simple, to say the least—they had no furniture to speak of, no stove, no refrigerator, no freezer. They kept beer, water, and soft drinks in an ice chest, and cooked dinner in the fireplace. Luckily, they were so madly in love that these radical inconveniences didn't get them down. Maybe ignorance was bliss.

All the grueling, low-pay gigs were beginning to pay off for Double Trouble. Although they still weren't in the money, they were earning something perhaps more useful—a reputation for the loud, butt-rockin' dance parties they hosted, the ballsy chick singer who could part your hair when she sang "Rocket In My Pocket," and the brilliant lightnin' boy guitarist, now billed as Stevie "Hurricane" Vaughan.

Ron Young, pop music critic for the *San Antonio Light*, recalls seeing Double Trouble at the Old Reed's Red Derby on San Pedro Street: "Only a handful of people were in the place and there was no cover charge. But Vaughan rocked, giving all his heart, just like he came to do in arenas and concert halls around the world. After the show, I told Stevie his then-developing style was going to someday overshadow Eric Clapton's. He just grinned, shaking his head."

Mike Kappus, founder of San Francisco's Rosebud Agency and manager for Robert Cray, John Lee Hooker, and John Hammond Jr., remembers seeing Stevie for the first time in 1978. "Myself and some friends had driven some distance to check out this guitarist with the growing reputation and arrived during the last number," Kappus told *BAM* magazine. "We went backstage and somehow convinced Stevie to do one more song. There were about 6 people in the club when the final note rang out."

Kappus was involved in promoting the annual San Francisco Blues Festival with Tom Mazzolini, and invited the band to come out for next year's show. The T-Birds had just done the massive outdoor gala, and knocked the crowd dead. "The impact the Thunderbirds had was s*tunning*," Mazzolini emphasized. "After seeing them, Bay Area bands realized their potential more. They shaved their beards, wore ties and clean clothes, and started emulating the Texas scene…almost overnight."

Lou Ann's reputation was spreading like wildfire; she appeared in a picture in *Rolling Stone*, sharing a warm hug with Muddy Waters while sitting on his lap. And once the band started playing major blues festivals, it was Lou Ann the critics and fans tended to gravitate toward. They found it so ironic that a 25-year-old white woman would take to the blues in the age of disco, and would do it so well. Stevie didn't understand why Lou Ann was getting so much attention, and found it hard to swallow that she was the star of the show.

Stevie's "look" had evolved from the scraggly long-haired hippie Nightcrawler to the smooth polyester pimpster of the Cobras. Now that "Hurricane" had Double Trouble, he streamlined his fashions to skin-tight double-knit trousers, pullover shirts, and Japanese kimonos, topped by a beret that covered his already balding head. He sported a "soul tip," the little patch of hair that started at his lower lip and pointed at his chin. Sometimes, he'd even slick back his hair like Jimmie, donning a leather jacket if he wanted to look really tough. Austin laughed out loud and the in-crowd complained he was still trying to be like his big brother.

Stevie shut their mouths in August 1979 when Double Trouble put on a galvanizing performance at the Austin Blues Festival, starting off with a slinky, sensuous version of "Natural Born Lover," then charging through Lou Ann's medley of Slim Harpo songs like "Ti-Na-Ne-Na-Nu," and "Scratch My Back." Lou Ann gave Jimmy Reed's "I'll Change My Style" a pout-and-squeak reading that even Betty Boop would admire. Stevie's playing may have been a little restrained here, but what makes it refreshing is how much care and study he put into not damaging a blues song's fragile integrity. This rare display of taste and control was magnificent. He didn't add anything new to the art form, but it's hard enough to keep the form alive and breathing, let alone to make anyone give a damn about it.

Luckily, Takoma Records gave a damn about the blues (one of the few labels that did in 1979), and signed the Fabulous Thunderbirds. Their self-titled debut album (subtitled *Girls Go Wild*) was soon on the streets, and helped them get a few more gigs, but otherwise didn't do diddly for their fledgling careers. The label didn't promote or distribute the album very well, and it was a commercial flop. The American market just couldn't get behind a roots record, although a second listen might have proved that this band was fine-tuned. Perhaps the only good thing that came out of the Takoma deal was that Chrysalis, a much larger record label, felt the album deserved another shot, and signed the Thunderbirds.

Stevie didn't exactly have a record contract like Jimmie, but at least someone wanted to pay him $7,000 for the tapes he'd cut with Joe Gracey earlier in the year. Joe and Stevie said yes immediately, then took it upon themselves to recut the whole project at Jack Clement's swank twenty-four track home studio in Nashville. In September, they loaded up all the gear and proceeded to spend the next week in a drunken Music City haze, fiddling around with the knobs for hours, and trying to cut something of worth, but coming up empty handed. Something about the record just didn't sound right this time; the tones were too sterile, and the fire was lost from the performance, leaving them in the end with a master that sounded even worse than the original demo.

When he got back home, he heard that Gracey had every intention of releasing the record. After all, he had to make back the investment. Stevie put his foot down. He would not hear of it, and refused to sign the contract. The investor, pissed off that his seven grand was going to go down the toilet, began to harass Stevie, sending henchmen to his gigs yelling threats and slitting the tires on the band's van. Stevie knew that the guy would get his money back someday, but there wasn't a damn thing he could have done about it then.

Stevie and Lenny's intake of alcohol and cocaine increased with every paycheck, every gig. Stevie got in the habit of carrying a bottle of Chivas Regal with him all day long, always polishing it off prior to showtime and sometimes following that with a shot in the arm. Even the band, who did their share, were worried about the large amounts that Stevie was doing. Yet, he seemed to handle it so well that, once onstage, nobody could discern that he was screwed up. But the words that Muddy Waters once told him still rang deep in his mind: "Boy, you could be the greatest guitar player that ever lived, but you won't live to see forty if you don't leave that white powder alone." How oddly prophetic the advice would turn out to be.

Stevie felt a little homesick around Christmas, and began to call up old friends. He talked to Doyle, whose life had taken a major turn for the better after some tough times spent in Dallas, when he met Barbara Logan, the woman who inspired him to quit drinking and supported him through his desperately needed rehabilitation. (Soon afterward, Bramhall was inspired to write a joyful shuffle one afternoon while watching Barbara plant flowers in her mother's garden. He called it "Lookin' Out The Window.") He also called up Rocky Athas, who just happened to be coming to town for a gig at the Armadillo. Stevie yearned to spend some time with his old friend, whom he hadn't seen in two years. "We were opening for Kansas," Rocky chuckles, "and Stevie came over in the afternoon while we were doing soundcheck. I showed him this '58 Cherryburst that I'd been wanting all my life, you know. He said, 'These are nice, but I just can't play Les Pauls. But I've got this Strat here that's just as old...'

"So he's sitting there playing it, and the representative for the local Musicians' Union decides to stop by and collect dues from the players. Stevie heard he was in the building and he told me, 'Look. I'm about three payments behind on my dues. I can't let this guy see me.' So he goes over and hides behind the couch. The union guy comes in and asks, 'Have you seen Steve?' and of course, I said 'No, sir.' After the guy left, I waved at Stevie to come out. He just seemed so confused. He said 'Man, I don't get this union stuff. We have to pay them dues, and we don't make any money.' I always thought that was funny. Here he was, hiding out over twenty-one dollars. But when

you've only got $1.80 in your pocket, what can you do?"

Stevie eventually traced his Christmas blues to the source; he was lonely, that's all there was to it. He and Lenny had been more off than on lately, due to too much cocaine-inspired bickering. Stevie was back to crashing on couches and Lenny was flirting with whomever she saw fit, but he missed her companionship something awful. Ever since Stevie was a child, he feared being alone more than anything else on earth. He couldn't even stand it for a few minutes. Some folks surmise that's why he really picked up the guitar. It was a faithful companion when Mom and Dad were at work, and Jimmie was out with friends. The guitar wouldn't leave him or break his heart like a lover; it only gave pleasure. As Stevie explained it himself: "The guitar is my first wife. She don't talk back; she talks *for* me. She don't scream at me; she screams *for* me—and she sho' have a sweet tone when she do." It was his one true love and confidante—not just for the day, but for life.

Yet, Stevie dreamed of getting married, doing the right thing for himself and the woman he loved. Trouble is, he had a hard time figuring out exactly *who* he loved. He still wanted Lindi after nearly two years apart and he proposed to her, but she said no way. While waiting in line for beer at a convenience store one night, he asked Mary Beth Greenwood to marry him too; she was shocked and flattered, but figured he had to be kidding and declined. That night he dreamed of Lenny sitting on Howlin' Wolf's knee while he sang the deepest blues Stevie had ever heard. She was having a natural ball, dishing out as much raunch and passion as Wolf himself. Then he knew it for sure; Lenny was "as mean as Howlin' Wolf," and she would be his bride.

On December 23, 1979, he saw Lenny before his gig at the Rome Inn, and told her that she was literally the woman of his dreams, and that he wanted to marry her—tonight! Miraculously, she said yes, so C-Boy summoned a preacher out of the phone book. Stevie and Lenny called their folks and friends, who were naturally bumfuzzled. Mary Beth Greenwood loaned Lenny a silk shirt so she could at least look somewhat orthodox for the wedding pictures.

Stephen Ray Vaughan and Lenora Darlene Bailey took their vows between sets on the dance floor of the Rome Inn, slipped rings (made out of scrap wire off the ground) on each other's fingers, and proclaimed love everlasting. A few close friends bore witness: W.C. Clark, Gretchen Barber (who was dating Billy Gibbons at the time), Chris and Jackie Layton, Cutter, and the rest of the band. Jimmie arrived late, missing the wedding but just in time for the reception. Lou Ann and Diamond Joe stood back and watched the happy couple kissing, opening the hastily purchased wedding gifts and feeding each other wedding cake, wondering what was to come next. Lou Ann was especially worried about the future of the band; she had lost her man, but was she losing her guitarist, too? Although the band was constantly rocked by ego clashes, both Stevie and Lou Ann knew that the onstage chemistry worked. They had come a long way in less than a year, and yet they nearly hated each other.

"Stevie was so funny when it came to women," Margaret Moser observes. "He had a lot of girls, but I think he was a lot more interested in playing guitar than chasing pussy... I really don't like what she [Lenny] did to Stevie. But he seemed to be really nuts about her... Stevie's management desperately wanted Lenny out of the picture—she was an embarrassment."

Stevie's cousin Connie Trent held a totally different view of Lenny: "The Lenny that I *first* met," Connie clarifies, "I started hearing about her from my aunt. She said that Stevie had met this girl in a club and that he was going to marry her—in a club! Jimmie said he liked her, that she was a nice girl, real sweet. And back then, she was an innocent, shy little girl. Very...religious. She was in no way prepared for what was to come. She didn't know then that Stevie was going to hit the big time, and what the pressures of that would be like. She was really in love with him, too."

When Connie spoke of Lenny's strong religious interests, she wasn't necessarily referring to a "traditional" faith. Lenny was obsessed with the occult, psychic phenomena, casting runes, astrology, voodoo, and other sundry superstitions. Stevie also was infatuated with the supernatural all his life, and toyed with various religions and beliefs, constantly seeking the oracle but never quite finding it through any other channel but his instrument. When he picked up the guitar and magically rubbed his hands across the strings, he talked to angels, flirted with demons—and kissed the sky.

Newlyweds Stevie and Lenny at his parents' house in Oak Cliff. Courtesy of Connie Trent.

A cassette tape still exists of a soundboard recording done at a short-lived Austin club called Peona's in late 1979 that finds Stevie clearly taking the wheel, leading the band with true force and power through "Love In Vain" (not the Robert Johnson composition), a swinging blues tune that really sounded like the Double Trouble Thundershuffle the world would later come to love. It was apparent by the audience's reactions and his increasing presence, that he didn't need some female singer prancing around in a halter top to thrill a crowd. He didn't need a saxophone player either, and Johnny Reno knew it. Reno split the group, claiming that he wasn't getting paid enough money to put up with all the headaches of working for two irrational, irresponsible leaders who had no game plan and were winging it through life.

Stevie admittedly needed help when it came to running a band. He wasn't prepared for the responsibility of booking gigs (much less tours), negotiating with flaky clubowners, and handling all the promotional stuff a bandleader is expected to juggle. All he wanted to do was play his guitar, so these crucial duties often went neglected. That problem was solved when Joe Priestnitz asked Double Trouble to join the roster of bands under his new booking agency, Rock Arts. It was a simple agreement; they kept Double Trouble working and in return took fifteen percent of the pie.

Priestnitz sent them out to California to play the San Francisco Blues Festival as promised, routing supporting dates through Santa Fe, Berkeley, and Palo Alto, California. When they finally reached the festival, Double Trouble burned with an intensity that impressed even the hardcore purists in the audience that day. During their 45-minute set, Stevie noticed a handsome brown-eyed black man standing backstage, his eyes fixed on Stevie's flying fingers. He was smiling.

The man turned out to be Robert Cray. Stevie's Hendrix bit had really blown his socks off, being that he also hailed from Seattle and worshiped Jimi Hendrix. "We did four or five dates together in the Bay Area and Santa Cruz, switching opening slots, and we became pretty good friends," Cray later told *Rolling Stone*. "We had barbecues together down in Santa Cruz. We went to pick him up one afternoon for a barbecue, and he was dressed up like Jimi Hendrix—had a Jimi Hendrix wig on and a little short Japanese kimono. We were just rowdy youngsters then."

While in the Bay Area, Double Trouble did a live radio broadcast in Gilroy that captured Stevie playing slide, along with Robert Cray on second guitar, Curtis Salgado (from Roomful of Blues) on harp, and Lou Ann singing. The people out west were truly wowed by these crazy kids from Texas, by the way they dressed, drank like fish, loved the blues, and talked like southern farmhands. Double Trouble had conquered the City by the Bay.

On the way back to Texas, the van's engine burned up primarily because Stevie altogether forgot that it required oil to operate. While the band was stranded somewhere in the desert, he phoned Priestnitz and begged him to wire money to get the whole band and their equipment back home.

They barely had time to unpack before they were onstage at the Armadillo opening for Randy Hansen and Machine Gun, a Jimi Hendrix tribute band. Lou Ann was wearing tight blue jeans with a gold sequined stretch halter top, and caught Hansen leering at her from offstage. Although Stevie thought Hansen was an overstuffed bag of tricks, Stevie did learn a valuable lesson from him that night; if you can actually play Hendrix's demanding style and get that monster tone, then you might as well do it. Why hold back?

As Stevie grew less inhibited on guitar, working up the nerve to play Hendrix songs like "Manic Depression," "Third Stone From The Sun," "Little Wing," and "Voodoo Chile," the Austin blues crowd turned up their noses at him, opting to go see the Fabulous Thunderbirds play traditional, sweetly understated down-home blues. Thus the line was drawn by everyone, especially Lou Ann, who was heard telling him backstage: "Little Stevie, if you want to play that bullshit, do it somewhere else."

They Call Me Guitar Hurricane

STEVIE BEGAN to claim that the spirit of Jimi Hendrix had not only spoken to him, but it had seemingly entered his body and was taking over the way he played. Whether such statements were founded in truth or coke-induced fantasy isn't important; all that really mattered was that Stevie resurrected Hendrix's ideas, meshed them with his own, and it worked.

Stevie went junking in local thrift and secondhand shops, looking for long, colorful scarves, tighter trousers, kimonos, paisley vests, and the right lid to top it all off. It had to be a Spanish bolero hat—nothing else would do. The old apple jack cap was turning into a real pain in the ass anyway; it kept falling off when he played, and the thing tended to subtract ten years off his already boyish face. Stevie grew long, freaky sideburns like Jimi's, even sported a soul tip beneath his chin, and borrowed turquoise and silver jewelry from every woman he knew. Friends noticed him talking funny, too. He would go off on these bombastic stream-of-consciousness lectures about music or art or the news or anything, just to hear himself prattle. It was as if he had changed overnight; yeah, he had always liked Hendrix, but wasn't this a little much?

The problems were worsening between Stevie and Lou Ann. As if the musical preferences weren't weird enough, the main difference between them was personal. Stevie could handle his shit and Lou Ann couldn't if it had been handed to her in a box. The booze was getting to her, affecting her performance so much that the poor girl was literally falling down drunk onstage. An ill-fated southern tour only accelerated the tension, and everyone in the band knew it was only a matter of time before the pressure cooker blew its top.

Cleve Hattersley, an Austin musician (formerly of Greezy Wheels) and business manager, had moved to New York in 1978 to book the legendary Lone Star Roadhouse, and gave Double Trouble their first Manhattan gig in 1980. "We booked them for $100," Hattersley told *Guitar World*. "They drove all the way up from Austin, and crashed on friends' couches. The gig went alright, but afterwards, Lou Ann got out of hand. She was real drunk and throwing beer glasses and screaming at the waitresses. And Stevie, of course, was upset. That was the final gig that band ever had together."

Double Trouble was booked to play Lupo's Heartbreak Hotel in Providence, Rhode Island, the next evening and Stevie was troubled. He had no idea how he was going to fire Lou Ann in the middle of a tour. Luckily, she quit that afternoon, informing Stevie that she was joining the Providence-based band Roomful of Blues, and that he would have to carry on without her. He packed up the gear and drove home to Austin with his mind on the future. He was relieved to be free of the albatross, but didn't know what he was going to do. Lead his own band? Stevie laughed out loud at the preposterous notion. Yeah, right.

That notion, much as he feared it, festered in his mind constantly. Why couldn't he do it? He already had a tight band that promised to stand by him, a good booking agent, a few songs, and a whole lotta attitude. By now he could play any blues or R&B classic blindfolded, but what he really wanted to do was turn up his damn guitar and go for it, just like Hendrix did. Stevie was, after all, a restless, questing spirit, and knew he could never be satisfied playing studio gigs for chump change the rest of his life. So why not? He had nothing to lose...except his freedom.

Stevie came dangerously close to the slammer his very first night with the new, streamlined Double Trouble when he and Lenny were busted for cocaine in Houston. The band had just opened a show for Muddy Waters at the Palace, where an off-duty police officer caught the lovebirds having too much fun backstage, and promptly carted their happy asses to the city jail. Priestnitz bailed them out that night, allowing Stevie to make a gig in Lubbock.

Meanwhile, things were rapidly changing in Austin. The scene that had given life to Double Trouble and other great blues bands was crumbling fast; Antone's was forced to move out of the building on Sixth Street to make way for a parking garage, finding a temporary location in a shopping center on far north Anderson Lane. The Soap Creek Saloon also fell to the wrecking ball, and relocated in North Austin inside the building that once housed the legendary Skyline Club. The Armadillo closed down too. The cosmic cowboy movement that it built its reputation on was dying, the shed was losing money fast, and the owners could only watch sadly as the Austin institution was razed to make way for a highrise.

Nothing as wonderful as the Rome Inn could last forever either, and the doors closed for good in March 1980. "The woman who owned the building was getting old," C-Boy explained, "and she sold it to some guy. He didn't want no music, he didn't want no whiskey or beer. He *did* want $2,000 a month rent. So we just had to get out. Man, I got calls from up in New York, Chicago, everywhere, people calling me I never met before saying 'Keep the Rome Inn going. Don't let it go!' "

The Rome Inn heralded their closing with an incredible final week of rhythm-and-blues, featuring all of the bands that gave the club its infamous reputation; Double Trouble (who played "The Sky Is Crying" for C-Boy), Lewis and The Legends, W.C. Clark, Angela Strehli, and Kathy and The Kilowatts all played farewell shows that week. The last concert played inside those walls was, of course, the Fabulous Thunderbirds. All accounts say they cooked that night, bringing in their sizable local following, making a load of money and giving it all back to C-Boy, who had been so generous to the band when they were struggling. They promised a long time ago that they would someday pay him back, and they did—with interest.

Although its closing signaled the end of a decade and the end of an era, the spirit of the Rome Inn continued to live on in the hearts of its musicians and patrons. (C-Boy passed away some years later, on January 25, 1991, at age sixty-eight.)

With the closing of the Rome Inn, Stevie took to spending his nights at Antone's. He got to know Hubert Sumlin, Mel Brown, Lonnie Mack, Bonnie Raitt, and Buddy Guy, who all nearly established residency there.

Although Antone's closed at two A.M., Stevie said it wasn't unusual for the music to last until 4:30—when it had started at midnight.

A family snapshot (1980). *Left to right:* Jimmie, Big Jim, Stevie, Lenny, and Tina (Jimmie's daughter). Courtesy of Connie Trent.

That's how it went at Antone's, night after night. Stevie and Lenny turned into the proverbial lounge lizards, taking in the blues. Stevie had the rare opportunity to not only play with the masters but to drink with them and hear their stories firsthand, and he made lasting friendships with them years before the rest of the world ever heard of Stevie Ray Vaughan. "One night, B.B. King scared me to death," Stevie later recalled in an interview with *Guitar Player.* "He sat on his amp and played rhythm for me for about four songs. And then he stood up and played one note—you know, one of those B.B. notes that makes you go 'Hauugh!'" From that night onward, Stevie could count the King of the Blues as one of his personal friends.

On April 1, Stevie Vaughan and Double Trouble played a now-legendary concert at Steamboat 1874, a two-story club on Sixth Street whose name alludes to the historic building's age. The performance was broadcast live on FM rocker KLBJ's now-defunct "Better Late than Never" program. Stevie and band arrived at six P.M. for the soundcheck, and although this new lineup was only two months old, they felt confident that the show would be a breeze. That night was recorded on a multitrack recorder, and mixed down to two tracks. The tapes were offered to Double Trouble after the show, but no one bothered to claim them, and the reel-to-reel multitrack masters were subsequently erased. Luckily, the two-track mix master still exists, and that is what fans now hear on 1992's *In the Beginning* CD (Sony/Epic).

After a brief introduction by host Wayne Bell, Stevie blasted into the open with his trademark Freddie King instrumental, followed by another favorite, an Elmore James-influenced boogie titled "Slide Thing." "The Sky Is Crying," and "I'm Leavin' You (Commit a Crime)" were performed next, but were edited out of the album (although the entire broadcast can still be found on various bootlegs). He exploded on Otis Rush's "All Your Love (I Miss Loving)," singing with a mighty command that shocked the Austin audience because his improvement as a vocalist was so significant. "Tin Pan Alley" is a masterpiece, and for several years was the most requested song on KLBJ, even ranking above "Stairway To Heaven."

"Love Struck Baby," "Tell Me," Howlin' Wolf's "Shake For Me," and Stevie's own "I'm Cryin'" (mistakenly retitled "Live Another Day" on the CD) closed the show. Actually, Stevie played a lot longer, but the station ran

Hurricane takes the wheel. The new, improved Double Trouble in 1980. Photo by Daniel J. Schaefer. Courtesy of Epic Records.

out of tape, and failed to capture the entire performance.

Later that month, Stevie and Lenny had their court date in Houston, pleading guilty to possession of cocaine. Stevie somehow managed to skate with only two years' probation; Lenny got five. Part of his probation included drug abuse treatment, but it is not known whether Stevie even set foot inside a clinic. He was also told that under no circumstances could he leave the state of Texas, and that he couldn't hang out with "persons of disreputable character."

By happenstance, Stevie was making new friends of a more respectable nature. He had known Edi Johnson, an accountant at the Manor Downs racetrack, for several years. She knew a little about the music biz through an association with Frances Carr, the owner of Manor Downs who not only loved the blues but also had friends in high places—namely the Grateful Dead. When Double Trouble was offered a record contract from Takoma Records (who released the T-Birds' first album), Stevie asked Edi to play the role of manager and review the long legal document. She admittedly didn't know what she was doing, but looked it over before passing it on to another Manor Downs music buff, an Irish entrepreneur/concert promoter named Chesley Millikin.

Chesley told Stevie not to sign it. He felt a better deal could be secured with a bigger record label, and furthermore, he was going to be the one to do it. Millikin wanted to be Stevie's manager, with a little help from his friends Frances and Edi. They formed a company called Classic Management, signing Double Trouble as their prime act in May, 1980.

Classic Management put the band on a salary of $225 a week plus per diems (although Stevie didn't realize this money was recoupable), hired Cutter Brandenberg to road manage Double Trouble, and recruited publicist extraordinaire Charles Comer to help promote them. The team knew that making stars out of raggedy blues players wasn't going to be a waltz in the age of punk rock, new wave, and MTV hair bands. Stevie was no matinee idol—none of the guys were exactly dreamboats—so Chesley figured the band should try out another female vocalist. That idea failed, and Classic finally realized that Stevie's talents were already so well-directed that their best approach would be not to try and squeeze him through the star machine, but to amplify what was already there. An important, almost poetic component of his existing persona was the middle name Ray, which Stevie rarely used. Chesley wanted to push Stevie out front as the undisputed leader, and hereby christened them Stevie "Ray" Vaughan and Double Trouble.

The T-Birds toured widely in the U.S. that year, but were an even bigger hit in blues-crazed Europe, where they traveled the U.K. in support of Rockpile, a group led by Dave Edmunds and Nick Lowe, both ardent Thunderbirds fanatics. The Fabulous Thunderbirds returned home triumphant, and played their biggest Dallas concert to date at the Agora Ballroom on Sunday, June 22, 1980. Within a few months, drummer Mike Buck left the band, and was soon re-

Stevie Ray with his beloved Number One. Photo by Daniel Schaefer. Courtesy of Epic Records.

Rare commemorative poster for Stevie's birthday party at Antone's, October 3 and 4, 1980. Art by Danny Garrett. Courtesy of Danny Garrett/The Center for American History, The University of Texas at Austin.

placed by Fran Christina (nicknamed "Franny"), a former member of both Roomful of Blues and Asleep at the Wheel.

The summer of 1980 was the one Texas could never forget. Boiling hot 100°-plus temperatures cooked the Southwest for two consecutive months, making the masses crazy from the heat. *Houston Chronicle* critic Marty Racine recalls those long, excruciatingly hot weekends when Double Trouble would rock Fitzgerald's: "Sometimes at night when the waitresses were picking up empty glasses and soiled napkins and fallen chairs, he would plop alone on the lip of the stage exhausted and tap out a sublime instrumental to chase the stragglers home. ['Lenny'] The stragglers understood. It was church in the honkytonk, the silence that follows every storm, and it played out forlornly in the humid Gulf Coast night when the rest of the city slept and the restless souls who remained would make their peace, still sweating from ripping up the joint."

Stevie was visiting Dallas when he heard that Albert King was in town. He went to the hall early, around soundcheck time, so that he could get the best seat in the house and maybe get a chance to talk to his spiritual godfather for a few minutes. As Stevie waited there in the dark bar, he saw the door open, and there was Albert King, standing in the bright white daylight. Albert walked right up to him, pointed his long, mighty finger at Stevie, and spoke plainly: "I remember you, 'bout three-and-

a-half years ago we met, right?"

Stevie was dumbfounded. "He started calling me by name, telling me where we met, what happened and everything," Stevie recalled. "Later on that night, I was sitting in the audience, and he starts talking about this 'little kid, ninety-eight pounds soaking wet,' you know…then all of a sudden I hear my name. He called me up to the stage with my guitar and I thought I was gonna play one song with him. But I ended up sitting in for the rest of the night. It was amazing, you know? Nicest guy I ever met."

Double Trouble was playing a saloon on Dallas' Greenville Avenue that same weekend when a familiar face walked in the door. Stevie recognized him as Ronny Sterling, Jimmie's best friend when they were kids. "They were playing to a grand total of around twelve people," Ronny remembers. "Nobody was even paying much attention to him then; but then again, some of us knew that he was going to make it, it was just a matter of time."

The next night (August 30, 1980), Stevie and Double Trouble were playing in Fort Worth at a little joint called Blossoms' Downstairs, smoking the blues in front of a small, wild crowd of about forty people. He opened with "Wham," and "They Call Me Guitar Hurricane," and for the next few hours, rocked the house with songs that would later wind up on Double Trouble albums. Amazingly, the arrangements would change little over the next ten years; even "Tell Me Darlin'" sounds exactly the same as it did on "In Step," Stevie's final record. The set at the time included "The Sky Is Crying," "Empty Arms," "I'm Leavin' You (Commit A Crime)," "I'm Cryin'," "Love Struck Baby," "Tin Pan Alley," and "Tell Me." Stevie and the band were in rare form, ripsnorting through these and undiscovered classics like Wolf's "Howlin' For My Darlin'," as well as a delightful take on Albert King's "Crosscut Saw," which Stevie sang so well, it's a shame this jewel was never recorded professionally during his lifetime.

Stevie was shy when it came to onstage chatter; throughout the show, his only spoken words were not to the crowd, but to a waitress: "Can I get a snot of Shapps, please?…Er, excuse me—a shot of Schnapps?" he asked with chagrin. "Oh well," he mused off-mike as he knocked back the peppermint-flavored spirit, "I may not be able to pronounce it, but I can sure as hell drink it!"

On Halloween night, Stevie played a private party at the Ark Co-op dormitory on the UT campus, and blew everybody's mind when he showed up dressed just like Jimi Hendrix in blackface and an Afro wig. He played the part of a black prince all night, never breaking character—even reprising most of Hendrix's songs before the evening's end.

Michael Ventura was a friend of Stevie and Lenny's, and also wrote for the *Austin Sun*, an obvious plus to his musician friends. He included Stevie in many of his works, even basing a character on Vaughan in a novel he wrote years later. Ventura moved to Los Angeles after the *Sun* folded in 1979, but made frequent trips back to Texas—once in particular, just to see Double Trouble play. "I drove twelve hundred miles in one stretch to get to Lubbock in time to see his gig," Ventura recalls with a laugh. "Chris and Stevie said 'Hey, isn't that Ventura?' And I was so touched that it mattered to them. I told them that 'I could win a Pulitzer Prize, and I still wouldn't feel as good as I feel right now.'

"Stevie influenced me as a writer in the sense that he gave me an example of how I wanted to write," Ventura explains. "I wanted to write the way Stevie played." The three shared a certain affinity, and might spend entire nights listening to O.V. Wright records, making salsa, talking, and drinking. Ventura didn't dig coke, but stayed near Stevie as much as the social climate would allow.

Chesley and Joe Priestnitz started coordinating the band's maiden voyage of the northeast in the fall, but ran into a major snag with Stevie's probation rules—he still wasn't allowed to leave Texas. After several futile attempts to convince the parole officer, Chesley called a lawyer. Within hours, the parole officer was out of a job and Stevie was free to hit the road.

Although he'd played several of the venues before with Lou Ann, this time he had to stand or fall on his own. They were important gigs: New York, Washington, DC, Philadelphia, Boston— major eastern cities. One of the band's favorite stops was a Baltimore club (read: dive) called No Fish Today, located by the fishing piers in the most dangerous part of town—the

same neighborhood that Billie Holiday was born and raised. Dale Allen, a good-natured southern boy was a co-owner of the joint, and always tried to give Stevie Ray Vaughan and Double Trouble special treatment when they came to play, meaning that the band slept at Dale's house instead of in the van.

Stevie and bass player Jackie Newhouse got soused at the gig and were later seen duking it out in the parking lot, marking Stevie with an attractive black eye the next day. No Fish Today "mysteriously" burned to the ground a few years later, but it's still legendary among area blues hounds as one nutty, happening little haunt.

Shortly before Christmas, Stevie Ray Vaughan and Double Trouble played another successful two-night stand at Fitzgerald's in Houston. They were paid a visit that night by an old familiar face. Tommy Shannon had been hanging out in Houston, laying bricks by day, looking for the right inspiration to make music again. He found it sitting in the audience watching the "little midget" he knew from way back in Dallas. That's right, the kid that everybody used to snicker at was now the hottest guitar man he'd heard since Johnny Winter.

Tommy said he "saw his destiny" that night with Double Trouble, and when he sat in with them later, it felt better than he'd ever imagined. Two weeks later, Newhouse was fired and Shannon was in—permanently. Stevie was elated. He had worshiped Tommy Shannon since the Progressive Blues Experiment days with Winter, followed him around with Krackerjack, and now this cat was in his band. He had finally found the perfect combination of musicians, discovered the elusive thundershuffle that would catapult them into fame one day soon.

Stevie thought he had found the record deal of his dreams when he met Mindy

Newspaper advertisment for the shows at No Fish Today, the infamous dive that Stevie took a liking to on his first Northeast tour. Courtesy of Thomas Kreason/Rockabilia.

Stevie Vaughan and Double Trouble

february 12-13 DESPERADO'S washington d.c.
february 15-16 NO FISH TODAY baltimore, md.

east coast tour direction: Tom Carrico Studio One Artists po. box 5824 bethesda md. 20014, 301-279-5911

66

Getting serious about the
music, 1980. Courtesy of
Thomas Kreason/Rockabilia.

Giles, then the national
sales rep for Alligator
Records. Stevie loved
Alllgator's Chicago-based
roster; he thought that
Johnny Winter, Koko Taylor, Albert Collins,
Son Seals, and Lonnie Brooks were pretty
damn good company to share a label with.
He was as wild about the idea as Giles was
about his talent. She went back to Chicago
and tried to rustle up a gig for the band with
intent to schmooze the label into seeing and
signing Stevie Ray Vaughan. Chicago
clubowners protested. Unimpressed, they
asked who the hell was this 'Stevie Rave On'
anyway? She finally booked a showcase at
Jawbone's, a tiny neighborhood juke joint.
Unfortunately, label president Bruce Iglauer
thought Stevie was just another white boy
bluesman, and left before the band had
finished their first set.

Stevie returned to Austin with a
crushed ego, but his spirit was still stronger
than ever. These guys didn't know what
they were missing. He had the gift. He knew
he had it. He had a manager, a financial
backer, a band, a secretary, a roadie, and a
wife that knew it too. "It was just a matter
of time," he liked to say. But each new
disappointment made him want to drink,

smoke, and snort more to ease the discouragement
and keep his confidence from crumbling altogether. For a while, he didn't even bother coming
home if he had too much fun on the town; he'd
sleep in his car, on a couch, anywhere he happened
to finally pass out.

Danny Thorpe remembers Stevie from that
period as an all-night lounge rat, too wound up to
sleep or even relax due to his ever-increasing
consumption of cocaine. "More often than not,
Stevie didn't have anyplace to go," Danny glumly
recalls. "He went through a lot of rough times
with Lenny, and didn't always feel like going
home. I used to go to work at Heart of Texas
Music every morning at eight-thirty and Stevie
would be there, waiting for me to open up. He'd
head straight for the bathroom to snort some coke
or shoot something stronger. Ray [Hennig, the
store's owner] was a little bit naive to what was
really going on here, and he'd turn to Stevie and
say, 'My, but you're up awful early today.' I just
thought to myself, 'Well, he probably hasn't slept
in four days.'" Stevie began to use heroin to ease
himself down. It didn't work;
the combination of drugs only
made him a more erratic pain
in the ass.

In 1981, the T-Birds re-
leased their second album, *Butt*

Stevie with his prized
1928 National Steel
guitar. Courtesy of
Christian Brooks.

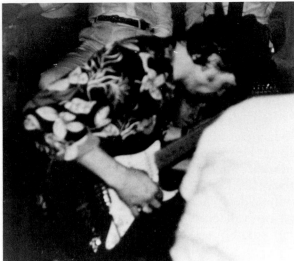

Rockin', which reunited them with the Roomful of Blues horn section. The Austin record release bash was held at the Paramount Theater downtown, and Stevie was invited to open the show, but he surprised everyone by politely declining, explaining that Jimmie played to a blues crowd and that he wanted to rock. *Butt Rockin'* garnered the Thunderbirds heavy praise from luminaries like the Rolling Stones, Eric Clapton, and Tom Petty, who offered the band opening slots on their tours that year. Even with celebrity endorsements and critical acclaim, the record still didn't sell.

Michael Ventura came to visit in the spring of '81, and after one particularly long night for Stevie, Michael and Lenny sat in the kitchen having breakfast. Lenny divulged that Stevie had played his guitar all night, came to bed at sunrise, then played in his sleep. She was awakened by his picking hand moving so hard and fast. She looked closer and observed that his face was scrunched up tight like onstage when he was really into it. She didn't wake him. "I just kinda listened, if you know what I mean," Lenny told him.

"Stevie told me once that he dreamed about Jimi Hendrix a lot," Ventura wrote in "Blues for Stevie" (a posthumous news article). "Jimi would teach him special changes in his sleep, but when Stevie woke up, he couldn't remember the lessons. He figured that was justice."

Stevie was booked for a two-night stand at Antone's that weekend, and Michael relished the opportunity to hear the new, improved Double Trouble. He and Lenny stood together (the joint

Left: Snapshot of Stevie and Lenny goofing off at Antone's in the spring of 1981. Courtesy of Michael Ventura.

Right: Stevie plays "Lenny" on Lenny (red Strat) for Lenny, who peers up at him from the awestruck audience. Courtesy of Michael Ventura.

was packed to the rafters) near the stage and watched Stevie rip and roar. "There's nothing but my half-dozen snapshots to record that night," Ventura says. "Stevie called a break, watched his band leave the stage, and pulled out an acoustic twelve-string. Lenny's eyes were wide, and she said, 'I never saw that guitar before!' Stevie jumped off the bandstand, asked someone for their chair, and sat down hunched over the twelve string. He closed his eyes and played like he was all alone. The club was packed, but it got real quiet. And stayed quiet, while Stevie went deeper and deeper into that twelve-string sound; he must have played for a half hour. 'Throw it all to the firewall' a woman near me said softly. I don't know quite what it meant, but it sounded exactly right. When he finally put the guitar down, nobody applauded, and few people moved. It was quiet as a church.

"I was honored to be one of the people Lenny would call for donations when he needed a new guitar," Ventura digresses. "He was real hard on guitars, and rarely sat in with another band if he hadn't brought his own for fear he'd break somebody else's instrument—not break the strings, but break the guitar. He never smashed one, he simply held the thing so hard the poor babies would just crack. Anyway, he came back on stage with the Fender that we'd chipped in for his birthday present. He sat in the chair again and played the pretty melody called 'Lenny' that he had just written for his wife. I have a snapshot of Stevie looking at Lenny, whose head is resting on her arms at the foot of the bandstand. There are others in the photo just standing, rapt, with eyes closed or heads down, the music taking them far into themselves. The song was timeless that night—not just longer but in another world. Then he called the band back and rocked us home. He played that night nonstop for three more hours.

"I went back the next night," he continues, "but something had happened and he was really upset. He played with a desperation that was unusual even for him.... I was there until after the place had closed, the chairs were up on the tables, and suddenly here was Stevie walking haltingly across the dance floor sobbing, sobbing and talking, talking quickly and to himself about love. How important it was to him, that through his playing people would know he loved. He loved them. That's what the music was for, it was for *love, love, love*. I cannot duplicate the shudder with which he said the word.

"I never found out what was eating him— my impression was that it had to do with his wife or his brother, but—it was none of my business and I didn't ask, because I felt like this was a moment I walked into. This wasn't a moment that was being given to me by him, you know. But he was weeping, and he looked at me and started talking. That was our last talk. It wasn't really a *talk*. He needed somebody to talk at."

That troubled evening left an indelible impression upon Michael's soul; he had witnessed the darkest side of Stevie Ray Vaughan, and it frightened him. In "Blues for Stevie," Ventura called it "the open wound, the raw and never-to-be-healed place that was the well-spring of his blues. The thing that was under the cockiness, the flashy hats, the drinking, the drugs, and later the abstinence."

At a Fitzgerald's show in Houston on October 14, they played two nights to packed houses, rollicking through "In The Open," "Come On (Pt. III)," "Look At Little Sister," "Close To You, Baby," "You'll Be Mine," "Thunderbird," and Guitar Slim's coy "Letter To My Girlfriend." Stevie was hot both shows, closing the second night with a rousing rendition of Hendrix's "Manic Depression," and "Little Wing," which featured a slice of "The Star-Spangled Banner" thrown in at the last few measures. Throughout the show, a man's voice was heard above the crowd, uttering only one word over and over again: "*Unbelievable!*"

Let's Dance

IN THE EARLY MONTHS of 1982, Lou Ann Barton released an album called *Old Enough*, which was her major label debut (recently reissued on Antone's Records). Glenn Frey of the Eagles had fallen in love with Barton's voice, signed her to Asylum Records, and produced the record along with vaunted R&B magic man Jerry Wexler.

Although the record contained a few gems, many of the songs were complete throwaways, limp pop numbers recommended by Frey. Reviews were not kind to Barton. *Rolling Stone* rock critic Deborah Frost called the album "dreary" and posed the question: "Did she do it for love? Did she do it for money? Did she do it for spite? Did she do it 'cause she had to, honey? She probably did it in one take." The album quickly fell out of sight after Lou Ann failed to show up at concert dates. Her record contract was canceled, and she was soon back on Antone's stage doing what she did best: singing rowdy blues and rockabilly songs to nominal crowds.

Oddly, Stevie Ray Vaughan and Double Trouble benefited greatly from Lou Ann's association with Jerry Wexler. While the producer was in town for Barton's record release at the Continental Club, he witnessed an all-star Austin jam with Lou Ann, Doug Sahm, Charlie Sexton, and Jimmie and Stevie Ray Vaughan. He liked what he heard, especially Stevie's wild guitar. Wexler attended Stevie's show the next night, and had a little talk with Chesley Millikin about the possibility of

The top local names joined together for the 1981 Austin Blues Heritage Festival, including Vaughan and Double Trouble. Poster courtesy of Jane St. John.

booking Stevie onto the Montreux Jazz Festival.

Claude Nobs, the producer of the festival, was convinced by Wexler that Double Trouble would be just right for a blues night, and told Classic Management the band could play if they covered their own expenses to get there. Ten thousand dollars later, the band had airline tickets and cartage arrangements to Lake Geneva, Switzerland, and started telling all their friends that their big break was finally coming on the stage of Montreux Jazz.

Stevie returned to Chicago in late March, this time making a much-ballyhooed performance with Albert Collins at the National Association of Music Merchants (NAMM) convention. He raised a few eyebrows, including those of a *Musician Magazine* critic who raved, "Vaughan and his two flame-throwing sidekicks reduced the stage to a pile of smoldering ashes." Still, no record contracts were offered.

In the spring, Chesley Millikin was paid a visit by his ex-employer, Mick Jagger. Jagger had come to Manor Downs with his girlfriend, Texas-born model Jerry Hall, to buy some quarterhorses. Chesley couldn't resist the opportunity to turn Mick on to his little discovery. He gave Jagger a videotape of Stevie playing a flood relief benefit at Manor Downs, and asked Mick for his honest opinion of the act. Jagger didn't watch it right away, but the Stones' drummer Charlie Watts did, and called Chesley immediately asking if the band could come play a private party at New York's Danceteria. The showcase was arranged especially for Stevie Ray Vaughan and Double Trouble to see if they might be appropriate as a new act on Atlantic/Rolling Stones Records.

The posh disco was packed with big-name stars, expensive groupies, beautiful models, and members of the pop elite. Even Johnny Winter attended the show after hearing what little Stevie Vaughan was up to. "There were all kinds of people," Stevie recalled, "everybody from Johnny Winter to—who's that blond-headed guy—Andy Warhol?" It was an exclusive party, however; the doors were closed to the general public, leaving Double Trouble alone with the Rolling Stones and about fifty intimate friends. They were afraid to stare too hard across the lights, because each face they recognized made them even more paranoid. Then things started going wrong.

The band was terrified. This was The Big Audition. "Yeah, we were nervous, no doubt about that," Stevie chuckled as he remembered the moment. "We were playing on rented equipment that was pretty shabby. Amps were blowing up and shit! (laughing) And then my strap holder came off. Not just the strap, but the holder itself popped off! I thought, 'Well, I guess I'm gonna have to just hold my guitar up for the whole show.' Fortunately, somebody was there who could fix that and we got on with it."

"Got it on" would be more like it. Stevie Ray brought the roof down, eliciting sensational rave reviews from *The New York Times* and even *Rolling Stone*, which ran a picture of Stevie, Mick Jagger, and Ron Wood laughing together. This was really big noise.

"Yeah, well, they liked it all right!" Stevie said. "We were supposed to just play 30 minutes, but everytime we were going to stop, they were yelling for us to keep on, screaming, 'We'll buy the whole goddamn club if we have to!'"

"I kept seeing this guy jumping up and

down, acting like he was playing along," Stevie told *The Dallas Morning News*. "With all those bright lights you could hardly see, and I thought it was somebody I knew from Texas. Come to find out it was Jagger that I'd been playing to the whole time, and I didn't even know it."

Stevie saw Ron Wood standing off to the side of the stage, his eyes as big as saucers. "Come on up and jam with us," Stevie offered. All Wood could say was, "What could I possibly play after *that*?"

After "that," the buzz on the street was that Stevie Ray Vaughan was to be signed to Rolling Stones Records and furthermore, the band would tour with the Stones in Europe on 1981's so-called "Farewell Tour." Unfortunately, the tour was canceled due to heavy riots in several cities.

Of course, the record contract from the Stones never came, although Stevie still spoke optimistically of it in an interview with Houston's *Zest* magazine. "We're negotiating a contract right now. I can't say when or who it is right now. I think it might be a good one. We're just trying to get something that *means* something to us when the record comes out. And means something to the guy who produces it, other than bucks. It's got to mean music to him and the same music to us, or it doesn't make any sense. I figure if they put out a record and promote it, it'll work. Because my soul is in it, you know."

Stevie Ray Vaughan and Double Trouble began to parlay more lucrative gigs around Austin, grabbing opening slots that promised high exposure. On Memorial Day, 1982, the band opened for Bobby and the Midnites, an R&B side project for the Grateful Dead's Bob Weir and his celebrated cast of players that included Billy Cobham, Dave Garland, Alphonso Johnson, and Bobby Cochran at Manor Downs. On Saturday, June 5, Stevie appeared as a special guest "star" when the Fabulous Thunderbirds opened for Jerry Lee Lewis at the racetrack.

On Monday, June 7,

Double Trouble shared a bill at the Austin Opera House with Dave Edmunds, Nick Lowe, and the Fabulous Thunderbirds, playing to a wildly appreciative audience. It was a blues/rock extravaganza and dance party that made headlines all over the region. But what made even bigger headlines was what happened the next night when Stevie was booked to open for the Clash's "Combat Rock" tour at City Coliseum—a strange pairing to begin with. As soon as the punk audience saw this Jimi Hendrix wannabe walk onstage, the beer cans and spitballs started flying. They heckled him through the entire set, but Stevie acted *professional*. He was gonna play his music and he didn't give a damn it these assholes listened or not. When the hellish set was over, he told Chesley to book another band for the second night—he wasn't going to let these ignorant punks make a fool out of him again.

That summer, Chrysalis released *T-Bird Rhythm*, the Thunderbirds' third effort. It was a much more focused, radio-ready album, produced by Nick Lowe. The label even made a video for "How Do You Spell Love?" But again, the best-laid plans were not enough. The album was lost in a corporate distribution shuffle, and the T-Birds were dropped by Chrysalis for good. For the next two years, the band would flounder without a record contract, caught in the crossfire Jimmie fired Keith Ferguson over a personal dispute, and hired another Roomful of Blues alumni, Preston ("Pinky") Hubbard on bass. They began recording another album with Dave Edmunds producing, and manager Mark Proct shopped it to every label in the U.S., only to be rejected. They just weren't the right stuff for the video genera-

Austin's Home of the Blues

Tommy Shannon   Stevie Vaughan

Chris Layton

Stevie's appearance at Montreux '82 brought him attention from John Hammond, Jackson Browne, and the Rolling Stones. Stevie returned triumphant, playing a welcome-home bash at Antone's. Courtesy of Keri Leigh.

tion. One A&R rep reportedly remarked, "The band I love, but how do I sell a fat, balding, forty-year-old vocalist who wears a turban to kids who watch MTV?"

Meanwhile, Stevie was on his way to Montreux XVI. On July 17, 1982, Double Trouble played the lavish Montreux Casino Stage to several thousand jazz and blues buffs. They came on with a rather tame "Hideaway"—everyone had been forced to turn the volume down considerably—but Stevie looked *cool* with a cigarette buried deep between his lips as he played an astonishing crossbreed of both the King and Clapton versions of the song. He stopped on a dime, and launched into "Rude Mood" for a few minutes, then slid right back into the last chorus of "Hideaway." The Swiss hippies thought he was righteous, dancing atop their seats while the more reserved, sophisticated jazz snobs sat motionless and puzzled. Some began to boo. Loudly. The reaction was even more mixed during "Pride And Joy," and Stevie was visibly shaken by their disapproval. He turned the guitar down even more, losing all tone in an effort to please the persnickety foreign audience.

Clad in a shiny red button-down shirt with silver pin-stripes against black dress slacks that were held up by a side conch belt around his tiny waist, Stevie looked every bit the part of the tough Texas Thunderbolt, and made "Texas Flood" a sacramental offering of Lone Star culture. "Love Struck Baby" was met with a profound amount of boo-hiss, and poor Stevie didn't know "whether to shit or go blind." His first European experience had turned into a nightmare. Stevie wasn't sure whether these people were yelling out insults or compliments. The tone of their voices didn't sound sympathetic, and the language barrier confounded him. He knew he wasn't on his turf anymore, that this wasn't the usual slew of Austin alkies ready to cheer him on no matter how he did. He had something to prove to these people—that he was a fierce new blueblood with a lot to offer.

Stevie summoned the courage to continue his set despite the jeering. After all, it was only about a quarter of the crowd that was howling for mercy—the other half was blown out of their socks by Stevie Ray Vaughan and Double Trouble's ass-wallopin' brand of heavy blues. He played "Dirty Pool," "Boilermaker," and included a surprise, too—Hound Dog Taylor's jumpy "Give Me Back My Wig," a blues classic that Stevie copped from Lightnin' Hopkins. He sang: *Give Me Back My Wig/Baby, now let your head go bald/Give me*

back that wig I bought you babe/Let your doggone head go bald/ You don't have no business/ Honey, wearin' no wig at all..." Montreux is the only known recording of this great song done by Stevie—an odd choice at an even odder time—but it worked very well and why it was permanently "lost" remains a mystery. He walked offstage to the roar of equally mixed hisses and hurrahs, turning his back instead of obliging the bastards with a final bow, and the band solemnly sulked away through the curtains, surely thinking to themselves, "Well, guess we really bit it this time."

Stevie was the first act in history to play the Montreux Jazz Festival without a record contract. Although this is considered the gig that give him his break, it almost destroyed his reputation—this was a jazz festival, and Stevie Ray Vaughan didn't play no jazz. "I got the feeling a few times that a couple of jazz musicians felt me and the boys were invading their turf," he said matter-of-factly, pulling his hat down over his eyes and fidgeting in his chair. "Now, I don't know about that. The blues and jazz come from the same place, now don't they? So these two music forms ought to get along if any two can."

It was not only Vaughan's rough-boy image and choice of rockin' material that bugged the elder statesmen of jazz, but his volume level was something the old-timers found particularly irksome. "They thought I was too loud," he complained, "but shoot, I had four army blankets folded over my amp, and the volume knob was on two. I'm used to playin' on ten! I don't mean to hurt nobody by playin' loud," Stevie added, apologetically. "But I've learned that an amp only works right when you turn that thing up to ten. Anything less, and you're stopping it from working. Guitar amps are made to overload."

Stevie always found it funny that the show that brought him the greatest international acclaim (and even won him a Grammy) was the only night in his life he was ever booed. "It wasn't the whole crowd," he was quick to point out. "I don't know if you've ever been to Montreux or not, but the room there was built for acoustic jazz. When five or six people boo—*wow!* It sounds like the whole world hates you."

For the next two nights, the band hesitantly accepted an impromptu booking inside the festival's basement after-hours bar, where the producers, musicians, and industry types would congregate. He worried that it might turn into another bummer, but his fears were abated on the first night when he heard David Bowie was in the house, was knocked out, and had asked to meet with Stevie if he could. *If he could?* The two ended up talking for hours about old blues records and the way Stevie played guitar. Bowie was ecstatic, and took Stevie's phone number. Said he might be calling.

The second evening, Jackson Browne and his entire band attended Stevie's show (after much prodding from Chesley), and were also blown away by this meat-and-potatoes rock and roller from the South. Chesley went to bed that night satisfied. The Montreux Jazz experience had indeed paid off for Stevie. He had no idea how well until he got up at seven the next morning and found Stevie and Jackson still in the bar, jamming away. Browne told Stevie that anytime he wanted to make a record, he should feel free to come to Los Angeles and use his home studio anytime—free of charge.

When Double Trouble came back home, the locals were foaming at the mouth. Everybody had heard about the superstars he'd been rubbing elbows with, and newspaper headlines reflected Austin's full support for Stevie Rave On (jealous fools called him "Stevie Ray Asshole" behind his back). His local gigs quickly turned into five-thousand dollar affairs (one Auditorium Shores' concert drew 12,000 people!) and Stevie felt like his time was near.

In November, he called Jackson Browne to check on the offer of studio time, and managed to burrow in at L.A.'s Down Town Studios for two days; not a lot of time to cut an entire album, but the band streamrolled through ten tracks, rarely stopping for overdubs unless Stevie busted a string. Luckily, Stevie had the foresight to bring along Richard Mullen, his favorite recording engineer from Austin's Riverside Sound, because Browne's house engineer apparently had no interest in doing anything for the band, and spent his time watching TV and eating microwave popcorn until Stevie politely asked him to leave.

The making of *Texas Flood* was no glamorous affair; the band had lined up only a few concert dates in California to support the trip, the budget was thinner than a shoestring (to say the least), and the studio itself was located in an alley behind a Goodwill store. Inside, it was no-frills all the way. Using Persian floor rugs and tapestries for baffles in the small concrete cutting room, the band managed to get decent sound quality, although it didn't begin to stack up to the big budget sound of Double Trouble's later records. Nevertheless, Stevie and the boys certainly made the best of what was available to them, producing a first effort that captured all the fire of a live show.

One night, recording was interrupted by a phone call from Chesley Millikin who informed Stevie that David Bowie had finally called. "Is the lad busy for, oh say, the next year?" Bowie had asked Chesley. Ziggy Stardust himself wanted Stevie to play on his upcoming album and accompany him on his next world tour as featured guitarist. Bowie even offered to hold off the recording sessions until January to ensure Stevie's availability. Chesley asked a stunned Vaughan what he thought of the proposal. Stevie paused, then accepted the unexpected invitation.

The next night, Stevie got another unbelievable phone call from Chesley. This time, it really was incredible news: legendary record producer John Hammond Sr. had heard about Stevie Ray and was interested in buying the album Stevie was recording at the moment. He wanted to sign Stevie Ray Vaughan and Double Trouble to his own Hammond Music Enterprises label. The elder Hammond had been a talent scout for Columbia Records since the 1920s, and was credited with discovering Bessie Smith, Count Basie, Aretha Franklin, Charlie Christian, Billie Holiday, Bob Dylan, and Bruce Springsteen, among a long list of others. "*Jesus Christ*," Stevie mumbled, astonished, "*And this guy digs ME?*"

For the rest of the night, Stevie tried to concentrate on the mixes of the demo they had just cut, but if John Hammond signed him to Columbia, they'd probably just re-record the whole thing anyway. He let Richard Mullen do his thing, totally unable to concentrate on anything but the flurry of opportunities that were suddenly landing in his lap. It was Thanksgiving night, 1982, and Stephen Ray Vaughan had a lot to be grateful for. He called his wife. He called his mother.

Bowie hired Vaughan immediately, long before he had hired the rest of the studio band or producer Nile Rodgers. From the late December night that Bowie telephoned Rodgers' Manhattan apartment to the album's final mix, the entire project took just five weeks, only three of which were spent actually cutting and mixing at New York's Power Station Studios. Stevie played on six songs, but took only two hours of studio time to overdub all the lead guitar tracks. The rest of the band consisted of drummers Omar Hakim (Weather Report) and Tony Thompson (Chic), Carmine Rojas (Nona Hendryx) on bass, and percussionist Sammy Figueroa and keyboardist Rob Sabito (two Chic alumni).

"He had this certain aura around him,"

producer Nile Rodgers told *Rolling Stone*. "He had this certain vibe. He and I hit it off right away. He picked up some of the guitars and started playing and making his comments. Then he noticed that we were eating barbecue. He says, 'Nile, man, I know where the best barbecue in the world is.' I said, 'Yeah, where, Stevie?' He says, 'A place called Sam's Barbecue, down in Texas.' And he gets on the phone, and within a few hours there's a box of ribs on its way from Austin to New York. That's the kind of guy he was.

"Another time, when I wasn't around, he was playing with one of my guitars, and he broke one of the strings," Rodgers laughs. "He wrote me the sweetest little note—it was just very Stevie Ray Vaughan. It said—I'm doing his voice, you know, 'cause he's got this accent—it said, 'Nile, I love your guitars. Sorry, brother, didn't mean to break no *straaaang*.' "

Bowie raved about Stevie to the press, mistakenly heralding him as a great blues purist: "I think he considers Jimmy Page something of a modernist," Bowie insisted. "The lad seems to have stopped at Albert Collins." The two were a fascinating, if unpredictable combination: The Thin White Duke meets The Texas Thunder.

Stevie learned a lot from the Bowie sessions about recording techniques for the guitar, and playing heavily stylized, intricate parts to Bowie's often treacherous chord structures. He even learned a little about reading sheet music, something he had never before tackled in his twenty years of guitar playing. "It was more an experience of looking at music in different ways, of looking at big arrangements and fitting the parts in," Stevie clarified. "I learned a lot about how songs are built. But the Bowie sessions were easy because I was basically free to do what I wanted. I really enjoyed the Power Station." (Stevie returned there in 1984 to record *Couldn't Stand The Weather*.)

While in New York, Stevie was invited by Houston-born blues legend Johnny "Clyde" Copeland to come spend a day in the studio playing on his *Texas Twister* album (Rounder Records). "I did three songs," Stevie told writer Bruce Nixon in 1983. "The two of us were just playing back and forth with the solos, with the horns and everything—the full band. It was great playing with him." A down-home dump near Times Square, it sure was a switch from the Power Station, which was the most high-tech thing Stevie had ever seen. Copeland had always been one of Vaughan's idols, especially as a vocalist; his mid-sixties hits "Break Off My Right Arm" and "Down

On Bended Knees" were very influential in teaching a young SRV how to growl the blues. "It sounds dumb, but I found playing with him very inspiring," Stevie confided. "He's an amazing guitarist. We just tried to kick each other into doing something. But we'd played together twice before onstage, so I know a little bit of what to expect."

Stevie was also summoned to join John Hammond in the studio at Manhattan's Media Sound to re-mix *Texas Flood*. Hammond thought the original mix was awful, and wanted to add his skilled touch to the tapes to make them really sparkle. "When you mix and mix and mix, sometimes you get off balance about how the record really sounds," Stevie later said. "He would come in, and if things were going real smooth, he'd just listen and come back later. If we had the echo turned all the way up because we'd gotten used to the sound of it, he'd come in and say, '*Turn that damn echo off!*' and then laugh, and you'd know it was okay. The record is real consistent in sound and tone because of that. It's hard to say just how he influenced the album. When he walks into a room he has a whole effect just by himself, just his being there smiling. If something was not as good as it could have been, he'd give input, and his support was incredible."

Hammond's record label was in the midst of financial difficulties, and John wanted the absolute best for Stevie, so he took the tape to CBS/Columbia. They passed, but a sister company, Epic Records, liked what they heard and took the bait, offering Stevie Ray Vaughan and Double Trouble a long-term record deal. This was it!

Dallas Morning News' music critic, Joe Rhodes, traveled to Austin on a cold March night to interview the soon-to-be-famous Vaughan at his home, and found Stevie buried in a pile of rhythm-and-blues records that covered the entire linoleum floor. A rented black and white TV was on, but the sound remained off while Stevie played jazz organist Groove Holmes' *Live From Harlem* LP on a stereo with blown-out tweeters. "Look out," he said, his fingers dancing across an imaginary keyboard. "*Here comes the good part....*"

Stevie munched on 6-hour-old pizza and tried to concentrate on the interview, but appeared to be more interested in spinning albums by Ray Charles, Al Green, Buddy Guy, and Jimi Hendrix—and that's just what he did—all night long.

The David Bowie Serious Moonlight tour was due to begin May 16 in Brussels, Belgium, and would have lasted for six months, carrying Stevie

Ray from Wembley Stadium in London to the US Festival in Southern California before ending up in Australia and Japan. Showco, a Dallas-based production company that had previously staged tours for the Who, Rolling Stones and Led Zeppelin, had been awarded the contract, and went full-tilt to prepare the sets (which cost more than $200,000) for the two-million-dollar tour.

The band went into intense rehearsals at Dallas' Las Colinas complex, and the rough tapes from those sessions indicate that Vaughan could have easily handled being the Spiders from Mars' new star guitarist. He reprised some of his greatest work from "Let's Dance" (the title cut), the sensual dalliance of "China Girl," and the funky "Modern Love," and added exciting new twists to Bowie classics like "Jean Genie," "Heroes," "Fashion," and "Ashes To Ashes." Too bad the world never got the opportunity to hear the two play together live; it was a fantastic sound.

After a month of rehearsals and a slew of flattering press, Stevie backed out of the tour two days before it was due to begin, saying he couldn't sign the contract offered by Bowie's management. He was quickly replaced by veteran Bowie sideman Earl Slick. According to Stevie, the problem was that Bowie's contract would have conflicted with his newly inked Epic Records contract. "They offered a contract I couldn't legally sign," he said. "I was told that they owned my image while I was on the tour, which meant I couldn't do any interviews on my own thing without getting written permission from them first."

A spokesman for David Bowie told the story differently: "I just think he (Vaughan) got too cocky with his good reviews. He thought he deserved more money than the other guys in the band and he started making additional demands at the last minute and David called his bluff. It was David's decision."

Stevie didn't deny asking for more money but "the money wasn't it," he insisted. "I had decided to blow off the the money. They had told me that if I needed more money I should ask for it, that it wouldn't be any problem. So I asked for some." The reasons are understandable: With a debut album of his own due out soon, Stevie had been promised an opening slot on the Bowie tour with his own band, meaning that he would be putting in extra time and money of his own. He was to be paid $300 a night to play with Bowie, but no extra pay was allotted for him to open the show. When the Bowie camp reneged on this offer at the last minute, Stevie's management sent back a biting response. The press had a field day with it,

asking who does this little smart-ass think he is, turning down an offer from Major Tom?

The story does go a little deeper. In all fairness to Bowie, Stevie wasn't always as professional as he could have been, showing up for rehearsals high as a kite and dragging Lenny with him; she proceeded to meddle in his business constantly. Bowie told Stevie not to bring his wife along anymore—*period*. Stevie was furious. Bowie heard that Stevie was already getting TV offers for his own band, and instructed Vaughan not to accept them under any circumstances. Bowie insisted that Stevie would not be allowed to do any promotional appearances whatsoever with Double Trouble for the duration of the tour, and furthermore, he wanted Chesley Millikin to surrender his management stake in the band. That was the last straw.

Martha was trying to get her son to reconsider the tour, and not walk away so angry. But Stevie was insulted and pissed. Martha went after him like Mother Superior, gently reprimanding and telling him not to give up such a golden opportunity. After all, she reminded Stevie, he's a very powerful man. Stevie looked her straight in the eye and told her, "Mama, he doesn't mean anything to me. I never even listened to his music. I couldn't care less." Stevie made up his mind that the whole arrangement was just more heartache than it was worth.

What hurt Stevie the most about the Bowie tour debacle was that he never heard from Bowie himself. "I still haven't gotten to talk to him and that's a drag, 'cause it seems like after all that, at least we could talk. But I can't get through to him," he told writer Joe Rhodes. "Things just got confused between business people...things that were offered weren't there, and David was the one who offered them. I don't want to talk bad about anyone. I'd just as soon leave all this behind and talk about the future."

The future was in his album, and the tour dates that were already rolling in for Double Trouble. He loved his band dearly; he couldn't just give them the big kiss-off when some British rocker in tight pants gave him the high sign, could he? He had dreams to remember, and Stevie Ray Vaughan always dreamed big.

When *Creem* magazine called *Let's Dance* "totally engrossing," and predicted that it "just may be the future of pop music," they probably didn't know the significance of their forecast. But the future was coming faster than a locomotive at full speed; the future of pop music, at least in Stevie Ray's case, was the blues.

Texas Flood

MUSICIANS spend their entire lives slaving over songs, moving from one lowly gig to the next and trying to duck industry snow-jobs, in hopes that someday the "real thing" might come along—something that will not only pay the bills, but that will give them a lasting pat on the back for all the struggles they've endured. Fame comes like a thief in the night and exits the same way, stealing souls and confining them to a timeless vacuum. Suddenly stars find that they've no time for love, family, friends, writing songs, or doing any of the things that make life sweet. Money comes flooding in faster than a star can count or spend it, as do the lawyers and accountants eager to handle the job. Agents and managers will plan every minute of every day of eternity for the star, sacrificing their own families in the pursuit of money. To this industry, the smell of money is as pungent as a steak cooking in a far-away neighbor's backyard. Inviting themselves to the cookout, they feast on the juiciest hunks of meat they can find, ripping the meat off the bones like dogs who haven't eaten in weeks.

Stevie Ray's success came rolling in like a flood; news of his escapades pelted the industry like heavy rain. His performances knocked audiences senseless, as if zeppelin-sized chunks of hail had fallen on them in the concert hall. The publicists' spin centered on this bad-ass Texas guitar slinger who could easily do battle with top guns like Clapton, Beck, Page, and Eddie Van Halen and come away unscathed. Furthermore, this unknown kid with friends in high places was going to change the face of pop music by playing the blues through a simple guitar and amp. He didn't need two keyboards, quirky pop songs, or a rooster hairdo to do it either. Stevie Ray Vaughan was going to do it on his own terms, with his own merit.

Texas Flood opened with the stinging Strat work of "Love Struck Baby," an original Chuck Berry-type rocker which featured Chris "Whipper" Layton's genius new rock beat; it was totally unlike the straight-on approach most drummers would take on this type of number, syncopating the rhythm into an unusual, impossible-to-play signature. "Pride And Joy" was the first thing American radio heard, those raw, familiar John Lee Hooker chords screaming out over the first four bars. Joined by Double Trouble on the turnaround, they laid into the thundershuffle even MTV techno-poppers could get into. "Texas Flood," "Tell Me," "Dirty Pool," and "I'm Cryin" sound just as they did the many nights at the Rome Inn. The nights Austin took for granted were now the rage of the country.

Side one closed with "Testify" but Stevie's approach bore little resemblance to the Isley Brothers' classic (it's a little closer to the version that George Clinton did with Parliament Funkadelic). He turbocharged it with a superfunky down-south fatback beat, and flaunted every show-off lick that fit. One might think that this would be an obvious nod to Jimi Hendrix, but Stevie indubitably slapped his stamp on it. This was the definitive recording of "Testify"; if Hendrix were alive, even he would probably scratch his head a little at Vaughan's fluidity, especially at this breakneck speed.

Stevie's take on Buddy Guy's "Mary Had A Little Lamb" actually owed as much of its groove to an early Freddie King instrumental called "Just Pickin'" (King Records) as it did to Guy's version.

Stevie's vocal work was smooth and sensual as he sang words that hinted at what Mary did after school. (The song was dedicated to "Rockin'" Robin Brandenberg, Cutter's new daughter, born on Halloween night.)

The album ended with "Lenny," the magnificently moody piece that Stevie wrote while "serenading my wife in bed." It was like Wes Montgomery playing Hendrix's "Castles Made Of Sand." His tone was warm and round, his imagination ran away, and he left each listener wondering what other kinds of music SRV might have up his sleeve besides the blues.

The cover art for *Texas Flood* was created by Brad Holland, and depicted Stevie as a Clint Eastwood-type macho axe-slinger with a bolero hat and scowl. In *Guitar World* writer Bill Milkowski recalled, "Stevie Ray was already swathed in mystique before I dropped the needle on the track. The beady eyes, splayed nose, and killer gaze depicted by Holland suggested an arrogant, mean son-of-a-bitch who had slept on pool tables and participated in his share of barroom brawls. This was the renegade Texas gunslinger— the anti-Buck Owens. The back cover of *Texas Flood*, however, told a different, far more accurate story: Stevie Ray, laughing happily—caught in a candid moment with his band (and John Hammond Sr., grinning over his shoulder like a benign vulture)—a twenty-nine-year-old man-child in the promised land."

Within a week of its release on June 13, 1983, *Texas Flood* sold out of its first pressing and had gone into the second. Neither Stevie nor Hammond could be more excited about what was to come.

John Henry Hammond Jr. was born around the turn of the century in a mansion on New York's Fifth Avenue. He was a direct descendant of Vanderbilt and

Embarking on his first major tour, Stevie is featured on the cover of *The Austin Chronicle*, June 1983.

heir to the family estate. A Yale Graduate, Hammond was a jack-of-all-trades throughout his early years, working as a controversial newspaper columnist, a concert promoter, record company talent scout and outspoken civil rights activist (one of the only white men courageous enough to speak out in the segregated 1920s). Hammond's strides toward an equal society did not go unnoticed; as an outstanding member of high society, his views were widely recognized around the world. Hammond was the first white man to serve on the NAACP's Board of Directors, and continued to serve most of his life, all the while singing the praises of the blues, jazz, and gospel music that he adored so much.

Perhaps John Hammond's greatest contribution to our world was his exceptional talent for recognizing a real star when he saw one. Stevie always called John "the man with the golden ears." He worked closely with Columbia/CBS Records throughout his distinguished career. Hammond always had a weakness for great guitarists, and placed Stevie amoung the ranks of Robert Johnson and Charlie Christian.

Hammond gave jazz guitar legend Charlie Christian his career, taking him to Los Angeles to introduce him to clarinetist Benny Goodman. Goodman just happened to be Hammond's brother-in-law, and also happened to be leading one of the hottest swing bands in the country. Hammond also had designs on recording delta blues master Robert Johnson, but by the time Hammond learned of Johnson's whereabouts, the mysterious bluesman was dead—murdered after playing a juke-joint party in Three Forks, Mississippi. Hammond's guitar discoveries share some striking similarities; Charlie Christian, Robert Johnson, and Stevie Ray Vaughan were all consummate, nearly superhuman players, all had recorded in Texas, and all died tragic deaths at an early age.

Stevie and the band had been advanced $65,000 on the first album. This kind of figure is

Playing in " The Twilite Zone," New Haven, Connecticut. Photo by Lisa Hill.

peanuts for most large record labels, but, to this pack of Texas boys, it was more moolah than they had ever seen. Word hit the streets in Austin that Stevie finally had some cash, and back debts and favors were called in. One of the first to stick his hand out was the guy who invested in Double Trouble's first studio demos. The investor threatened to release the sloppy Nashville tapes if he didn't get his $7,000 back—pronto. He got it, and seemed pacified, quietly fading away into Stevie's past.

Joe Priestnitz was formally dismissed as Double Trouble's booking agent now that Stevie Ray was playing in the big league; the band was now represented by the Empire Agency of Marietta, Georgia. Empire was owned by Alex Hodges, a genial southerner who counted Otis Redding, the Allman Brothers, the Charlie Daniels Band, the Marshall Tucker Band, Asleep at the Wheel, and Hank Williams Jr. among his former clients. Coincidentally, tragic accidents claimed the young lives of Duane Allman and his bass player Berry Oakley (both died on motorcycles in the same neighborhood within a year of each other), and Otis Redding was taken at the height of his career by a plane crash in (of all places) Wisconsin.

Stevie Ray Vaughan and Double Trouble were immediately off on the road, supporting acts like Linda Ronstadt, the Moody Blues, Steppenwolf, Men at Work, Huey Lewis and The News, and the Police. He did a showcase at New York's prestigious Bottom Line opening for Bryan Adams, and all of Manhattan's media elite were on hand. Stevie was worried that the show might flounder; he got no soundcheck that afternoon, and no respect from Adams or his crew. Nevertheless, he came on and smoked. *The New York Post* warned the rest of the world about the oncoming flood with "Fortunately, Bryan Adams, the Canadian rocker who is opening arena dates for Journey, doesn't headline too often. As a result, he doesn't have to endure being blown off the stage by his opening act."

A few days later, Stevie was playing a club called Toad's Place in New Haven, Connecticut, sharing the bill with Albert Collins and Koko Taylor. Koko didn't recognize the boy she had seen five years earlier backing Lou Ann Barton at the Houston Juneteenth Festival. "I didn't even know who this child *was*," Koko remembers, "but *oh, man!*—him and Albert Collins were swappin' guitar solos onstage, he was goin' after Albert like crazy—and you know," Taylor adds with a sly laugh, "Albert *was* enjoying it."

Stevie's guitar arsenal at that time was a colorful collection of vintage Strats. The tattered '59 that he lovingly called "Number One" had been repaired and modified to make it "road-ready." He kept a hollow yellow '64 Strat (formerly owned by Vanilla Fudge guitarist Vince Martell) that he liked to use for a trebly, ringy tone on songs like "Tell Me." His red '64 (named "Lenny") was the one that guitar tech Byron Barr had found in an Oak Cliff pawn shop and purchased with love-and-happiness donations from friends.

Other guitars that he used for fun were a 1958 dot-neck 335 Gibson and a National Duolian Steel-body acoustic (serial number 0704), which Stevie swore was once owned by country blues guitarist Blind Boy Fuller. He still had his old '48 Airline, a bright orange '60 Strat, and blonde '57 Strat that he bought from Jimmie. He was given a rare prototype Rickenbacker (which he in turn gave to Hubert Sumlin), and a Cherryburst Hamilton Lurktamer with his name plastered across the neck in a custom mother-of-pearl design. The guitar was a gift from ZZ Top's Billy Gibbons, a nod of appreciation for the little kid he'd been carefully watching since 1970. Stevie also kept a Kay Barney Kessel model guitar around (a personal favorite) for informal picking sessions, but he couldn't use it on stage because, as he said, "It don't stay in tune worth a shit."

He used GHS custom strings in these sizes (top to bottom): .013, .015, .019, .028, .038, and .056.

Roadies liked to joke about Stevie "playing on telephone wires," a reference to his fetish for the biggest strings known to mankind. As a result, all of his guitars had to be modified with bass frets to reduce wear on the instrument and the man, whose fingers usually resembled a red, tenderized steak after a two-hour gig. He had his whammy bars installed upside down like Hendrix, giving him greater ease and control. His amp collection included two Fender Vibroverbs ("numbers five and six," he boasted proudly), two Super Reverbs, a Marshall with two 12-inch speakers, two Studio Master Valve Lead Masters, and a Dumble amp. (It was legendary amp builder Howard Dumble who first introduced Stevie to Jackson Browne.) As far as effects, Stevie had a general disdain for them, but he kept staples like a Vox wah-wah and an Ibanez Tube Screamer running, and let the Fender built-in reverb or tremelo do the rest.

On July 27, 1983, Stevie joined Buddy Guy for a live broadcast over Chicago's WXRT-FM, and the two raged on for hours, just having a natural ball playing together. Of course, this *was* at a club (the Checkerboard Lounge), so Vaughan and Guy had more than a few drinks together, and it showed—many of the jams were long and sloppy, but the recording brimmed with character anyway.

SRV did get to cookin', and challenged Buddy to a call-and-response duel; amazingly, Stevie damn near creamed Buddy at his own game during "Long Distance Call," after which a humbled Guy swore, *"Now here's a guitar player who is one bad*

Albert Collins in action. Photo by Harold Dozier.

Backstage with Matt Dillon and record producer Steve Lilliwhite at the Bottom Line, New York City. Courtesy of Epic Records.

mutha...!" Buddy's quivering vocals soared on "Don't Whup Your Love On Me So Strong," and the two sang together on "Mary Had A Little Lamb." By the night's end, Buddy couldn't stop preaching about Stevie Rave On.

Clarence "Gatemouth" Brown, a Texas blues guitarist (and fiddler!) once explained his rather planetary approach to the blues, which seemed to also describe Stevie's revved-up, experimental attack: "Where I see my music going is where the modern blues player is afraid to go," Brown said in *Meeting The Blues*, "a vortex on the other side of Mars, beyond that. In order to get there, you have to suspend the G-Force. Then, if you do that, you might get a chance to stop in the twilight zone, a rest period. But the ultimate part of this trip is the nine giant steps," Gatemouth says, his speech sounding more like a Jimi Hendrix space-rap than a bluesman's testimony, adding that "you got to go at supersonic speed and not many can get there."

Vaughan's career was flying at supersonic speed. He was no longer in the ranks of his fellow bluesmen—Stevie Ray had graduated to rock star status. Along with that came the obvious pluses and minuses of fame. The money was great, but Stevie had no idea how to handle all the spare cash that was always in his pocket. He'd been on the road before, but never like this: Now he enjoyed plush tour buses and hotels, and hanging out with celebrities like Matt Dillon, tennis star John McEnroe, and Tatum O'Neal. He had people to clean up after him, people to pay his bills for him,

people to bring him lots of cocaine.

Lenny traveled with Stevie a lot on that first tour. It may have been the biggest mistake of their marriage. The couple made every day a party, doing all the free coke that had been offered the night before on the bus and often hiding out in hotel rooms until show time. Lenny tried hard to put a distance between herself and the band, the management, and especially the road manager. She and Cutter were always at odds over what was best for "their Stevie," whether it was haggling about who did or didn't get on the guest list or because Lenny insisted that Cutter write large quartz crystals (used for luck, purification and healing) into the band's stage rider. Cutter finally got his fill and left the tour in Berlin. The pressure of obeying his star's wife, dealing with coke attitudes, and not getting paid enough finally got to him. He did not go quietly. He let all the frustrations go at the hotel, smashing his room to bits and leaving the madness and his anger behind.

In early winter Double Trouble got a call informing them that *Texas Flood* had just gone gold, and as they sat in their respective hotel rooms that night, they all began to realize that this was not a dream anymore. They really had made it, and life would never be quite the same again.

On December 4, 1983, Stevie was presented with three Readers' Poll awards from *Guitar Player* magazine at San Francisco's Kabuki Theater. Before Stevie, only Jeff Beck had taken home a triple win (in 1976). SRV was awarded Best New Talent, Best Electric Blues Guitarist, and Best Guitar Album. When he arrived in Austin, he cleaned up at the *Austin Chronicle* music awards (an easy catch) as Musician of the Year, Best Blues Band, Best Electric Guitarist, Best Texas LP, and Song of the Year ("Love Struck Baby"); Double Trouble took Band of the Year. In addition to several other various and sundry awards he received around the nation that year, Stevie Ray Vaughan was nominated for two Grammys: "Rude Mood" was up for Best Rock Instrumental, and "Texas Flood" for Best Traditional Blues Recording. Although he did not win, SRV was noticed within the industry for getting so much attention off of a debut album. That, indeed, was quite a coup.

Chesley Millikin got a call from Margaret Moser informing him that Stevie had swept the Chronicle Music Awards. Chesley flew the band down from New York for an unannounced set at the close of the ceremonies. The T-Birds came on and rocked for an hour, and were joined by Stevie at the end of their set. The brothers played a mean headcutting game on "The Crawl"; first Stevie would play with his teeth, then Jimmie would follow suit. Jimmie played behind his head, and Stevie did the same. Then Jimmie went off on a stream of uncharacteristically flashy licks, but this was Stevie's territory and of course, he did them better. In their own set, Double Trouble offered rough new songs like "Couldn't Stand The Weather" for the hyped-up hometown crowd.

After the awards, local media types staged a backstage interview that was a little too late for anybody, including the drunken camera crew and reporter, to concentrate on the business at hand. The Thunderbirds gathered on two fat white sofas and waited for someone to start asking questions. Nobody did. Five minutes passed. A party was raging all around them, the cameras were rolling, and no interview took place. Finally, a frustrated Jimmie barked, "So, what the hell are we doin' here?"

"Oh, yeah!" The interviewer exclaimed. "Roll the cameras!"

An inebriated cameraman focused on the ceiling. Poor Charlie Sexton happened to walk right into the middle of this confusion, his trip to the beer cooler intercepted by a pointed insult from Kim Wilson: "Here comes Charlie with his new hair. He's such a pretty boy, don't you think? Come here, Charlie!" Wilson beckoned him into the lion's den. Good-naturedly, Sexton obliged.

"Hey, man," Ferguson piped over to Kim, "I'm not sitting next to the Henna-head!"

"How ya' doin, Charlie?" Wilson teased. "You know, the least you could do is get a jacket that matches you hair."

"Just call him 'Rhubarb Charlie'!" Ferguson remarked to uproarious laughter.

Stevie was called into the "interview," taking a seat next to Charlie and brother Jimmie. The three had their arms wrapped around each other, and Charlie leaned into Stevie—he knew that Stevie understood how it felt to be ridiculed by the crowd, and that the teasing often wasn't easy to shrug off.

Everybody'd had a few drinks, but the interviewer was beyond hope, stumbling over words and finding it difficult to construct a coherent sentence. The band eyed him suspiciously. "Okay, so I'm fucked up," the reporter finally admitted, doubling over in a loud laughing fit. "Hey! Take it away, Jimmie," he yelled. "It's the Jimmie Vaughan show." The cacophony grew louder, and the only words that could be heard were Kim Wilson's, who was asking "Where's the producer? Someone needs to be asking us some questions. Obviously, you can't do that."

"I don't even wanna try!" came the stuttered reply.

"Try," Someone urged.

"O.K." The reporter conceded, trying to assemble a halfway relevant question. "So—you guys been around a long time, huh?"

Fran took the ball, joking, "Yeah, Charlie knew me when I was just a kid."

Stevie had remained diplomatically quiet through the whole ordeal, trying to conceal his own alcoholic intake in front of the cameras. After some friendly chiding from the guys that he was the only one in the room with a record coming out, he spoke his mind. "What it is," he sputtered, "is that we're all trying to help one another. If one makes it, everybody gets listened to." All conversation ceased; everyone in the room was visibly stunned by this subtle, tactful answer in the face of being bullied. "That's what it all boils down to," Stevie smiled shyly, "believe it or not!"

Chris Layton approached the group and wanted a seat, electing Charlie Sexton to play interviewer, who directed a question at Stevie. "What is your next album going to be like, Stevie?"

"Probably dangerous," Stevie chuckled.

"Thunderous!" added Layton.

"So, Jimmie—how long have you played guitar?" Sexton chided.

"Oh, about ten years," he said with deadpan delivery.

Turning to Stevie, Sexton asked, "So I guess that means you've played twenty years?"

"Twenty-two, actually," Stevie quipped. (He was telling the truth.)

Tommy Shannon got into the picture, standing behind Chris and Stevie, and decided to join in the tongue-lashing competition with, "I'd just like to say that I'm glad to see that Keith Ferguson is still alive!"

"Stevie, how long has Tommy been in your band?" Charlie asked.

"Since we got him out of the Moses Tour!" Stevie wisecracked.

"So, Kim, how does it feel to be voted Best Miscellaneous Instrument this year?" Sexton questioned.

"Pretty good, I guess." Wilson said. "The guy last year played a toilet paper roll, so I think this is an improvement."

"Now, Kim, you're not telling him everything," Ferguson reminded. "Last year, you were voted Best Male Organ." The room fell apart laughing, as Keith continued, "In fact, we'd like to present you with this award," he giggled, taking off his shoe and handing it to Kim. Kim sniffed it, grimaced, and passed it on to Double Trouble.

"Are you guys really shooting this?" Layton asked, embarrassed.

"Hell yes, we are!" the interviewer exploded, snatching the microphone back from Charlie. He focused on Stevie, trying to get under his skin by asking, "So, Stevie—the Grammy Awards—how'd you get into that deal?"

Stevie rolled his eyes, and shot back the best possible answer before getting up to leave. "Well, my mother had me and I just kept tryin'."

"Well, you're still no Buddy Holly!" the interviewer told him in one last attempt to piss Stevie off.

Stevie stopped in his tracks. "We're just doin the best we can, man," he shot back, irritated. "That's all Buddy Holly did." He walked away with a look on his face that said everything he didn't dare—*goddamn, what an idiot...so this is fame.*

Voodoo Chile

IN JANUARY 1984, Stevie Ray Vaughan and Double Trouble went into New York's Power Station Studios to begin recording *Couldn't Stand The Weather*. This time, the band took it at a more relaxed pace; there was no need to charge through the tracks as they had done with *Texas Flood*. The sessions took nineteen days but were not lockouts, meaning that they had the tedious job of lugging all their equipment in and out each day. John Hammond was present during most of the sessions, but wisely stayed out of the way, speaking up only when he felt he had the right track. Again, overdubs were kept to a minimum, and the songs were cut mostly live. For the first time, Double Trouble was faced with the problem of having too much material to squeeze into one disc; several cuts were inevitably shelved, later turning up on the posthumous *The Sky Is Crying* CD. "Wham," "Little Wing," and Kenny Burrell's 1963 cool jazz classic "Chitlins Con Carne" all came from the Power Station sessions.

In an interview with *Guitar for the Practicing Musician*, Chris Layton remembered how "Cold Shot" was recorded: "We never had a real arrangement on it. We did, but it kept changing. We did it at like five o'clock in the morning. Tommy had been passed out on the couch, and Stevie comes in and shakes us. 'Hey, wake up. Ya'll want to play?' And we walked in the studio, wiping the sleep out of our eyes. And we just cut it that way. That's why it sounds so lazy like that, the groove's so laid back," he laughs, adding, "that's where the real art of performance comes in."

The title cut is Stevie's own little masterpiece; it's his best song to date, with powerful lyrics, a funky riff, and a thoughtful arrangement. "I wrote all the parts to that song myself." Stevie bragged. "It was the first time I'd ever done that. Most of it was done between gigs, on the bus going from town to town. I had a little Fostex 4-track recorder. I would record one track and go back and play bass or something and work with it until I found something that fit. That way, it's much easier to show the band what I need. I was trying to do something completely different from what I'd done before."

"Stang's Swang," the jazzy little ditty that closed the album, features special guests Stan Harrison on sax and Fabulous Thunderbirds drummer Fran Christina, who got the tricky drum part in one take. The song was not named after saxophonist Stan Harrison, but after Stevie. "My nickname was 'Stingray,' " Stevie revealed, "and the tune was 'Sting's Swing.' "But I decided not to spell it that way—what the hell, I figured Sting (of the Police) had already gotten enough publicity this year, right? *Stang's Swang* is the way I always pronounced it, anyway."

The elder Hammond was not in great health during the album's making; he had already survived five heart attacks and a stroke, and was under strict orders from his doctor not to work at night. To accommodate Hammond, Stevie tried recording during the day, but the experience was doomed. Hammond defied his wife and doctor and sat in on several evening sessions. "Stevie wrote six new songs just before we started recording," Hammond told *New York Magazine* in April. "It was like the early days with Dylan, when he was writing five tunes a day."

John's favorite song on the album was "Tin Pan Alley," which he described as "a tremendous, dynamic and haunting song." It was Stevie's first time actually recording with John Hammond and, wanting to please him, he cut "Tin Pan Alley" first. The song was done in one take, and as Stevie stared into John's eyes through the glass divider, chill bumps rose on everyone in the studio— Stevie's love and respect for the man was that intense.

Stevie attended the Grammy Awards ceremony in February to claim the Best Traditional Blues Recording award for "Flood Down in Texas," a track off of the Atlantic Records' compilation of Montreux Jazz '82 called *Blues Explo-*

sion. He joined George Thorogood onstage that night for a salute to Chuck Berry, but Stevie was less than pleased with the way it turned out: "He (Thorogood) told me that he was going to turn all the way up, and if I didn't, I wouldn't be heard. And I figured, '*Just let him go.*' There was a lot of respect there that Chuck Berry should have gotten that I'm not sure he got. The whole point was to have him perform and give him an award for being Chuck Berry. That's what I thought was the disappointing thing. I'm not trying to run Thorogood down, but I thought he was real disrespectful to Chuck Berry in doing what he did. We were there to say thanks to him."

On March 19, 1984, Stevie Ray Vaughan and Double Trouble appeared at the worldwide CBS Records Convention in Hawaii. Stevie was dressed to kill in a flamboyant getup topped by his faithful blue kimono. SRV blew the suits away with his inspired vocal performance of "Cold Shot," leaving many executives to whisper that his singing was indeed a formidable match for his guitar skills. Of course, Stevie had been talking to CBS about signing some other Austin talents, namely Angela Strehli and the Fabulous Thunderbirds. This was an audition of sorts for them, and Jimmie paired up with Stevie during his set, adding some extra muscle to "The Things That I Used To Do."

Stevie seemed particularly jacked up that night—a combination of little sleep, too much cocaine, and sheer adrenalin. He was taking more chances on the guitar, reaching for the heavens but only making the stars. His solos were uneasy, and he made tons of mistakes, missing several key riffs during "Third Stone From The Sun." He even attempted "Stang's Swang," with Franny recreating his challenging drum part from the album, one of the only times this song was ever performed in public. Angela Strehli joined Stevie and Jimmie to sing Jackie Wilson's "Lonely Teardrops," and a mean shuffle called "You Were Wrong."

Stevie announced Jeff Beck with his usual Texan bravado; this was the first time they've ever met onstage—and it just happened to be in front of the entire record company. Beck was obviously frustrated as he grappled for a tone throughout "Wham," and Stevie wasn't in the mood to play nice guy tonight; he pumped up his volume, stared his idol down, and floored it. The friendly camaraderie that would later develop between them was absent here—this was a serious showdown, and even the mighty Jeff Beck was a little nervous. They segued into Beck's "Hawaiian Eye," a very difficult piece that they had only re-hearsed once earlier that day. Beck was greatly impressed by Stevie's knowl-edge of his work; hell, this kid was using his licks and tricks that Jeff had forgotten or discarded years ago. Stevie called "Jeff's Boogie," the Yardbirds classic he had cut his teeth on at the Cellar. SRV pulled out every gimmick he had, daring Beck to go faster and faster still, leaving poor Chris and Tommy (who eventually gave up and stopped playing) behind. The two duked it out like giants, and came out of it smiling, sharing a genuine hand-shake. (Although Beck did cringe a little when he felt his hand being crushed in Stevie's vise-like grip!)

Angela Strehli returned to the stage with Beck, Stevie Ray, and Jimmie Lee to sing her own "Lost Cause Blues." She crooned it so sweetly, bringing her Texas barroom blues twang to these important international ears. Stevie was always there for Angela; he admired her from the first time he ever laid eyes on her. Her heart and soul were true to the blues, and she was what he always envisioned in a female singer. It made him mad that she couldn't seem to find a decent record deal, but putting her in front of the CBS bigwigs seemed like a good way to help her out. Unfortu-nately, the suits passed on Angela, but were very impressed by the Thunderbirds, and began nego-tiations to buy the tapes the T-Birds recorded with Dave Edmunds in 1982.

Double Trouble spent the next two months on the road, jetting from Charlie Daniels' Annual Volunteer Jam to Scandinavia, Finland, Sweden, and Norway, where they played the Voss Jazz Festival in late March. Their set consisted of mostly old material, but did include "The Things That I Used To Do" and "Tin Pan Alley" from the new album, which had still not been released. When they came home, they taped a broadcast of "Austin City Limits" with the Fabulous Thunderbirds. Now that Stevie was becoming a bonafide star, he reached out to Jimmie as often as possible, wanting only to forgive and forget past rivalries and arguments. He wanted the best for his big brother—after all, Jimmie was the one who taught him everything, so Stevie figured he should be the one getting all the acclaim. Stevie went on an evangelical mission to talk him up in all his interviews, insisting that "Jimmie Vaughan is the best guitar player I've heard."

SRV and Dr. John rehearsing for the Carnegie Hall show, 1984. Courtesy of Dr. John/ Barbara (B.B.) Becker.

Couldn't Stand The Weather was released in May, 1984, and reached #31 on *Billboard*'s pop albums chart. Stevie had finally realized his dream of recording a Hendrix song by including "Voo-doo Chile (Slight Return)" on the album, which drew mixed reactions. Some thought his version was masterful and long overdue; others called it blasphemy.

"There's this automatic thing that happens to Hendrix music when you say you're gonna play some of it," Vaughan observed in 1984. "People put it on a pedestal and say, '*Don't touch it.*' I don't understand the logic behind that. Hendrix did everybody a favor by showing us you can put all these styles of music together and make it work," he points out, growing more heated with every word. "What I want to know is why isn't that just as accessible as Chuck Berry's music, Bo Diddley's music, or anybody else? That's a ques-tion I'd really like to know the answer to. But in the meantime, I ain't gonna lose any sleep over this thing. I'll probably put a Hendrix song on every record I ever make 'cause I like him so much." He hesitated and then added, "And also to spite a few people, too.

"I think he and Django Reinhardt pretty much played the same....I think they were prob-ably two of the most free guitar players I've ever heard in my life. To me, it sounded like Jimi was playing everything that ever excited him. That's pretty much the way I look at playing myself. That's where I get ideas. I'm not necessarily copying anything to a tee, but I've tried to incorporate everything that I've ever heard that excited me. I want to be *excited*, it's more fun that way...When people say I play too close to Hendrix, I'm not offended. I consider that a compliment!"

Although the album sold very well, and the videos for "Cold Shot," and "Couldn't Stand The Weather" were in regular circulation on MTV, not all of Stevie's critics were impressed. *Rolling Stone* hated *Couldn't Stand The Weather*. Writer Kurt Loder chalked the record up as another tired blues bar band trying to follow in the footsteps of Johnny Winter and ZZ Top. Loder called Stevie's version of "The Things That I Used To Do" "pointless," and lambasted him for trying "Voodoo Chile (Slight Return)" sarcastically writing, "When Vaughan sings 'Lord knows I'm a voodoo chile,' you wonder if the Lord's ever heard the Hendrix original." He summed up his review admitting that the album would still find an audience among those starved for guitar heroes, despite "the lack of crackle in the rhythm section and the absence of any interesting tunes."

In early July, Stevie was in St. Paul, Minnesota, and a long ways from home. He stormed into his brand-new tour bus after the show, tossed his hat into the corner, and threw himself on the rear-cabin couch, his aqua-green kimono drenched with sweat. He was angry and embarrassed, apologizing to well-wishers. "I'm sorry you had to see that," he kept saying, genuine anguish crossing his face. "You people deserved better than that."

He was speaking of the night's constant sound problems that nearly overshadowed the show itself. The room he was playing didn't help, either—a fifties hangar-style ballroom that had the acoustics of a fallout shelter. His stage monitors kept blowing out, and every so often, the main P.A. speakers would blast a low rumble that sounded like the Incredible Hulk belching into a microphone. The crowd didn't seem to care; they knew he was struggling, and understood. It wasn't his fault, anyway. Nobody was blaming Stevie Ray Vaughan except Stevie Ray Vaughan.

Chicago Bluesman Otis Rush, whose song "Double Trouble" made such an impression on Vaughan that he gave his band the same name as a tribute to Rush. Photo by Ralph Hulett.

Stevie was back in Dallas on July 12 to play the Bandshell at Fair Park with Angela Strehli opening. He had the chance to spend time with Martha and Big Jim, who by now had been confined to a wheelchair due to his battle with Parkinson's Disease. He could see the excitement in their eyes when he played, and watched sadly as his father tried to dance again—the way he did when he and Martha were young—but to no avail. Never in their wildest dreams had they imagined that little Stevie would be the star of the family. Big Jim and Martha had always placed their bets on Jimmie, but now they saw that Stevie deserved every bit of the accolades they had only read about. "I can't tell you how much that means to me," Stevie remembered warmly. "That's probably what I need to pay back more than anything."

A few days later, the band was in Houston, and Stevie met with *Houston Post* reporter Bob Claypool, who he considered an old friend by now. Claypool knew him back when, and congratulated Stevie on his success, but related how much Houston missed the old once-a-month shows at Fitzgerald's. "Yeah, all this touring is nice...up to a point," Stevie told him. "I still like seein' new places, but it gets weird when you have to look at a piece of paper to see what day it is, and what place this is. It's also gettin' harder bein' away from home. I miss my wife, Lenny, but she'll be coming up pretty soon. Otherwise, well, I haven't gotten tired enough of it to stop yet," he said with a laugh.

Stevie also talked about adding an acoustic segment near the end of every live show on that tour. "I'll be playing my 1928 National Steel guitar," he fantasized. "From what I can tell, this guitar originally belonged to Blind Boy Fuller (others said he was crazy)...the guy who does our guitars on the road (Byron Barr), brought it to me.

He owned it and I was using it. But I gave him a Stratocaster copy awhile back, and he later came around and gave me the National…It's a wonderful guitar—wait'll you hear it. I use it at the end of the show." If, indeed, this delta blues idea ever really materialized, history was not privy.

Stevie then returned to Austin, and heard that Otis Rush was playing at Antone's. Because this would be his only night at home for several weeks, he resisted the urge to go and told himself he was gonna stay home and relax this time. After an hour of twiddling his thumbs, Stevie couldn't take it anymore—he grabbed his guitar, jumped in the car and headed for the Home of the Blues.

Of course, Stevie could hardly order a beer before being called onstage. And what ensued was pure double trouble; Otis and SRV were quite a match, trading licks back and forth as if it were a private lesson. Stevie's heart soared when Otis insisted that he take a solo on "Double Trouble," the Rush composition that Stevie Ray loved so much he had named his band after it. When the jam finally concluded, Stevie was still pumped up. He grabbed the mike and announced, "*Otis Rush is the greatest, ya'll!* Man, I could do that all night long, Otis, how 'bout you?" Rush, who had played better than any human could expect to, wiped away the bullets of sweat and said, "No way, Stevie. I can't keep up with you anymore."

The most important concert to date was still a few months away: Stevie Ray Vaughan was going to play Carnegie Hall. The legendary New York venue traditionally featured opera, symphonic music, and Shakespearean theater; its plush aisles were usually filled with socialites wearing rare diamonds and expensive cologne. John Hammond had introduced this crowd to the blues once before when he staged the "Spirituals to Swing" concerts there in 1939. Dedicated to the legacy of Bessie Smith and Robert Johnson, the show put Big Bill Broonzy, Sonny Terry, Big Joe Turner, Charlie Christian, and Count Basie in front of a whole new, very white audience. History was repeating itself as

Hammond was again preparing the highbrow debut of his latest discovery—except this time, John was giving the purists a white man playing the blues and wondering if they would take him seriously.

Stevie prayed that he wouldn't fall flat on his face and disappoint his mentor. He rounded up the best all-star band he could muster, calling Angela Strehli to sing, his brother to play second fiddle, Antone's house drummer George Rains, the Roomful of Blues horn section, and Dr. John, who filled in at the last minute for Booker T. Jones (of the MGs) on keyboards. They rehearsed for a week in Fort Worth before flying to New York. Stevie wanted to make sure the band looked sharp—dressing them all in deep blue velvet Mexican mariachi suits with silver studs down the pants. They looked awful silly, but at least everybody's threads matched.

It was the day after his thirtieth birthday—October 4, 1984—and Stevie Ray Vaughan was playing the biggest gig of his life. Yet, he was so broke that his phone had been disconnected back home, leaving Lenny to wait for his call at a neighbor's house. It finally came: "Sweetheart, I'm standing backstage here at Carnegie Hall, and I'm scared and I just want you to know how much I much I love you," Stevie managed to say before he heard his name being called over the P.A. "I'd better go now—wish me luck, baby. I guess this is it!"

He was still nervous through most of his set with Double Trouble, but his tensions eased a little when he noticed audience members wearing T-shirts printed with Stevie Fucking Ray instead of tuxes and evening gowns. Moreover, the crowd response was polite, but lukewarm. Stevie bore down harder during "Voodoo Chile," hoping to get the crowd on their feet. He was positively amazing, but still, the people sat. Finally, a kid jumped up and turned to the reserved crowd, and

Stevie's first *Guitar Player* cover, October 1984.

shouted, "STAND UP! This ain't *La Traviata!*"

The show was completely sold out, and the reviews the next day were fantastic. The *New York Times* said that Vaughan had transformed the famous hall into a "stomping roadhouse," but mistakenly took Stevie for a "honky-tonk guitarist and singer." *New York Newsday* put Stevie on a level with Hendrix and B.B. King. In addition to the show, Epic Records and MTV threw Stevie a big birthday party in midtown Manhattan. The star-studded bash included guests like Whoopi Goldberg, Sean Penn, and Matt Dillon—all confirmed Vaughan fans—as well as Martha and Big Jim, flown in for occasion.

While hanging out in New York City, Stevie met Liza Minnelli in an elevator, and the two wound up jamming together at an after-hours restaurant. "It was fun," Vaughan told a reporter. "She would do swing-jazz tunes, and when she'd sing with me, I'd just play straight blues and she'd make up words." Liza was crazy about Stevie, nearly falling in love with him until he finally explained that he was a married man in love with his wife, and thanks, but—no thanks.

Stevie journeyed to Japan for the first time that month, and to his pleasant surprise, the Japanese audiences went crazy over Double Trouble. Plans were made for a film company, called Black Box, Inc., to document the Tokyo concert, but the video was never released in the

states. SRV came on "Scuttle Buttin'," with his Albert King corncob pipe smoking away. He bent over his guitar, concentrating hard on the notes whirling out from his fingers. He swung his axe, punctuating the punchy intro to "Say What!" with his wah-wah whirring away, and found the highest bend possible, pinching the strings with a mighty force while his right hand danced effortlessly over the pickguard.

Tommy was smiling more than usual tonight, looking buzzed and happy (actually they were all tanked) as he nervously paced with his tobacco-burst Fender Precision bass. Stevie bowed his head, finished the song in a reckless flurry, then addressed the crowd: "*Hello, Tokyo! Ya'll ready to get it?* Let's go to Texas—yeah, you got it—real nice and personal, uh, is what we call it...by way of Seattle." The band ran head-on into "Voodoo Chile" to wild Japanese screams that sounded about as American as Amarillo on a Saturday night. He rocked his torso, hitting a stingingly high B note, then tossed his head back, allowing the piercing sound to ring out over the beat. His legs were quivering beneath him. He'd gotten the guitar singing, wiggling it in front of his pelvis like Hendrix did—and sure enough, the girls lost it. He fell out of the sky for the next verse, Whipper broke it down, and the guitar scratch started again. Shaking his wet hair and panting a little from the workout, Stevie was supposed to be singing but opted for another solo because it felt so good.

Later on, during "Cold Shot," the overtly heavy chorus effect was eating his tone up, and he paused before the solo, waiting for just the right scream to set him off. Someone yelled and he was gone, his left leg wagging like a rubberband. Seguing into "Couldn't Stand The Weather," Stevie worked that pile-driving funk groove. He flubbed the lyrics, thinking only of his guitar, taking too many extended rides when one or two would do. These were common (and understandable) criticisms of Stevie's shows from this period. He was too excessive a guitarist, lacking the material and the voice to stand the test of time—or so people said.

To prove more with less, he picked up the

white Strat (Charley) for "Tin Pan Alley," laid back and closed in on the groove, talking from his heart with tasty, light little blue notes. Voices cried out after every twelfth bar, encouraging him to take another turn. The blue lights tinted his red velvet suit a deep violet, and he took on a princely appearance. His vocals were smooth and coy; if the guitar histrionics were too much, he'd sure as hell have gotten the audience's attention when he sang: "*I heard a pistol shoot.*" A woman screamed wildly. He was telling it like he knew this place, and man, he'd been there. Stepping back, he whispered "*It's like this...*" howling on the high E string. Suddenly his blue-lit face was in terrible pain; he was crying silently to himself as the guitar heaved sobs. His eyes closed tight, his teeth clenched, his lips were saying "no, no, no." He stung a high note hard and quick, opening his mouth to let a big sigh rush out, audible over his vocal mike two feet away. Then another note, another sigh and he was all played out.

He called a stop and growled at the crowd jumping into "Love Struck Baby," the old Rome Inn barnburner. He snarled through the solo, tossing his hat onto the mike stand, ducking under his guitar strap, and playing the thing behind his head. The cameras revealed the unpleasant truth: Stevie Ray, barely thirty, was mostly bald. He busted a string on Charley, switching over to Number One for "Texas Flood," and his tone was blasting. The mojo bag that hung from his belt was most definitely working. He slipped into T-Bone's shoes, and they fit. He swung around, unplugged the instrument in mid-solo, and replugged it behind his back, playing the rest with both eyes closed. He finished the entire last verse behind his back, flipping the guitar back and forth, never missing a note. Then he introduced the band; Tommy kissed his bass and winked, Whipper waved. "*Domo Arigato*—to you!" Stevie bid the audience. A thick cloud of pot smoke hovered over the arena. Stevie took a deep whiff, a maniacal grin on his lips.

He returned for an encore of "Lenny." Stevie was sitting alone with her center stage, thinking of his woman back home, gently tugging her whammy bar, and making her quiver in his hands. He sat relaxed, smoking a pipe that he soon ditched, coughing. The song was his masterpiece for the night. This old girl was his steady companion when times were hard; her faded paint job and

smoke-yellowed crusty pickups had seen it all. He hunched over, touching her neck softly. His head was buried deep in her body, close enough to kiss her fretboard. He threw in a little Wes Montgomery, lost in the cool jazz and memories. Dueling bass lines with Tommy, his amp buzzed low as he turned the bottom E string down as far as it would go until it just died out. After all the whang-barring and de-tuning he was horribly clangy, but finished up with a beautiful precursor to "Riviera Paradise."

Jumping up out of the blues, he launched into "Testify." Here he went holding it like a violin, again tuning down the already appalling cacophony and wailing like crazy. Finally, the sound just became too awful, and he reached to Number One for some serious trickery; he played

Rare poster announcing Stevie's first Japanese tour, which was wildly successful. Courtesy of Don Ottensman/The Best of the Blues.

it backwards, forwards, upside-down and side-ways, one-handed, back-handed, and no-handed—he could do it with both hands tied behind his back. He was

PAUL DAINTY & CLIFFORD HOCKING

proudly present

STEVIE RAY VAUGHAN
AND DOUBLE TROUBLE

FIRST TOUR OF AUSTRALIA

MELBOURNE Concert Hall	Friday	October 26	
	Sunday	October 28	
	Wednesday	October 31	
ADELAIDE Festival Theatre	Thursday	November 1	
BRISBANE Festival Hall	Saturday	November 3	
SYDNEY Opera House	Monday	November 5	
	Friday	November 9	

STEVIE RAY VAUGHAN
Guitars/Vocals
TOMMY SHANNON
Bass
CHRIS LAYTON
Drums

— 1984 —

Stevie Ray Vaughan and Double Trouble's first trip down under. From Australian tour program, 1984.

reciting "Third Stone," and the rhythm section was rocking hard. While they went on, Stevie yanked off Number One and threw her to the floor, lunging after her as if he were going to rape the poor thing. Next he was humping it, whanging it to death, shaking it, throwing the controls past ten, making her whistle like a train and whinny like a horse. Stevie hunched over her, flipped her over by the whammy bar, jumped on top and rolled around the stage with her. Leaping to his feet, he tossed her in the air and caught her just in time to hammer the last...excruciating...note, and it was "Goodnight, Tokyo!"

Double Trouble dropped by the studios of MTV Japan for an interview the next day. They sat on a shiny-clean white leather sofa across from a female Japanese V.J. who misread Stevie as a real Texas cowboy, and decided to gussy herself as a cowgirl. After Stevie played "Wham" in the studio, she took off her cowboy hat and swung it in a circle above her hand, yelling out, " *Yeee-hooo!*

You are great-o!" She asked him about the Bowie album, and he told her that David gave him "a lot of freedom. He just let me plug in and go. It is not true that we called and canceled out two days before the tour started. That's just his press people tryin' to slander my name. They just weren't keepin' their promises."

When asked about Hendrix, Stevie became pensive. "He was a very strong man," Stevie responded quietly, softly stroking the guitar. "His music and his life influenced my music and my life—a lot."

"Did you cry when he died?" the V.J. asked.

"Of course I did," Stevie Ray acknowledged, then paused to look out the window, reflecting aloud. "I didn't realize I was supposed to laugh. I cried real hard for the first few days afterwards. I was trying to play my gigs and suddenly little pieces of Hendrix started coming out of me. I didn't even know...but it came out right." His mind drifted away, his hands moved absently up and down the strings. Stevie's fingers found the opening lines of "Testify," the Isley Brothers' classic that featured a young Jimi Hendrix on guitar.

Double Trouble's first tour of Australia was a smashing success, with three sold-out shows at Melbourne's Concert Hall near Halloween, then moving on to Adelaide and Brisbane before concluding with two climactic nights at the Sydney Opera House November 5 and 9. While in Sydney, Stevie saw God—Clapton, that is. He had been Stevie's hero since he was tall enough to reach the record player. Unfortunately, Stevie was so far gone that the words Eric told him didn't register until years later. "He was leaving the hotel, and I went out to talk with him, hangover and the whole bit, you know?" Stevie recalled with a forlorn chuckle. "He was sober, of course, and was really calm the whole time while I sat there downing two, three shots of Crown. And he just sort of wisely looked at me and said, 'Well, sometimes you gotta go through that, don'cha?'"

A few days later, he got a call informing him that he had won two W.C. Handy Awards for Blues Instrumentalist of the Year and Blues Entertainer of the Year. Stevie was thrilled—he had finally been recognized by his friends, peers, and idols in the blues world, and nothing was going to stop him from getting to Memphis and accepting the award personally.

In the blink of an eye, the band was sitting in the lobby of Memphis' Peabody Hotel, watching the parade of ducks (that's right, ducks) marching through the hotel lobby. (Since the turn of the century, a collection of ducks have taken a daily walk through the hotel's lobby.) Even more amusing was the late-night jam following the awards ceremony at the Orpheum Theater; Stevie was so nervous sharing a stage with all his heroes at once that he could barely play his guitar. Every time he'd look up, there was B.B. King or Albert King or Hubert Sumlin next to him. All Stevie could play was rhythm guitar, and it was with a giddy smile upon his face.

Another dream came true when SRV got the opportunity to film a two-part "In Session" television special for CTV (Canadian TV) in Hamilton, Ontario, with his "spiritual godfather," Albert King. It was an intimate setting; the two were seated on stools, casually talking and swapping licks back and forth. Albert reminded Stevie of the early days when they first got to know one another: "I often think of how you'd come in, draggin' your little guitar, and they'd say, 'Stevie's here—let Stevie sit in!'—and I'd say, '*Who is Stevie?*'"

"I's who I is," Stevie remarked with a smile.

"You'd get up there and hit two or three good licks," Albert recalls, "and then you'd back off. I used to tell you, 'stop standing over there looking' at me all out-of-whack and play your guitar!'" Both guitarists laughed at the memory. "I still don't see how you got so baaad!"

"I'm a bad boy," Stevie informed him.

"You just can't let your head get big on me now, Stevie," King laughed, "'cause I got me a whip back here..." Stevie went into the opening bars of "Texas Flood," and the two jammed for a long time before shifting over into "Stormy Monday," which featured Albert's smooth, smoky tenor singing the old standard. The first time these two met on stage, Stevie was shamed by an out-of-tune guitar. This time the

curse was on King, who was hideously out of tune after several mind-blowing string bends. Stevie chuckled quietly under his hat.

The two rambled on and on, playing favorites like "Outskirts of Town," "I Dreamed I Was Lucky," and "Don't You Lie To Me, Baby." They gave each other the utmost respect. Even Albert, a surly sourpuss at times who has never been known to particularly like anybody, had let Stevie Ray warm his heart.

"You know, Stevie," King said warmly, "I wouldn't have missed this for anything in the world. I mean that." Stevie could have died right that moment and had no regrets; he had played on TV with Albert King, and no reward could be greater in his eyes.

Stevie remembered that night fondly: "During the lunch break, Albert went around to everybody in there looking for an emery board," he says, his eyes growing wide. "I didn't think anything of it. We were jamming on the last song, 'Outskirts Of Town,' and it came to the solo, and he goes, 'Get it, Stevie!' I started off, and I look over and he's pulling out this damn emery board, filing his nails, sort of giving me this sidelong glance (laughs). I loved it! Lookin' at me like, '*Uh-huh, I got you swinging by your toes.*' He's a heavy cat."

A stop in Victoria, British Columbia, during the last week of June yielded a sweet surprise; a 15-year-old kid showed up wearing the trademark

"Gettin' it" in Wichita, Kansas, 1984. Photo by Dave Ranney/ The Wichita Blues Society.

92

A boyish smile, captured by legendary photographer David Gahr.

Fistful of Dollars hat, a kimono and a conch belt. It was the first time Stevie had encountered someone who worshiped him the way he did Hendrix. The boy had come over 300 miles dressed up just like his hero and it blew Stevie's mind. Stevie made a point to find the kid, bring him backstage, and even gave him a few pointers on the guitar.

"We just wanted to make him understand that we had as much respect for him as he does for us," said a flattered SRV. "It's kind of strange when people treat me that way. You want to be careful; you want to be sure somebody's not idolizing you so much that they don't see themselves clearly. It's easy to do. I know, 'cause I did it, too."

After nearly six straight months on the road, the entire band was tired, lonely, and homesick. So many good things had happened on the road, and it was all fun, but this schedule was brutal. They wanted nothing more but to spend a week at home with their girlfriends and spend some of that big money they'd been making. It hit them like a ton of bricks in 1984 on Thanksgiving night when the band went in search of a holiday dinner and ended up in a two-bit diner eating cardboard turkey.

"It's hard" Chris Layton recalls, "trying to find that balance between living out of a suitcase and all the hardship that comes from eating crappy food, and not being able to sleep in good beds sometimes, and try to combine that with inspirational playing and feeling healthy and rested—when you don't feel either one. In my book, that was probably the toughest trick of all."

Rude
Mood

SRV

IN EARLY DECEMBER, Stevie went to work producing Lonnie Mack's *Strike Like Lightning* album at Cedar Creek Studios in Austin. Stevie and Lonnie had wanted to work together since 1980, when Lonnie first saw SRV playing at Austin's Rome Inn. The young fireball ripping through "Wham" stopped him dead in his tracks. Lonnie told Stevie that night that he would like to produce Stevie's record someday. As fate would have it, Stevie's career took flight, and now Mack was turning the tables. Plans were delayed while Lonnie was plagued with a variety of personal problems; first, his piano player was killed in a car accident, then Mack's own health took a bad turn.

Stevie even played a benefit concert to help with Mack's medical bills. "Then one day I saw him, and he told me, 'You watch, Stevie. In six months I'll be getting younger.' Wouldn't you know it? Six months down the road, hair started growin' on his head again. His beard started losing its gray and it was turnin' black instead," Stevie recalled with a smile. "God bless him."

"Lonnie's something between a daddy and a brother," Stevie said. "He understands. He's real deep—a warm kind of deep. The way I look at it, we're just giving back to him what he did for all of us. It wasn't a case of me doing something for him—it was me getting a chance to work with him."

Stevie had somehow convinced Mack to move to Austin about the same time Lonnie inked a record contract with Alligator Records. This was the same label that had rejected Double Trouble back when they were young and desperate for a deal. A&R rep Mindy Giles asked Stevie if he would get involved as producer. Stevie held no grudges against Alligator, and besides, it was the chance of a lifetime. Stevie did find it tough to deal with label president Bruce Iglauer—he kept remembering how Iglauer had walked out on his set without giving him a chance. Nonetheless, Iglauer knew that having Stevie's name on the project meant sales; Stevie knew that meant money for Lonnie Mack, and he wanted to see Lonnie make some good money for a change.

"We [SRV and I] weren't especially close," Iglauer recalls. "When I was dealing with him, he was still into drugs and alcohol, which I'm not judgmental about, but it did make him distant—and *changeable*. It was a typical Lonnie fly-by-the-seat-of-your-pants, get your old friends around and have-a-party-and-make-a-record project. Stevie had come in off the road, and had done absolutely no preparation whatsoever. Basically, his approach was to walk in and ask Lonnie what he wanted to do. His attitude was 'If Lonnie's happy, I'm happy.'

"It was so weird trying to figure out '*who's in charge, here?*'," Iglauer laughs, "I mean, everybody was kindly deferring to Lonnie, who really just wanted to be one of the guys and didn't want to make all the decisions. And I was like, walking on eggshells, because Stevie was sometimes irritated at me, and I really

Recording Lonnie Mack's *Strike Like Lightning* with Engineer Steve Mendell in Austin, 1984. Courtesy of Studio D.

didn't want to make that worse. Stevie really didn't see himself as a producer."

Stevie looked on his producer role as something kindred to bodyguarding: "I tried to keep other people from telling him how to do it, y'see," Stevie told *Music And Sound Output* magazine. "That was my job as producer, was to let Lonnie Mack sound like Lonnie Mack. Hell, Lonnie knows what he's doing. That's what I'd tell people who wanted to butt in." Stevie played on five of the ten tracks and sang on one, the candidly biographical "If You Have To Know." He also contributed his '28 National Steel on Mack's "Oreo Cookie Blues" (A hilarious ode to Oreo addiction), the entire song cut live in one take. Stevie did not force himself in the least upon Lonnie; but Mack was begging him to play more...and more, and more.

So Stevie did. When he and Lonnie re-cut "Wham" as "Double Whammy," Stevie became a little upset at Lonnie wanting to cut the song a lot faster than the original. "To hell with the original record," Mack announced. The crew of hangers-on left at 2 A.M. and Stevie spent the whole night tirelessly recutting guitar parts—the same solo a hundred times—until he got it right. When Iglauer returned at noon the next day, Stevie had just left, and the exhausted engineer was passed out at the mixing board.

Although Stevie kept his nose out of the production, he certainly had it buried deep in something else. "I wasn't used to people doing coke in front of me," relates Iglauer. Running a blues label usually put him in contact with a different generation of musicians who preferred to drink. "Stevie had this jar, like a mason jar that he kept the stuff in," Bruce remembers, sheer amazement in his voice, "and he would pour coke into the top of the jar, and do the whole capful—which was *a lot* of coke." Iglauer tried some when the mirror passed under his nose, and was terrified at the potency of the nose candy Stevie was putting away like sugar. "I did just a little bit...my heart was racing, and I felt like I was going to die." That incident was enough to scare Bruce Iglauer away from cocaine for good.

Lenny was constantly hanging around the studio, which didn't help matters any. "I didn't get it," muses Iglauer, "She was always trying to drag him away, get him separated from the group. They spent a lot of the time doing coke in the bathroom. The only time that things were relatively cool when she was there was the day she brought her masseuse friend with her to relieve everybody's tension—and by that time, there was a lot that needed to be worked out!"

In the middle of recording, Stevie flew up to Dallas to perform a "Christmas Bash" concert with the Fabulous Thunderbirds at Fair Park Coliseum on December 15. The concert didn't sell out, but SRV's guitar filled the coliseum to capacity. And then some. Unfortunately, Stevie's vocals were down in the house mix most of the night, but he seemed confident and strong as he charged through the new and old with gusto. He called Jimmie out to join him on an encore of "Love Struck Baby," and after the concert the brothers spent the rest of the night reuniting with friends and family. They were home for the holidays together, just like the good old days, and for a few days he was Steve Vaughan again, hanging out with his family—he didn't have to play Stevie Ray Rockstar.

When Stevie returned to Austin to mix the Lonnie Mack album, the project was moved to Austin Recording Studios, located in a modified garage. The dilemma that faced them was severe; two of the songs they had recorded didn't even have words written yet. Desperate, they called in expert lyricist Will Jennings to help deliver some words on the spot. A shocked Bruce Iglauer watched as Stevie, Lonnie, and Will raced against the clock to write "Strike Like Lightning": "The track they cut was actually 'Watch Your Step,' the old Bobby Parker song, but then they decided to write over it," Bruce says, shaking his head. "Then Lonnie cut the vocal track, and he sang so hard, he started coughing up blood. His health wasn't great, but this pressure really wasn't helping. I think at that point he just wanted to get it over with."

Everybody did. Iglauer went back to Chicago with the tapes, but was dissatisfied with the way the album sounded. He arranged for a re-mix of the master tapes to be done in Chicago. Lonnie washed his hands of it, and Stevie began to prepare for the next Double Trouble album, booking a month at Dallas Sound Labs. The recording studio was located inside the Las Colinas Complex, where he'd rehearsed the ill-fated "Serious Moonlight" tour with David Bowie. But before he

Stevie and Lonnie Mack. Photo by and courtesy of Randy Jennings/Captured Live.

did anything else, by God, he was going to have a vacation.

He had been working awfully hard for the last three years nonstop, and Lenny was running just as fast as she could to keep up with him. They could see that the marriage was falling apart; they had both been unfaithful to each other, falling prey to the selfish indulgences of the rock and roll life. For Stevie the music was filling his pockets and his soul; for Lenny music was the thing that kept her man away for months at a time. They vowed to try and rekindle the flame, and embarked on a real Caribbean honeymoon in the Virgin Islands.

Stevie and Lenny sunbathed on the beaches of St. Croix and shared some sweet moments together, but Stevie's thoughts would always drift back to the music. "He handled it," Lenny said. "I couldn't believe it. No 7-Elevens, no cassettes. But of course, he talked music. The uh, *work mode* is always there. He gets that look, you know?"

The romantic rendezvous didn't seem to change their mounting mutual anguish once Stevie and Lenny returned to Austin. Lenny continued to sit in on business meetings, driving the management team nuts with her questions about where Stevie's money was going, why they didn't take better care of him, etc. Lenny was jealous of any and all women that crossed Stevie's path, knowing how hard he found it to resist advances from beautiful, doe-eyed young groupies. Anybody who wanted some of Stevie's time was a nuisance to her, so she gradually shut them all out. She would ditch phone calls from his mother and his cousin Connie, Classic Management, and his friends. She insisted

98

ride. It was the show's high point.

The special guests couldn't save the show, either; Stevie reunited with ex-Cobra Joe "Blow, Joe, Blow!" Sublett on "Honey Bee" and "Texas Flood," but the sax and trumpet were badly out of tune with each other and the rest of the band. Stevie rightly dismissed the horn section, and strapped Charley on for a version of "So Excited," singing lyrics that were never heard before or since. He appeared to be making them up as he went along—in fact, he blew the words to nearly every song tonight; in the middle of "Pride And Joy," he got mixed up and started singing "Boot Hill." He repeated himself on the guitar, only going through the motions; only on "Rude Mood" did the sheer speed of the piece inspire him to play some impressive licks at last.

After "Love Struck Baby," Chesley, Delbert McClinton, and Jerry Jeff Walker joined Stevie onstage to present him with a new hat, christened "The Black Texas Cowboy Hat." (Stevie can be seen wearing it on the cover of *Family Style*.) The horn section returned (in tune this time), for the

Immersed in the music. Photo © 1985 by Cindy Light.

old Triple Threat arrangement of "Cold Shot." Stevie took the opportunity to debut a new song—a still-unshaped instrumental version of "Life Without You." In the middle portion, he brought it down and explained to the audience, "We don't really know what this song is about yet; everytime I write some words, it's about something else. But it all boils down to this—without you all, I sure wouldn't be here. Thank you."

Soul To Soul also saw the addition of keyboardist Reese Wynans, who was hired as a permanent member of the band. A veteran of the Delbert McClinton, Joe Ely, and Jerry Jeff Walker bands, Wynans brought a fatter, smoother sound to Double Trouble with his pumping Hammond B-3 organ and rolling barrelhouse piano styles. He also made Stevie's job a little easier onstage, giving him a solid rhythm bed to play off of and freeing him to concentrate on soloing and singing. And best of all, Wynans liked to play jazz, one of Stevie's greatest passions. The two had known each other around Austin for years, and Stevie had offered Reese the job before, but kept losing Wynans' phone number. "Every time I'd get another number, it'd be disconnected," Vaughan said.

"We were cuttin' Hank Ballard's 'Look At Little Sister' when he walked into the studio. I said, '*Hey, wait a minute!*' I hadn't seen him a long while, y'see. He asked me if I still wanted him in the band, and I said, 'Yup.' Then he asked me when I wanted him to start, and I said 'Right now.'" With a third member in the Double Trouble rhythm section, Stevie joked "*now we're Serious Trouble!*"

While in the studio, he started thinking of his own little sister, or the closest thing he ever had to one—his cousin Connie Trent. They'd never gotten to see each other much in the first place, then he moved to Austin and married Lenny and his star began to rise—for too many years they had hardly seen

As his popularity was spreading worldwide, Stevie garnered praise from even the most unlikely organizations. He was made an Honorary Admiral of the Texas Navy in 1985. Courtesy of Connie Trent.

Stevie and Tommy buddy up onstage at the
Sandstone Amphitheatre in Bonner Springs,
Kansas, in 1985. Photo by Dave Ranney/The
Wichita Blues Society.

each other at all. Stevie missed her
gentle strength and reassurance,
and felt like he needed to talk to
her. He went to great lengths to
track her down, calling several
old friends in search of her new
phone number. "He surprised me
to death!" Connie recalls. "He
called me at work, and said 'I'm
here, I'm in town—how 'bout
dinner tonight? I'm dyin' for some
Tex-Mex!'" He kept her on the
phone, excitedly telling her that
Eric Clapton had been by last
night. Clapton was rehearsing a
tour at Las Colinas, and had
dropped by to jam.

"I went to the rehearsal studio and proceeded to get loaded waiting for him," Clapton
told author Ray Coleman in his biography. "He
didn't show up 'til four in the morning, fresh as a
daisy having slept all day and into the night. So he
was ready to *go*, and I was *gone*. It was almost the
same situation as Australia, except that I was
checking out and he was checking in. And I tried
to play, and I made such a fool of myself. It was
really horrendous. That feeling of postponement
is still there...next time I see him, we'll try to play."

Stevie wanted to bring Connie up to date on
all the news, good and bad, in his life, and made
plans to come pick her
up. "Stevie drove up in
this white Cadillac, Photo ©1986 by Cindy Light.

which belonged to the studio, to pick me up,
asking me like, 'Is this okay?'" Connie laughs.
After dinner, he stopped at the hotel flower shop
and picked up two roses, to begin with. He kept
adding to it, you know. So he walks back up to me
with this mangled menagerie of roses, because he
couldn't make up his mind, and handed this—
glob—to me. I just died laughing.

"This was around the time when he first
realized that he was really making it, and he had
noticed that a lot of his friends were starting to act
different toward him, so he...really just wanted to
use the roses as some way of saying 'thank you for
being there, for caring, for letting me call you at
two in the morning and bend your ear.' And for the
first time in our experience, he had enough money
to actually pay for it.

On April 10, Stevie played "The Star-
Spangled Banner" at the Houston Astrodome for
the opening day game (also the twentieth anniversary of the stadium). Mickey Mantle, who had hit
the stadium's first home run, was there to throw
out the first ball, and autographed SRV's Number
One guitar. The field resembled a three-ring circus
during pregame, then SRV took centerfield and
played "The Star-Spangled Banner" a la Jimi
Hendrix. The crowd was shocked. They were
used to hearing opera singers; what the hell kind
of gag was this? They threw cups of beer and
popcorn at him, a roaring boo echoed through the
stands.

During this time Stevie Ray Vaughan and Classic Management were growing apart. Stevie still didn't quite understand that his weekly salary and all the bonus money advanced to him was just a loan. Music money doesn't just disappear into the black hole; loans have to be paid back. It bugged Stevie when he realized that his money was paying the roadies, the publicist, his management staff, his producer, everybody. When they bought gear, clothes, even office supplies, it went on his tab. It was a very rude awakening when he heard that his producer, Richard Mullen, was suing him for back payment of engineering fees. Even worse, his old buddy Cutter also wanted his piece of the pie, filing a lawsuit over the royalty points he'd been promised on *Texas Flood* and never received.

Photo © 1986 by Cindy Light.

Stevie was always generous with money, often to the point of foolhardiness. He would always shell out a few bucks to anybody who had a hard luck story, and he loved to shop. Most of his change was spent on sharp new threads or expensive guitar toys, but he threw away as much as he invested on partying sprees with friends. Cash seemed to sprout wings and fly out of his pocketbook whenever he'd stop at a truck stop or an airport gift shop. Stevie would keep the bus waiting while he bought T-shirts, coffee mugs, and meaningless souvenirs for pals back home.

Around 8:30 P.M. on a warm spring night in 1985, Stevie prepared to go onstage at the second annual Chicago Blues Festival. The three-day concert rounded up the country's premier blues talents, from masters like Sunnyland Slim and Jimmy Rogers to newcomers like Vaughan. Chicago's Grant Park was stuffed with over 100,000 people, swarming around the bandshell like ants stalking a slice of bread. Stevie was nervous. He paced in a circle around his dressing room, sucking on a bottle of Crown Royal and talking to himself. Although there were others in the room, Stevie hardly even noticed their presence. He was trying to psych himself up to actually go out and headline a blues festival, to follow a full day of performances by the artists who had inspired him all his life. What if the mostly black crowd hated him for stealing their music and making a fortune off of it? What if they threw bottles?

Stevie took the stage in total darkness, his white suit and white hat a dead giveaway. The crowd roared its approval. His fears floated away into the brisk evening air, and he broke into "Scuttle Buttin'," not even stopping to look up at the audience, which was on its feet. Their screams sent chills up his spine. Nobody in this crowd gave a damn what color he was. Off in the distance, a black man sat on a blanket with his eyes closed, his head nodding back and forth in sheer delight. He was smiling, loudly repeating, "Stevie Ray. Blow me away, Stevie Ray...all I can say....Stevie Ray!"

Two months later in New York, Vaughan was sipping a drink at the Mayflower Hotel, which overlooks the west side of Central Park. Journalist Robert Santelli brought up the subject of a blues revival. Stevie took off his hat—something he rarely did in public—ran his hands through his hair nervously, put the hat back on, and grinned.

"There ain't no blues revival goin' on," he drawled, swirling the straw around in his drink. "The music has always been there. Never really gone anywhere. The same cats have been makin' the same great music all along. What is different now is there's a chance for the music to be listened to by a lot of people again. And that, let me tell you, is good news for everyone."

Stevie took his blues gospel to MTV for an hour-long guest host spot on the "Rock Influences" program. SRV sat in the bar of The Lone Star Cafe, one of his favorite old haunts, and discussed the Texas artists who laid the groundwork for his own music. Like any devout Texan, he proudly referred to home as "The Country of Texas," and told stories about Bob Wills, Buddy Holly, Willie Nelson, Janis Joplin, Johnny Winter, Lightnin' Hopkins, and T-Bone Walker. He picked up his guitar and revealed the secret to playing T-Bone properly: "Hold the guitar flat across your lap and away from your body." He flew through an inspired "Rude Mood." When he finished, he just laughed and humbly remarked, "But that's just a white boy tryin' to play Lightnin' Hopkins."

The program also featured a great performance recorded at The Capitol Theater in Passaic, New Jersey, where Stevie turned in blistering versions of "Look At Little Sister," Come On (Pt. III)," and perhaps the most beautiful, personal reading of "Ain't Gone 'N' Give Up On Love" ever recorded. Stevie played forcefully throughout, looking sober and totally in control.

But he wasn't. Stevie Ray was falling apart emotionally. He grew more distant from the band, his family, his wife, his manager, and even the press. When he refused to grant an interview to an important AOR station in Philadelphia, the program director threatened to boycott his records. Chesley badgered him into going through with the interview, and Stevie showed up, but he didn't offer anything but curt answers. The irritated deejay finally asked him, "Who do you think you are to blow off an interview with our radio station?" Stevie flew out of his chair and bellowed '*You go straight to fucking hell!*' into a hot microphone, slamming the door behind him.

Meanwhile, Epic was preparing the release of *Soul To Soul*— some record company insiders compared the experience to trying to inflate a hot air balloon with a big hole in the side. A video was filmed for "Change It" at the old Coupland Tavern in the tiny hamlet of Coupland, Texas, about twenty miles out of Austin on old Highway 95. The rustic, old-west setting of the nearly abandoned ghost town was the perfect setting for the song's stark feel. The video opens with a south wind howling across the plain, rattling the steel shingles on the old cotton gin, and blowing dust across the street leading to the old dance hall. Stevie comes busting through the swinging wooden doors, a guitar slung over his shoulder as tarantulas and lizards crawled beneath his feet. Stevie just adored the place, and took along several buddies as extras in the video, re-opening the old tavern for one day to let the cameras roll.

Soul To Soul was released in September, and although arguably his best studio record to date, and maybe his finest ever, sales were sluggish and reviews were mixed. *Rolling Stone* panned him again, commenting "there's still some life in their blues rock pastiche—it's also possible that they've run out of gas." SRV and Double Trouble were soon off to the U.K. to play a series of concert dates. While in London, Stevie visited the famous wall where the Clapton Is God graffiti first appeared. Scrawled right below it in big, black letters was Stevie Ray Vaughan Is God. To which he responded, "Gimme a break."

Photo © 1986 by Cindy Light.

Publicity shot for *Soul To Soul*. Photo by Britain Hill. Courtesy of Epic Records.

Stevie played the mammoth German festival Rockpalast '85 looking radiant, happy, and healthy. This turned out to be one of his finest performances of the tour. He blasted through "Voodoo Chile" and turned in an ingenious solo on "Tin Pan Alley." He felt especially adventurous that night (maybe it was the uncharacteristic pair of tennis shoes he wore instead of his trademark boots), reaching further from his stock licks on "Texas Flood" and turning the boogie section of "Pride And Joy" into a full-fledged romp through these tried-and-true rhythm patterns. He found some new sounds in these experiments, but it all came out sounding almost premeditated. He became especially possessed during an absolutely bone-chilling "Little Wing," followed by "Third Stone From The Sun."

In Toronto, Canada, Stevie was introduced to up-and-coming guitarist Jeff Healey through Albert Collins. Healey, who is blind, was just sitting in at local jam sessions, and didn't have a band together. A jam was arranged with Stevie, and the two came out of it with mutual admiration for each other. "How could you *not* be impressed by him?" Stevie later said about Healey, who counted Vaughan as one of his biggest influences.

Stevie gave one of his more coherent interviews that year to journalist Wolf Marshall for *Guitar*:

WM: What would you like to be musically remembered for?

SRV: For taking the color out of blues.

WM: What about playing with James Brown on "Living In America" (from the *Rocky IV* soundtrack)?

SRV: We ended up with seven different versions because of different mixes. I don't know whose idea that was. I didn't know whether James Brown didn't like it himself. He didn't have too many flashy guitar players on his records. He was already on when I went in. He's real tough. I went

through it two or three times, 'cause they wanted wild stuff....There is a dub version, an R&B version, a R&B version, a rock 'n' roll version, and there's a Stevie Ray meets James Brown version. On the one in the movie you didn't even hear me at all.

WM: Who do you listen to now?

SRV: Whitney Houston. I'm in *love* with her. She's definitely got some soul in her throat. I love Rene Martinez, who is soon to be real well known. He plays classical and flamenco style guitar. We're best of friends and he's got soul. He opens shows for us and we sit down and gawk at each other. (Martinez later became SRV's guitar technician.)

WM: Do you think the blues as a form can be updated?

SRV: The Thunderbirds have already done it.

WM: Have you thought of making a record with your brother Jimmie?

SRV: Yep, it won't be too far off. It's going to be "ignorant hillbilly rock for the nineties."

Soul To Soul finally peaked at #31 on the *Billboard* pop albums chart, just like its predecessor, *Couldn't Stand The Weather*. However, "Say What!" was nominated for a Grammy in the Best Rock Instrumental category. Stevie Ray was doin' all right, at least as far as he was concerned.

David Brown, who had spent most of his adult life wrestling with the bottle, attained sobriety in 1985. He and Stevie had stayed in touch through Martha Vaughan, sending messages to each other, catching up on local gossip. "Martha told him that I had stopped drinking completely, that I had a new band, and basically had my shit together," says Brown. "She was trying to get Stevie to take the hint, I think. I often wondered if that didn't kinda kick Stevie in the *ass* a little bit, and make him want to get it together, too."

Danny Thorpe (from Heart of Texas) secured a string endorsement with GHS for Stevie that fall. Considering Stevie ate them for breakfast, it was a big help; busted strings had become

Photo by and courtesy of Randy Jennings/Captured Live.

a major expense for Double Trouble on the road. To show his appreciation, Stevie came in one day and bought two new guitars, an Epiphone that was later stolen in Europe, and his first Flying V. "He wanted a guitar like Albert King played, so we strung it up backwards, turned it upside down, and Stevie would commence to stingin'," Danny chuckles, his hands playing air guitar.

It was plain to Danny that Stevie and Lenny Vaughan were deteriorating faster than anyone could save them. "She used to come in screaming at us because Stevie was gone on the road, and she needed something," Thorpe recalls. "Like one time, he was on tour, and they left the equipment truck parked alongside the building. She wanted to move or something, and came in yelling at Ray because he didn't have the keys to the truck. She just lost it, all over the place....Whatever Stevie was, she was three times that in those years."

As anyone who's ever been there knows, junkies don't care too much for baths or wearing clean clothes. Danny used to visit the Vaughan house regularly, and was always shocked at what he saw. "He wasn't into personal hygiene much then. It was always kinda funny to me how he had all this notoriety and money, and yet, you'd go over to his house and they were living like pigs, basically. I recall this fringed leather jacket/western shirt-style thing that Hank Williams Jr. had given him, and he wore it everyday for weeks on end. Man, it just smelled like a barnyard.

"Stevie was really an example of how good success can be, and how horrible it can get," Thorpe stresses. "Because the way Stevie was living, we expected him to die any day.

Photo © 1986 by Cindy Light.

It just wouldn't have been a surprise. In all honesty, no one in this town ever though Stevie would do doodley-squat," he concludes, "because, realistically, what chance does a blues guitar player have of making himself a success today? Well, he proved to himself, us, and the world that he was really something. And consequently, he opened the doors for so many people. If it hadn't been for Stevie, there wouldn't be a market for Colin James or Jeff Healey or Robert Cray. They wouldn't have big record deals. He made the blues popular again in the eighties, and inspired a lot of young guys to go back and listen to the masters."

Through the success that Stevie Ray had shown them, Epic Records finally took his advice and officially signed the Fabulous Thunderbirds, releasing *Tuff Enuff*, the album they had made with Dave Edmunds. With Epic's promotion and distribution muscle behind them, the T-Birds were built for speed. A couple of videos yielded two big hits, "Wrap It Up" and the title cut. The T-Birds had finally hit paydirt, and the offers came rolling in. They spent time in the studio backing Carlos Santana on his *Havana Moon* album, contributed songs to the *Tex* and *Porky's II* soundtracks, and got hooked up on a national summer tour opening for REO Speedwagon. The tour was a bad idea for the headliner. Every night the T-Birds blew them out

Double Trouble takes a bow in Kansas City. The jacket Stevie wears was a gift from Hank Williams Jr.—roadies joked that it "smelled like a barnyard." Photo by and courtesy of Dave Ranney/Wichita Blues Society

Getting down to business, 1985. Photo by Dave Ranney/The Wichita Blues Society.

of the amphitheatre, and REO had to come onstage to the sight of people walking out.

The T-Birds hit the road with Stevie and Double Trouble in the fall of 1985, playing fifty-one one-night stands in rapid-fire succession. They blanketed the entire country before finishing up at Dallas's State Fair Coliseum. Stevie gave a stoned-out rap session/guitar clinic at Arnold & Morgan Music Store the day of the show, and turned in an even more confused performance that night. Word began to circulate around Dallas and Oak Cliff

that old Steve Vaughan was looking bad. What had happened to the guy? Where was all that energy?

Those who went backstage in Dallas were mortified. They saw a man with big dark circles under his eyes, looking away into space and talking nonsense. Scuttlebutt had it that if you wanted to see Stevie Ray, you'd better do it soon 'cause he might not be around much longer. Connie Trent wanted to see Stevie so bad she drove all the way to Fort Worth the next night and just showed up backstage. She explained to the rather large security guards that she was his cousin, and could she please just get in for a few minutes? Her request was ignored, and as she stood there wondering why Stevie's own family couldn't see him, she was relieved to see Jimmie coming around the corner. He hung his all-access backstage pass around her neck and kidded with her about the muscular bozos who had tried to turn her out. Jimmie threw his big arms around her and led her to Stevie's dressing room. "Did ya get in all right?" Stevie asked her, that childlike, innocent smile in his eyes. She and Jimmie exchanged knowing glances, and said nothing.

Stevie Ray Vaughan and Double Trouble were doing an unscheduled

Left: Fabulous T-Birds at a press conference in their hit-making heyday. Photo by Arlene Richie/Media Sources.

Right: After the show in Dayton, Ohio, on September 24, 1985. *Left to right:* John Beaulieu (WTUE radio's music director), SRV, Johnny Copeland, and Reese Wynans. Photo by Randy Jennings/Captured Live.

Jimmie, cousin Connie Trent, and Stevie take a minute from the backstage hustle for a family snapshot. Courtesy of Connie Trent.

one person and play to them for most of the night. It's easier to communicate that way—it's intimate," he stressed. "I get a certain intimacy goin' on with one person or a group of people. Of course, we're playin' to everybody, but you get a more immediate response to what you're doing that way." He spoke of his dream of someday having his own recording studio and record label. "I'd like to be able to help musicians who deserve some recognition and credit. Some of these artists have more to give then I do. I'd like to see them have a chance," Stevie told the reporter between autographing album covers for fans backstage.

Jill Savage was already a big SRV fan and a popular disc jockey when she moved to Dallas from Indiana in late 1985 to take the afternoon drive shift at Q-102, the city's leading album rock radio station. "The first thing they asked me was, 'Who do you want to meet first?' and I said, well, Stevie Ray Vaughan," Savage later recalled. "When I told them I wanted to meet Stevie, they laughed and said, 'Who, Green Teeth?'" (That was a nickname bestowed upon Stevie due to his fear of dentists.)

"Back then, Q-102 would still let you play what you wanted to, so I started playing Stevie or the Thunderbirds every half hour. One day the request line rang, and it was Uncle Joe Cook. He was just blown away,

date in Beaumont at the Montagne Center, and they did an interview with TV 12. Stevie explained his "soul-to-soul" method of playing live: "I'll pick out

and he said, 'Who ARE you, anyway? Where you from?' We struck up a friendship from that, and he kept me posted on everything Stevie did. I kept asking Joe to introduce me to him. So Joe started telling the brothers about me, I guess, and they finally came over to meet me. By this time, we already knew each other in a sense because we had heard so much about each other. The family kind of adopted me as a sibling daughter in time…Stevie always called me 'lil' sis.' "

Stevie turned in one of his most engaging performances ever in October, playing an all-acoustic show in Berkeley, California. Introduced as "some kind of incandescent meteor blast," Stevie walked out to thunderous cheering. It was a new experience for him. He was alone on the stage, but relaxed right into it; it was a rare opportunity for SRV to shed the heavy artillery and just play what was welling up inside his soul. He let it pour out, playing one long, brilliant instrumental after another. He didn't sing a word. His guitar spoke volumes about his journeys through hell and back, and his struggle against the devil's grip. No drug could take him higher than his guitar did. Barely teetering on the edge of heaven, it was apparent that Stevie Ray Vaughan was beginning to lose his balance.

Playing with the power he was known for. Courtesy of Thomas Kreason/Rockabilia.

Couldn't Stand the Weather

IN JANUARY 1986, Stevie Ray kicked off the New Year with John Lee Hooker, Robert Cray, and slide guitar wizard Roy Rogers at Rockefellers', a posh Houston club that often featured the blues. He was in the highest heaven onstage (aided by scotch and cocaine), but once he came off, he was struck with sharp, pinching pains in his gut. Stevie doubled over in the men's room, and threw up blood. Although he was alarmed, Stevie was simply too busy to pay it much mind.

Stevie Ray Vaughan and Double Trouble finally got their chance to play "Saturday Night Live" in February 1986. The gig might not have happened if not for guest hosts Mick Jagger and Jerry Hall, who insisted that not only must Vaughan be the musical act, but that he be allowed to bring his brother Jimmie on the show, too. Well, no under-assistant east coast promo man was gonna argue with the Mighty Mick, so Jagger got his way, and Double Trouble got the spot. SRV played "Say What!" illuminated by zooming red and pink spotlights, underneath a Radio City Music Hall marquee mock-up bearing his name. The band was joined by Jimmie Vaughan for a torrid "Change It."

This was the Thunderbirds' golden year (or their fifteen minutes of fame, depending on which direction you're looking). They put in TV appearances on "Solid Gold," "American Bandstand," the "Today" show, and "Good Morning America." By early spring, *Tuff Enuff* had climbed into a Top 20 position on the *Billboard* album charts, and *Downbeat* called Jimmie Vaughan "the finest and most authentic white blues guitarist of his time."

That year, both Stevie and the Fabulous Thunderbirds cut public service announcements for the highly successful "Don't Mess With Texas" TV campaign to clean up litter on Texas roads and highways. The Thunderbirds were shown standing in the middle of a Hill Country highway reprising their current hit "Tuff Enuff," but changing the words to "Don't You Mess With Texas." Stevie's PSA was tastefully shot against a huge Texas flag backdrop; he sat on a stool, dressed in red, white, and blue, and played a haunting 30-second slide rendition of "The Eyes Of Texas Are Upon You." He didn't speak until the end, when he leaned toward the mike and in his best Clint Eastwood tone whispered, "Don't mess with Texas."

Soon after, Stevie appeared on the internationally syndicated "Rockline" radio program, where he took phone calls from fans, answering their questions about his life and music. He performed a frantic "Rude Mood" and "Pride And Joy" live, all by himself. One caller asked why he played the blues. Stevie's answer was disarmingly succinct: "Because it's real, not somebody's formula to make money—it's real music." Another asked what his hobbies were. "I make sandwiches, hang out with my dog, you know, what everybody else does."

That same year Stevie talked with writer John Stix in New York City about the *Soul To Soul* album, and the changes that were occurring in his sound:

What kind of cushion does the addition of keyboard player Reese Wynans give you? Santana refers to his band as a big couch. Playing in a trio is like playing on toothpicks.

Photo by and courtesy of Randy Jennings/Captured Live.

Yeah, but toothpicks stand up. Reese is king of a lot of different things. He can be playing along and you won't necessarily hear him, but when he stops playing, you know it. He can stand up to the best of them, and stand tall. His ideas are straight ahead. He is free when he plays and he makes me free when I play.

What can a rocker learn from a jazz great like Kenny Burrell? A lot of rocking blues players might not want to hear him.

God, why not? There's a lot of finesse to be learned there. There's a lot of material. Kenny Burrell and Grant Green are incredible. It may be too laid back for some people but in a lot of ways it's not laid back at all. *Grant Green Live At The Lighthouse* is knocked out. It moves. A lot of people can't keep up with it. It makes fusion sound—not mild, but it doesn't rely on effects to get cookin'.

In late February, Stevie played The Easy Street in Des Moines, Iowa, testing out his new, improved set list. He had omitted "Third Stone From The Sun" due to all the annoying Hendrix comparisons, leaving only "Voodoo Chile (Slight Return)," which was getting better all the time. He also scrapped "Dirty Pool," "Honey Bee," "Mary Had A Little Lamb," and "Testify." "Lenny" was a thing of the past, for the obvious reasons; the two weren't getting along at all. They hardly saw each other anymore, and Stevie did not wish to be reminded of the fact.

On March 31, Stevie Ray and the Fabulous Thunderbirds played a triumphant hometown show in Dallas. Kim Wilson and Jimmie joined Double Trouble to play the T-Birds' rocking classic "Look At That!" Reese's boogie piano

---

Set list for
Stevie Ray Vaughan and
Double Trouble's 1986 World Tour

"Scuttle Buttin'"
"Say What!"
"Voodoo Chile"
"Lookin' Out The Window"/
   "Look At Little Sister" Medley
"Love Struck Baby"
"Tin Pan Alley"
"Cold Shot"
"Couldn't Stand The Weather"
"Come On (Part III)"
"Life Without You"

Encores:
"Rude Mood"
"The Things (That) I Used To Do"

108

was a great plus to the number, as was the dueling Vaughan Brothers, who went at it like gangbusters.

The SRV/T-Birds tour headed down under in April, where the two bands knocked Australian audiences senseless with a double shot of powerful Texas blues and rock 'n' roll. Stevie made himself a new fan of a more personal nature upon arriving in Auckland, New Zealand. As his bus was pulling up to the hotel, he jumped up as if possessed, and told the driver to stop the bus and let him off. He tore off down the street, in hot pursuit of a fine pair of legs. Stevie was infatuated with the woman from the second he saw her walking out of his hotel. But he didn't catch up to her that afternoon, and was seriously disappointed. All night long he talked about her to anyone who would pay attention, knowing that he would probably never see her again.

But they did meet again in what was either an amazing stroke of luck or a very elaborate plan on her part—in the hotel bar after the show. She took a seat and, feeling Stevie's powerful gaze on her, she smiled at him. They flirted with each other from across the room, and Stevie finally worked up the nerve to join her. She was a mere child of seventeen, not even old enough to be in a bar, but her flowing dark hair, almond eyes, and innocent smile enchanted him. Her name was Janna Lapidus, a native of Russia who had spent most of her life working as a model in New Zealand. Stevie invited her up to his room, and they talked until morning. Stevie even held up the tour bus while he bid her a long goodbye.

It wasn't the first time he'd spent the night with somebody else—except that he hadn't been technically unfaithful to his wife. They hadn't done anything, and besides, everybody knew the honeymoon was long over for Stevie and Lenny Vaughan. He called Janna on the phone almost daily, talking for hours on end and running up

Photo by and courtesy of Randy Jennings/Captured Live.

four-digit phone bills. When he called home to Lenny, he was usually more interested in talking to his dog T-Bone than her. "For $1.30 a second or whatever it is, the dog and he would have this big conversation," Lenny said.

A few days later, in Perth, Australia, Chesley Millikin closed the book on his six-year relationship with Double Trouble. He was tired of babysitting Stevie on the road, making apologies for sloppy performances and bad attitudes, and most of all, the constant feuds over money, money, money. To hell with the money; Chesley had to save his sanity. He gave official notice that effective June 1, 1986, Classic Management would no longer represent Double Trouble.

The change was actually beneficial to Stevie Ray. He and Chesley really hadn't seen eye-to-eye from the beginning. Chesley was a rock and roll starmaker but he didn't understand the blues, and Stevie wasn't going to be the one to teach him because, in his opinion, Chesley never listened to him anyway. The band interviewed several prospective new managers, but found no mutual love affairs. Finally, Stevie approached Alex Hodges, his booking agent, who was now at International Creative Management in Los Angeles. Hodges didn't really want to be a manager again, but he liked Stevie a great deal; seeing that Stevie needed help, he jumped in feet first, immediately lining up yet another tour for Double Trouble, the nonstop road machine.

Stevie had gotten to the point where he couldn't make it through a show without several bumps of cocaine and shots of whiskey. He'd drink more after the show to mellow him down, but the coke wouldn't let sleep come. He'd jumpstart his heart every morning with a few long lines of the lethal white powder, and the ritual would start over again. Touring with Jimmie didn't help—as always, Stevie tried to keep up with big brother, wanting to impress him with his party animal tactics, and Jimmie did nothing to discourage it, as he was stuck in the same sinking boat. Stevie liked to boast that he could do six to seven grams of coke a day, as if that made him cooler than everybody else.

Stevie and all around him knew that he couldn't take care of himself anymore. He needed someone to get him to gigs on time, someone to take care of his personal business (i.e. keep the wife away, do the laundry, handle the mounting stacks of paperwork)—Stevie Ray Vaughan needed an assistant. Enter Tim Duckworth, an old Houston buddy/guitarist who was now living in Los Angeles. After the Australian tour, Stevie didn't want to go home to Lenny, and asked Tim if he could crash at his pad. Tim could see that Stevie was in pretty bad shape, and proposed the idea of becoming his personal assistant.

SRV craved only rest and relaxation for a few days, but as word spread that he was hanging out in L.A., Duckworth's phone began to ring with requests for Stevie. He accepted an offer to contribute guitar to actor Don Johnson's album project, a bizarre move for Stevie Ray, but he was in good company, along with old pal Ron Wood (Rolling Stones) and Dickie Betts (Allman Brothers). He did find time to see some shows; Stevie witnessed jazz guitar great Kenny Burrell playing at The Continental Hyatt House (re-named the "Continental Riot House" by wayward rock and rollers) on Sunset Boulevard, and also sat in the front row for an Etta James concert at the Vine Street Bar and Grill.

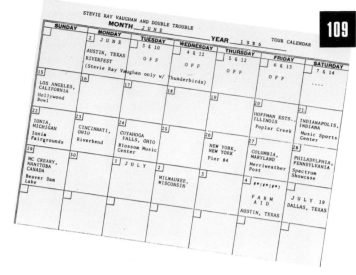

Stevie Ray Vaughan and Double Trouble's June 1986 tour dates. Courtesy of Thomas Kreason/Rockabilia.

Agenda for SRV and Double Trouble's first staff meeting with Strike Force Management. Courtesy of Thomas Kreason/Rockabilia.

```
                A G E N D A

       STEVIE RAY VAUGHAN & DOUBLE TROUBLE
            Meeting: June 3-4, 1986

1.  LIVE ALBUM
      a.  Listen and view
      b.  Mixing
      c.  Double or single
      d.  Price
      e.  Advance and credit at Epic

2.  FINANCIAL POSITION - Report from Joe Rascoff

3.  NEW SALARY RECOMMENDATIONS - Band and Crew
      a.  On tour
      b.  Off
      c.  Foreign tours
      d.  Isolated dates

4.  TAXES AND PERSONAL FINANCIAL PLANNING
      a.  Status of taxes in general
      b.  Withholding from royalties
      c.  Personal issues ... including wives traveling

5.  TOUR PLANS FOR YEAR
      a.  Summer
      b.  Europe
      c.  Remainder of year, '86-'87

6.  OLD BUSINESS
      a.  Gung Ho Contract
      b.  Don Johnson album
      c.  Merchandise - expenses and deal
      d.  Sponsor money
      e.  Ramsey
      f.  Other

7.  SETTLEMENT WITH CLASSIC - Review from Joel Katz

8.  NEXT STUDIO ALBUM PLAN

9.  RULES OF THE ROAD

10. REHEARSALS

11. RECORD SALES TO DATE

12. NEXT ROYALTY

13. GOLD RECORDS

14. OTHER
```

Epic Records needed another album, according to the agreement—the fourth (and last) per contract. But Stevie was in no shape to deliver one. He had been on the road for too long, leaving him no time to write new songs or even think about material or studios. It seemed like making *Soul To Soul* was just last week. The band wasn't real crazy about the idea of spending two months in the studio, either. It was agreed that Stevie Ray Vaughan and Double Trouble could make a live album—it was all they *could* do at the moment.

He already had a couple of tracks he felt were usable, recorded at last year's Montreux Jazz Fest '85, including his Grammy-nominated instrumental "Say What!" However, the rest of the Montreux tapes were not of use due to technical problems, so Alex Hodges booked them three sold-out nights in Dallas and Austin, complete with mobile sound trucks to capture the performances—unstable, unexciting, and mistake-ridden as they were. It was an honest way of doing things, Stevie said, not thinking how much the truth might hurt him later.

On July 17 and 18, 1986, Stevie recorded at the Austin Opera House to small crowds of about 2,000 per night. His old friends watched with bated breath, wondering if Stevie would even make it through the next song. He wore the black western jacket that Hank Williams Jr. had given him, and was joined by Jimmie on "Willie The Wimp," "Love Struck Baby," "Look At Little Sister," and "Change It." Stevie could still play fast and mean, but he appeared to have trouble

A weary Stevie Ray takes his final bow a few months before entering sobriety. Photo by and courtesy of Randy Jennings/Captured Live.

standing on his feet, swaying left to right and nearly falling over once or twice. "We had to devise ways of keeping Stevie going," recalls Danny Thorpe, who was working the Austin Opera House recordings. "Byron Barr was his guitar tech then, and he had to give him that stuff onstage just to keep him out there once the high wore off.... Byron was running out between songs and giving him a gram of coke in a shot glass of Crown Royal. And Stevie did two, maybe three of those a show," Thorpe says, bewildered. "It's a wonder he was alive at all."

The next night, Stevie was recording at Dallas Starfest, the biggest show he had played in his hometown to date. He was paid an unexpected, unwelcome visit from Lenny, who by now was on bad terms with Stevie's entire family. Although they had been unofficially broken up for months, Lenny was still pulling wild stunts to get Stevie's attention. Tonight was no exception. She appeared stage right in the middle of his show, and started yelling heated words at him. She was stoned, crying, out of control. "*You can't deny me, Stevie Ray! You can run but you can't hide*!" Lenny was heard bellowing at the top of her lungs. Stevie was

trying to keep his mind focused on the recording amidst Lenny's loud, hurtful ravings. He ignored it. Finally, Lenny started to walk onstage. Thankfully, two large security guards picked her up and carried her off, kicking and screaming like a wet hellcat. Upon seeing this, Stevie hit the opening riff of "I'm Leaving You (Commit A Crime)," and everybody knew what he was talking about. He looked Lenny dead in the eye as he sang, "*You tried so hard to kill me, baby/ But woman, it was not my time.*" Stevie Ray had finally had enough of that woman—this was more than he could take. He told the guards to get a limo and escort Lenny back to Austin immediately.

Lenny furiously tried to explain to security that she was only there to relay a message from Stevie's manager—"Be at the Stoneleigh Hotel for a private party after the show." Isaac Tigrett (founder of the Hard Rock Cafe chain) was throwing a bash in SRV's honor. Lenny said that Stevie was to be presented with a guitar that belonged to Jimi Hendrix. Stevie got the message after the show while talking with cousin Connie in his dressing room trailer. "We were actually alone for a few minutes, which was very rare," Connie recalls. Lenny had

Stevie Ray and Jimmie Lee recording *Live Alive* at the Austin Opera House, July 1986. Photo © 1986 by Cindy Light.

greatly upset Stevie and he was grateful for the chance to talk it over with Connie.

Then the rest of the family and friends began to filter into the dressing room, and Stevie and Martha disappeared into the bathroom for a long time to talk about his father's condition, which was getting worse. Stevie came out and saw his Aunt Mae Mae (Florence Vaughan), one of his favorite relatives, and spent lots of time hugging and talking to her. He kept telling her over and over, "You know I love Connie, don't you?" Mae Mae said, "Yes, I know," and he repeated, "No, I really do love Connie." She could only respond, "She loves you too, Stevie." Finally, he pulled his cousin aside and said, "I want you go to this party with me, Connie. I don't want to face these people alone." At that moment, all Stevie wanted was to be with his cousin, to cry on her shoulder and let her strength lift him up. But every time they'd manage to break free of the admirers, they would be interrupted by his limo driver, who kept asking, "Are we ready? Are we ready?"

Upon arrival at the Stoneleigh party, Stevie and Connie again tried to sneak away to a place where they could talk privately, but it seemed everyone there—managers, celebrities, and sycophants—wanted a piece of Stevie Ray's time. "Everybody was staring at Stevie and making him feel uncomfortable," Connie remembers. "Also, he had been using some kind of drug that night— I don't know what, but I could tell he had something. Dan Aykroyd was there with his wife, and lots of famous people, drinking and passing the mirror around, you know. And they all wanted to hear Stevie play his guitar for them. But he really didn't feel like entertaining."

Stevie signed the green Stratocaster (whether or not it ever belonged to Hendrix is questionable), played it for a while, then prepared to leave with it. As his entourage was leaving, Stevie became outraged when he discovered that Tigrett wasn't really giving him the guitar, as he had been led to believe. It was all a ploy to get him to the

Stevie leaving the Austin Opera House with the master tapes for *Live Alive*. Photo © 1986 by Cindy Light.

party. Stevie felt like he had been used. "So I'm standing there talking to his manager when all of a sudden we hear this big 'FUCK YOU!' coming from around the corner, and it was Stevie's voice," Connie remembers with a giggle. "Now, Stevie was the sweetest guy in the world, but by all means, don't mess with him. Needless to say, we got out quick!

"Back in the limo, Stevie sat across from me, and I just kinda took his hand and said, 'Stevie, there are people like that in this world, don't let them get to you.' And he was totally sober by this time. He just sat back and said, 'You're right, Connie. You're always right, Connie,' and kinda rolled his eyes a little. We just laughed and blew it off. We arrived at my house, and Stevie got out of the limo to walk me to the door, and his manager shut the door on his foot! Not meaning to, of course, but he thought I was getting out on my own. So Stevie limped me to the door, and we just stood there for the longest time looking at each other…it was the first time we had really spent time together in ages, it seemed. And it was really sad there for a moment that he had to get on a plane and leave. Then came all the vows— *'Yes, we'll stay in touch, yes, call me if you need anything,'*…but it was so hard just to find him! I wrote several letters, and of course, Stevie never saw them."

When Stevie came home to Austin a few days later, he noticed something funny-looking about his house. As he pulled into the driveway of his Travis Heights home, he didn't see any cars; his dog T-Bone wasn't in the backyard, and all the lights were off. He tried the door—it was padlocked. Lenny was gone. What about all the money he had sent her from the road? She had spent it impressing male admirers, having so much fun that she forgot to come home.

Stevie was working at Dallas Sound Labs, listening back to the concerts he'd just recorded,

Photo inscribed with one of Stevie's favorite sentiments for photographer and friend Randy Jennings. Courtesy of Randy Jennings/Captured Live.

when he realized how bad it really sounded. The drum sound was awful; he even asked Whipper to re-cut his drum parts on some songs. Stevie began over-dubbing his vocals and guitars, totally unsatisfied with what was already there. Bass and keyboard parts were redone, too. By the time they were finished toying with the tapes, the only original tracks left were the audience. But all the work they'd done didn't seem to help. Stevie still didn't like it. But he couldn't worry about the album right now; he had concert obligations to fulfill.

One show at Pier 84 in New York City with the T-Birds and special guest Stevie Winwood found Stevie upstaged by brother Jimmie. It happened a lot on that tour (although SRV was at a drug-addled disadvantage), and audiences across the country finally understood why Stevie kept saying that Jimmie was better than him—on several occasions, he was. The brothers worked up an encore medley of "Rude Mood" and "Pipeline" where they would play a double-neck Fender Strat together, Jimmie's arms wrapped around his little brother. It was a beautiful sight. Despite their sometimes bitter rivalry, JLV and SRV were closer than they'd ever been.

Stevie would use his days off on the road to fly into studios like Dallas Sound Labs, Sound Recorders in Kansas City, and the Record Plant in L.A. for all-night cutting,

splicing, and overdubbing sessions. To stay awake, Vaughan increased his dosage to two eight-balls of coke a day. When Stevie did sleep, it was usually under the studio console, where an engineer might find him the next morning, snoozing with a bottle of Crown Royal clutched in his hand. Neither Stevie, the band, or the engineers felt like a worthwhile album could be salvaged, but Epic was breathing down their necks to complete the album, which was running over budget. Meanwhile, Stevie Ray Vaughan was running out of gas.

The road was calling again. Stevie forgot about the record, and played a series of dates with Bonnie Raitt opening. The two spent countless hours together partying after gigs, rolling from city to city in a tipsy stupor. Stevie played the Greek Theater in Los Angeles, where he was joined by Hank Ballard on "Look At Little Sister," and Mitch Mitchell (drummer for the Jimi Hendrix Experience) on "Voodoo Chile." He was joined in Santa Cruz by Doyle Bramhall Jr., who was only sixteen but blew Stevie away with his knowledge of blues guitar styles. Stevie took little Doyle under his wing, even arranging a screen test for him at Paramount Studios. Hank Ballard joined him again in Berkeley, as did Albert Collins, and the three jammed on a long-winded, out-of-tune "The Sky Is Crying."

After a concert in Dayton, Ohio (where Stevie was joined by Johnny Copeland), Stevie met with fans backstage. One in particular stood out from the usual group of well-wishers, and was lucky enough to spend several hours with Vaughan.

Stevie gives "The Shining" grin. Photo by and courtesy of Randy Jennings/Captured Live.

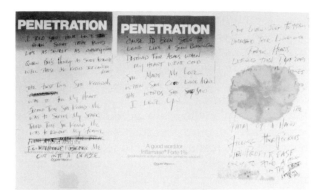

Rough lyrics and previously unpublished poetry scribbled on note paper and a napkin (far right). The spot on the napkin appears to be mustard. Courtesy of Thomas Kreason/ Rockabilia.

His name was Randy Jennings, and he was a gifted photographer. Randy and his date were speechless at meeting Stevie Ray in person, and the poor girl literally couldn't do anything but stand with her mouth open while Randy drilled SRV with questions. "He opened up a can of Bud," Jennings remembers, "handed me one, and says, 'Man, just take your time. We got all night.' And by the end of the night, of course, we were all just downright intoxicated."

Surprisingly, Stevie didn't lose Randy's phone number. Jennings traveled extensively with Double Trouble, shooting to his heart's content. One infamous shot happened after a Sunday night show in Columbus while SRV was signing autographs, still wearing his Indian chief's headdress from the performance. Jennings approached him, and Stevie flashed a deranged grin at the photographer. Stevie was blasted out of his mind, and didn't even remember the picture when it was shown to him years later. "He called it 'The Shining,' Jennings recalls with a soft chuckle, "because he said it's like when [Jack] Nicholson broke down the bathroom door in that movie, stuck his head

Still wearing each other's clothes: Stevie and Jimmie playing "Pipeline" together in 1986. Photo by and courtesy of Randy Jennings/ Captured Live.

through the little hole and yelled, 'Here's Johnny!'"

Vaughan's playfulness was something that Jennings remembers warmly, even in the heavy-abuse years. "He was usually real cooperative with me," Randy says. "He'd do anything I wanted for a picture. But he'd always notice when I was changing rolls of film, and that's when he'd do something real cool. He'd even stand there until he saw that I got the film loaded, then he'd turn around and take a stroll in the other direction. He loved to screw with me like that!"

Jennings couldn't help but notice the visible deterioration in Stevie's performances night after night. Due to his drug and alcohol consumption, not only was he losing fire from his burning soul, but his physical strength was going fast. Stevie played it cool. He knew what was happening to him, but he seemed content to keep going at the same destructive pace. "One image really sticks out from that time," Jennings says. "It was a shot of Stevie coming off stage swinging a big cup full of Crown Royal. He took his hat off, and he was all sweaty. Looking back at it, it's a real pathetic and sad picture. He's just standing there all alone and

State Street Jaycees
Oregon State Penitentiary
Salem, Oregon

Convicts have learnt to be content with less; therefore, we guard what we have against those who would take from us. That which we so zealously protect, we offer freely to Stevie Ray Vaughan. He has twice given us one of his most beloved possessions: his music.

So it is with a profound sense of pride and honor that the State Street Jaycees and the convicts of the Oregon State Penitentiary do hereby confer upon Stevie Ray Vaughan the title of "Honorary Convict." This title bestows upon Stevie Ray Vaughan the inalienable right to partake of the precious few liberties and privileges which we convicts hold dear. His gift to us prompts us to offer him our most treasured possession: brotherhood.

Signed this Aug. 6, 1986 ~ James Bernhard "Skinny Jimmy"

Oregon State Penitentiary's honorary convict decree, given to Stevie on August 6, 1986. Courtesy of Thomas Kreason/Rockabilia.

On August 6, 1986, Stevie played a free concert at the Oregon State Penitentiary. This was his second performance there; the convicts had loved him so much the first time that they felt moved to start a roadie training class. They even got a chance to prove their skills when Stevie's equipment truck didn't show up; it had gotten lost on the back roads of northern Oregon somewhere. They also presented him with an official proclamation that made him an "Honorary Convict," and Stevie Ray treasured it. They had offered him their only possession—brotherhood. Although he didn't know much about their lives or why they were in prison, he figured that these were just normal men like him who had listened to the wrong people and made the wrong decisions. Stevie—emotionally jailed himself—could identify with them. The prison experience stuck with him.

Stevie relaxes backstage after a hot summer show in Baltimore. Photo by and courtesy of Dale Allen/Killer Cases.

"People have got to realize that people in the pen are in there for reasons that were there long before they committed any crime," Stevie sermonized. "They're just as important as anybody else on the outside. Those people have to deal with laws, and the law can sometimes turn a thumbs down on people who really need help. But those people have so much heart, it's incredible," he marveled. "It's just *incredible* to see what goes on inside those walls; if you could go in and meet these folks, you'd be surprised at how many of them are in there just waiting for their turn to come out and show the world what they really have to give. They just want to be regular people again."

Vaughan rolled on to Memphis to tape a television pilot for the PBS network affiliate there. The show was called "American Caravan," and was being shot at the Orpheum Theater. Lonnie Mack was the star. Stevie was just helping out by lending his name and playing a couple of songs. But everything came to a screeching halt when Stevie got a phone call from Dallas. His dad was

it's just really, I don't know . . . it's pretty eerie now."

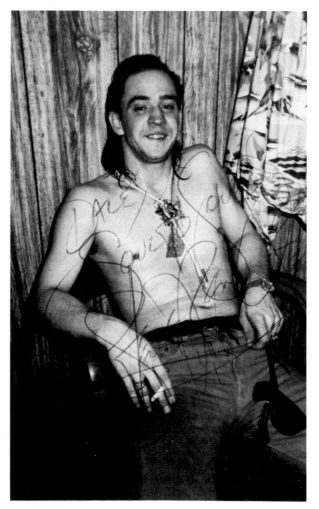

Handwritten list:
- ~~Dimple~~
- 2 4X12 MARSHALL CABINETS
- 2 HIWATT OR MARSHALL 100 WATT OLD STYLE — SUPER BASS, SUPER LEAD —
- PREFERABLY MAJOR HEADS
- 2 PRE CBS SUPER REVERB AMPS
- 1 LESLIE - FENDER VIBROTONE IF POSS.
- 1 IBANEZ TUBE SCREAMER
- 1 VOX ITALIAN WAH WAH
- 1 UNIVIBE
- ALL CABLES, ALL JUNCTION BOXES ETC...

Stevie gave this handwritten list of missing items to his Montreal promoter after most of his equipment was stolen on August 28, 1986. Courtesy of Thomas Kreason/Rockabilia.

attacks. He'd been confined to a wheelchair for several years, unable to work or even move around, and it saddened Stevie to see his father suffering. Even if Big Jim had made life tough on him growing up, even if he didn't want Stevie playing that "nigger music," Steve Vaughan still loved his dad very much.

The family stayed at Big Jim's bedside for three days after this last heart attack, knowing he was only sustained by life support systems and respirators, and that he had already given up the fight. On August 27, 1986, Martha signed the necessary papers to turn off the machines and end his life.

A funeral was held at Laurel Land Memorial Park on August 29, and Stevie attended. But within hours he was on the next plane to Montreal, where a lucrative festival gig awaited him. He threw himself back into his work, trying to ignore the pain of losing his father, his wife, and his manager within a year. He didn't want to think about how much his mother wanted to be with him now. He didn't think about his wife or little girlfriend overseas. Stevie had built his wall of denial with care, and he selfishly avoided feeling anything that might knock it down.

losing the battle with Parkinson's Disease in a Dallas hospital, and he'd better come home—quick.

His old man was in pretty bad shape. The once robust, brawny Vaughan had become thin and sickly, his frail body powerless against the disease that had been consuming him for so long, although he had no way of knowing until it was too late. Big Jim had asbestosis; it had started with coughing fits and ended up in seizures and heart

Itinerary for the 1986 European tour. All dates after October 3 were cancelled for Vaughan to enter a drug and alcohol rehab program. Courtesy of Thomas Kreason/Rockabilia.

STRIKE FORCE
10573 W. Pico Blvd./Box 201/Los Angeles, CA 90064
(213) 470-1986

ITINERARY WITH MILEAGES

DATE	DAY	CITY/COUNTRY	VENUE	MILES	HRS.
9/11	Thu	Production Day/Copenhagen	Saga		
9/12	Fri	Copenhagen	Saga	200	6
9/13	Sat	Off			
9/14	Sun	Hamburg, Germany	Grosse Freiheit	200	4.5
9/15	Mon	Berlin, Germany	Metropol	330	8
9/16	Tue	Offenbach, Germany	Stadthalle	130	3
9/17	Wed	Essen, Germany	Saalbau		1
9/18	Thu	Bonn, Germany	Biskuithalle	50	1.5
9/19	Fri	Kerkrade, Holland	Rodahal	60	2
9/20	Sat	Deinze, Belgium	Brielport	100	2
9/21	Sun	Utrecht, Holland	Music Centre	100	
9/22	Mon	Off			6
9/23	Tue	Paris, France	Olympia	300	
9/24	Wed	Paris, France	Olympia		8
9/25	Thu	Stuttgart, Germany	Sindelfingen	400	3
9/26	Fri	Munich, Germany	Circus Krone	150	
9/27	Sat	Off			
9/28	Sun	Ludwigshafen, Germany	Pfallbau	250	4.5
9/29	Mon	Zurich, Switzerland	Volkaus	230	4.5
9/30	Tue	Press in London	Air		

DATE	DAY	CITY/COUNTRY	VENUE	MILES	HRS.
10/1	Wed				
10/2	Thu	London, England			
10/3	Fri	Off	Hammersmith Palais		
10/4	Sat	Doetinchem, Holland	Markthal	274	?(5)
10/5	Sun	Utrecht, Holland.	Music Centre	40	1
10/6	Mon	Helsinki, Finland	House of Culture		
10/7	Tue	Off			
10/8	Wed	Orebo, Sweden	Park Theatre	670	
10/9	Thu	Lund, Sweden	Academiska Foreningen	350	6.5
10/10	Fri	Stockholm, Sweden	Concert House	380	7.5
10/11	Sat	Off			
10/12	Sun	Bergen, Norway	Oleana	650	16
10/13	Mon	Stavanger, Norway	Red Sea House	150 + 6 Ferries	
10/14	Tue	Oslo, Norway	Circus	300	10
10/15	Wed	Off			
10/16	Thu	London, England	Hammersmith Palais	980	
10/17	Fri	Newcastle, England	Mayfair	280	5
10/18	Sat	Manchester, England	Apollo	120	3
10/19	Sun	Off			
10/20	Mon	Dublin, Ireland	Stadium	368	

Mileages by Len Wright

Mileages per Eurotrax

Rare commemorative poster for the show in Paris, which took place just before Stevie entered Dr. Bloom's rehabilitation clinic in London. Courtesy of Thomas Kreason/Rockabilia.

Stevie was dealt a karmic warning when most of his personal equipment was stolen on the way to Canada. The Associated Press reported, "The day after the death of his father last month, he lost $20,000 worth of equipment and instruments to thieves, including a guitar once owned by Jimi Hendrix. The heist occurred in Albany, New York, where a man who claimed to be Vaughan's manager convinced the airline shipping Vaughan's equipment to load the gear into his trucks and off he went. A spokesman for Vaughan expressed shock that an airline would just hand over 20,000 dollars worth of gear without even asking the man for a claim check. A reward is being offered, no questions asked, to anyone who returns the equipment."

Stevie thought the stuff was gone for good, but was amazed when the police recovered most of the loot—everything but his prized Jimi Hendrix wah-wah pedal that his big brother had given him when he was twelve.

Stevie jetted back to L.A. to squeeze in more studio time for *Live Alive* before starting yet another European tour. He was running on auto pilot, cruising through shows as normal, thrilling crowds and letting his guitar get him off every night. He moved through sellout dates in Germany, Holland, Denmark, and Belgium before stopping for a celebrated two-night stand at Paris's Olympia Theatre on September 23 and 24. He was again visited by Mitch Mitchell, and the two

holed up in one of Hendrix's favorite bars nearby. He got a note at his hotel the next day from Billy Gibbons of ZZ Top encouraging him to "keep playing the blues." Little did Gibbons know that Stevie was letting the blues play him—for a fool.

On September 28, Stevie was in Ludwigshafen, Germany, out taking a walk with Chris Layton and Tim Duckworth, when he suddenly doubled over and threw up blood-specked bile on the sidewalk. His companions watched in horror as Stevie kept it up over the next few blocks, assuring them that he was okay—really, there was no need to be alarmed, he said. Chris didn't believe him this time. He'd known Stevie had a problem, but he hadn't known that things were this bad until now. Stevie put a quaking hand on Layton's shoulder and told him, "I need a drink."

"You can't drink like this, Stevie." Chris said firmly.

"I know, I know," Stevie admitted. "But I need one, though."

Back at the hotel, Layton and Duckworth watched Stevie down a few shots of whiskey, which seemed to calm him. But within a minute, Stevie's face became pallid, his eyes glazed over, his body began to tremble, and SRV realized he was in big trouble. "I need help, go get help," Stevie managed to say, gasping for breath. An ambulance came to the rescue, giving him a shot of glucose and saline before rushing him to the hospital. The doctor told him exactly what was wrong—he'd been drinking too much. He should lay off the stuff, go back to his hotel and rest. *Oh, if it were only that easy.*

Chris Layton says he will never forget the look on Stevie's face when he wanted that last drink. Layton recalls, "He had that hollow look in his eyes; like if you've ever seen a dead animal—like looking into a dead deer's eye, like nothing's there. Vacant."

Chris placed a panicked phone call to Alex Hodges from Zurich, Switzerland the next day. Alex was used to dealing with artists and their addictions after years of handling the party-hearty southern rock bands, but this time it was serious. It was life or death, and Stevie was leaning precariously toward the latter. "Stevie needs help," Layton insisted. "We've got to stop this thing. *He* said he needs help. Who's that doctor in London who helped Clapton and everybody get off heroin?" Hodges called Dr. Victor Bloom, putting Stevie in his care the very next day, and canceling all road obligations.

Dr. Bloom told Stevie Ray that the Crown Royal and coke he'd been ingesting for so long wasn't a very smart thing to do. All the alcohol had chewed holes in Stevie's stomach walls, and the cocaine was breaking him down even more inside, causing severe internal bleeding. Dr. Bloom told him that if he didn't stop right now—and he meant *now*—he'd be dead within a month.

Although he was far gone, Stevie Ray wasn't deaf. He took heed, agreeing to a four-week rest at Bloom's treatment clinic, and promised to follow up with more intense rehabilitation when he returned to the U.S. But he didn't want to go through it alone. He called home to his mother. She wasn't home. He left a message on her answering machine. "Mama, I'm over here in Europe somewhere and I'm in real bad shape," Stevie told her, his voice quivering like a frightened child's. "I've got some things I got to do. *I sure would like it if you'd come over...*" He gave Tim Duckworth the job of finding and bringing Janna Lapidus to his side.

The day before his thirty-second birthday, October 3, 1986, Stevie Ray Vaughan played his last concert as Stevie Rave On at London's Hammersmith Palais. He told the crowd, "I'm grateful to be here tonight—you don't know how grateful."

He donned his Indian headdress for the final encore, but he was so tired he couldn't even hold his head up enough to keep the thing on. As he was walking offstage, he became blinded by the darkness and lost his footing, missing the gangplank and falling several feet to the ground. He was bruised, vulnerable, and helpless. This was it, he realized. The message was clear—clean up or die.

"I woke up on a tour bus," Stevie remembered. "I couldn't hardly get up. I was scared of everything—my friends. Just being awake, I was scared. I tried to say 'hi' to my bass player, and I started crying. I was a wreck. And I realized right then the only way to win this thing was to give up. Thank God that happened. I had a breakdown—only then was I able to ask for help instead of telling myself 'I'll make it through this.' I'll make it through if I ask for help. People think that people on stage are bigger than life, stronger than life. That's what makes them so special to go see. But people on stage are not superhuman—that's a myth."

Stevie Ray Vaughan saved his own life by admitting that the problem was out of his control. No manager, girlfriend, buddy, or mother could make it go away. Stevie knew he had to trust a higher power this time.

He had finally placed his destiny in the hands of God.

The Things That I Used To Do

DR. VICTOR BLOOM'S clinic did not require its patients to abandon their addictions cold turkey. If one needed a drink bad enough, a small amount could be administered. But Stevie Ray knew that one drink would only lead to a thousand more, and somehow resisted the urge to indulge himself. Instead, he'd leave the clinic with Martha, Janna, and Tim to go shopping or sightseeing around London, experiencing the rush of discovering new places with his eyes open for the first time.

While in the clinic, Stevie received a surprise visit from Eric Clapton, who had been keeping a watchful eye on him, and wanted to let Vaughan know that he had support. Clapton had tried to tell Stevie years ago that he was in trouble, but his warnings went unheeded. "Back then he could sense that I wasn't ready, so he didn't push it," Stevie told *Guitar World*. "See, you can try, you can let somebody know what's going on, but if they're not ready to quit, you can't make 'em quit. You just can't. They're gonna despise you for it. They'll resent the fact that you tried to tell them how to live their life...All they wanna do is take this away from you, so you get defensive.

Stevie started looking into rehab programs in the States, and decided that he wanted to try the expensive-but-effective Charter method that stressed total abstinence from drugs and alcohol. Alex Hodges recommended the Charter Peachford Hospital in Atlanta—his office was in nearby Marietta, Georgia, and Martha's sister also lived in the area. Stevie could be near friends and family, but far enough away from Texas to escape temptation.

On the plane heading home, Stevie was petrified. He'd never flown sober before. He asked Martha to loan him ten dollars to buy some duty-free cigarettes. He slipped away to the bar and spent all the money as fast as he could on double shots of Crown Royal. He knew it wasn't right, and no sooner had he taken his seat next to Martha than he broke down weeping.

"Here I had just come out of the clinic in London," Stevie recalled guiltily, "had gotten some information about what was wrong with me...and *still* fell back into that old thinking. I mean, I was on my way to go into a treatment facility, and had a quick thought of, 'Wow, I've never done this straight before.'"

Stevie was amazed at how his mother silently accepted this and tried to comfort him. She could have told him he was a failure, and could have preached "I told you so," but she offered only love and encouragement to her son. "She even stuck around in Atlanta while I was in treatment," Stevie said. "It showed me how much she had cared all along, regardless of how far gone I'd gotten. When you get loaded all the time, you forget that people still care."

Stevie entered the Peachford Clinic on Wednesday, October 17, 1986, and was to remain there until November 31. He told Janna to stay in touch, and sent her back home. Double Trouble flew over to America, and Tommy followed his friend's lead by checking into an Austin rehab facility. He took his oath of sobriety the same day as Stevie. SRV also bid adieu to Tim Duckworth; he didn't need a personal assistant anymore. It was time for him to take care of himself. For the first time in a long time, Stevie Ray Vaughan was going to handle his own affairs.

As he went through admission to the hospital, a nurse handed him a list of an addict's typical symptoms. Each one described him to a T, and he was mortified. He really was a drug addict and an alcoholic. Stevie never had fully admitted that to himself before. He was going to have to learn. After shelling out nearly $20,000 to try this program, Stevie knew it was too late to turn back now. He just hoped it would work.

The clinic put him through a rigid routine that got him back in touch with life; first, they got the blood flowing by making him exercise every day, something that Stevie (a confirmed couch potato) had never done much of. Second, he was fed three solid meals a day, which most traveling rock and rollers don't bother with. And they made him open up and talk about his problems with counselors and other patients daily. He began to learn more about the medical effects of drugs on the body, and it scared him. *How could something so bad feel so good?*

All patients were required to keep strictly confidential journals, in which they could write down their thoughts as each day passed, keeping track of their personal progress on the path to recovery.

"This place is just intense," Stevie said of the Georgia hospital. "You don't have a lot of time here to slough off. There's a lot of work to be done when someone puts himself in a position where you have to go into one. Luckily, by that time, I had a real clear understanding that I needed some help...I obviously couldn't stop myself, and I pushed it to the point where I collapsed, man. It didn't take much suggestion from any doctor.

"I had conned myself into believing that I was controlling it—keep in mind that if I'm gonna roll that way, I'm damn sure gonna be a good con with it, too. I mean, doin' a quarter ounce a day, snortin' it. There's a lot of people that can go party socially and not run it into the ground, and I wish I was one of 'em, but I'd gotten to the point where I'd done my share and part of somebody else's. My brain was chemically changed. I didn't know when I was drunk anymore. Just before I quit drinkin' I could drink a whole shitload and not get drunk, and the next day with no warning take half a drink and get fucked up. And it was gettin' to where it was interfering with my playing."

Stevie said that although the physical craving for alcohol had passed, he still felt the urge to drink. "It's weird, 'cause it'll sneak up on me," he admitted. "I'll see a bottle and like, have to stop myself. Soon as I get past that urge, it's okay. But I go to meetings and just really pay attention and get on my knees a lot, man. It's true."

Jackson Browne visited him at the Atlanta clinic, and this meant the world to Stevie. He had always been flattered by Browne's charity towards him—Jackson didn't have to loan his studio to an unknown, struggling guitarist to cut his first record, but he did. Jackson didn't have to trek across the country just to let Stevie know that he cared, but he did. For once, Stevie could open up to Browne, sharing the details of his recent struggle, and was finally able to tell Jackson how much his kind deeds meant to him over the years. Browne wasn't the only one to offer support. Stevie also received innumerable letters and phone calls expressing similar sentiments. He later said that it was those well-wishers who sustained him in the clinic and stayed with him through his recovery.

Stevie remembered old Albert King, who had tried to set him straight so many times before, and he felt pretty foolish now for not listening to his hero. He thought back to the night Albert approached him backstage and said, "We gonna have a heart-to-heart. I been watching you wrestle with that bottle three, four times already. I tell you what, man. I like to drink a little bit when I'm at home. But the gig ain't no time to get high." Now Stevie realized that no problem was so bad that no drink or drug was going to solve his problems.

The Charter program was based around the Alcoholics Anonymous 12-Step method (as are most rehab programs today), and Stevie began attending AA meetings even before he left the Peachford facility. AA asked its members to maintain a code of anonymity—members were known only by their first names and last initial. It was preferred that Stevie not discuss AA publicly. This was something he found very hard to accept. He wanted people to know what it had done for him, that it saved his life every single day.

Stevie could have kept quiet about the whole rehab process. After all, the rest of the world didn't really need to know what he'd been through. It was still the mid-eighties, and cleaning up wasn't exactly in vogue; a hedonistic lifestyle had been the standard in rock and roll for twenty years. But Vaughan decided that he would talk about his drug and alcohol problems with the press; he bared all, telling the whole story so that others might learn from his mistakes. "I haven't kept it quiet that I'm sober," Stevie said, "and a lot of people just don't come around anymore. Those that do, most of them have sobered up, too. There's still people that are fighting the demon, still fighting to run with it. I hope they come around, 'cause you can only go so long or it kills you, or you go nuts, or go to jail.

"I sure would like to be a good example," Stevie stressed, a certain urgency in his expression. "Because it sure helped me. I know that. As fucked up as I was getting with it, if it helped me, it's bound to help other people. Fortunately, there are people who care. And I just had to remember that. And care about myself as well."

Stevie told *The Dallas Morning News* that in his heavy-abuse days, he was "throwing up, falling down, running into walls, and thinking people were after me...and running from other people,

the people who cared about me. I was treating people like drugs, too. If there was somebody that would put up with anything, that was fine. Luckily, there were people who still cared."

Stevie was not happy about the mixes of *Live Alive*, and took a little time out of his rehab program to look for a new studio to re-mix the tapes in. He found it at Stevie Wonder's private Wonderland Studios in L.A. "They welcomed us in, gave us a better rate than anybody else around, treated us well, gave us the studio for twenty-four hours a day," Stevie remembered. "...All of a sudden I would get these great phone calls in the middle of the night. Imagine this: being dead asleep, picking up the phone and Stevie Wonder is singing to you!" Wonder liked Vaughan's rendition of "Superstition" so well, he asked SRV to play on his upcoming (*Characters*) album.

At Wonderland, the band added the finishing touches, several overdubs, and a new mix to the project. Stevie explained the need for cosmetic surgery on the tapes by admitting he had "hamburger throat on several of the shows." He added, "The vocals had to be repaired. Some feedback was fixed, too—there's no sense in having that on a record unless you're Sid Vicious."

Chris Layton told writer Dan Forte, "Out of necessity, *Live Alive* became something we did at that time because we were so fucked up we couldn't have gotten it together to do a serious, good studio album....Mastering the album, Reese and I were in Los Angeles, Tommy was in Austin, and Stevie was in rehab in Atlanta, and we were all on the phone, going, 'What do you think about this?' Everyone's life was changing, everybody was getting clearer, so our views were different. We weren't listening to a song when we all had just done a big toot and a glass of whiskey."

Listening to the *Live Alive* tapes again, Stevie was amazed at how erratically he had been playing due to the drugs. It never really occurred to him before.

"The music has become really important now," Stevie acknowledged. "Music is really a way to reach out and hold onto each other in a healthy way. I'm finding that out now. It's helped me to open up more and take a chance on loving people, instead of just isolating and suspecting everybody that I run into."

Live Alive was released in November (while Stevie was still in rehab) as a two-record set, but only reached #52 on the *Billboard* Pop Albums chart. The reviews were not particularly good, but rock radio took a liking to "Willie The Wimp," written by the Austin team of Bill Carter and Ruth Ellsworth. The song was inspired by a newspaper article they had read about a Chicago pimp who had died and asked to be buried in his Cadillac—thus the chorus of "Willie The Wimp in his Cadillac coffin."

"Superstition" was also a hit, and Epic Records sprung for a video that depicts the band under the curse of a wandering black cat who electrocutes Tommy Shannon (by spilling a cup of coffee on his guitar cord), makes Reese Wynans disappear (by pulling the trap door under his keyboards), and crushes Chris Layton (by dropping a piece of heavy scenery on the drums), but Stevie plays obliviously on, and no harm comes to him. Stevie Wonder puts in a cameo appearance at the end of the video, stroking the dangerous cat and singing an a cappella chorus.

In late November, Stevie was visited at the hospital by Bonnie Raitt, who was in town to play a gig. She asked him if he'd like to come see the show, and he accepted. He didn't have any idea what she had in mind until later that night. Stevie was aghast when he heard her announce her special guest—Stevie Ray Vaughan. He'd never stepped on a stage sober in his life, but this was his chance to try. He might have been frightened at first, but it didn't take but one song for him to get in the groove. Nothing had changed, really. Music, playing the guitar, just felt better now.

Upon finishing his Charter program, Stevie was on his own. It was time for a change in all aspects of his life; he couldn't go back to the same old friends and habits. Stevie decided to move back "home" to Dallas in late 1986, ending his fifteen-year love affair with Austin. The chemical temptations and negative attitudes were just too severe for him to hang around. "We were playing the same kind of cards...and it was dirty," Stevie said. "Almost everybody I knew in Austin was who I got my stuff from, you know. Or hung out with because they had it. My mother still lived in Dallas. I figured I could be close by her and learn to know her again... I'd spent a lot of years trying to get away from (my parents), because I was scared of the fact that they could both see through my crap."

He didn't want to live in Oak Cliff again; that was still a little too close to the past. Stevie wanted to make a fresh start. He found a quaint condominium at 4344 Travis Street (just off the Central Expressway at Knox/Henderson) on the edge of the upscale Highland Park section of Dallas. He asked his girlfriend Janna to move in with him, and she accepted, much to the disapproval of mother Martha. She abhorred the thought of her full-grown son living in sin with an eighteen-year-old girl instead of waiting for a good Christian marriage. But none of that could happen until Stevie was truly free of Lenny and besides, he wasn't ready to rush into another marriage just yet.

He had asked Lenny to come visit him in the Atlanta hospital, making one last attempt to save the relationship, but she didn't show up. That was the last straw. It was really over. He filed for divorce. Lenny fought him every step of the way. The divorce proceedings turned ugly, taking over a year for their attorneys to reach a suitable compromise. This broke Stevie's heart so badly he found it impossible to concentrate on writing new songs—every time he did, he didn't like the dubious messages that emerged. "I couldn't write during that," Stevie expressed. "I wanted to, but divorces are sick. People don't treat people like people. Lawyers get together and try to trick each other."

In December 1986, Stevie and Janna took a vacation to Europe, even visiting the French Riviera, which Stevie said was "paradise." He phoned pal Bob Claypool at *The Houston Post* from Florence, Italy. "What are you doing over there?" Claypool asked. "Having the first vacation of my life," Vaughan laughed. "Just took some time off to relax and we're seeing the sights, having a great time. It's a real relaxing thing. I worried that too many people might recognize me," he confided, "and I'd have to deal with a bunch of autograph-seekers. But nobody cares, everybody's been real nice to me."

New Year's Eve found Stevie playing in Atlanta with Lonnie Mack, a live radio broadcast for FM-96. It was one of his first concerts as a sober man, and although his voice was unaccustomed to singing without the coke and alcohol coating, he put in a stunning performance. He blew his throat out in the first three songs, and was fighting so hard to sing the high notes in "Couldn't Stand The Weather" that it's still painful to listen to. His frustration and disappointment over his singing translates into one of the most incredible guitar solos the man ever played. It came out of nowhere; during Reese's normally placid piano solo near the end, Stevie just exploded. It was the wildest, meanest, fastest thing he'd ever come up with. The solo is otherworldly; of all the hundreds of tapes that exist of this song, there's nothing like this. The crowd was so flabbergasted they stopped cheering

Double whammy—Lonnie Mack and Stevie in Atlanta. Photo by and courtesy of W.A. Williams/The Image Works.

our lives with a true feeling of love for everybody and yourself. It's all you have to give—so give it freely. Do you understand?" The crowd roared its approval. Before he walked offstage, he told them, "Life without you sure would be a drag. Take care of yourselves. Happy New Year, everybody!" Those words meant more that night than ever.

One of Stevie's New Year's resolutions for 1987 was to stay true to Alcoholics Anonymous. He joined the Aquarius chapter in Dallas, and was pleasantly surprised to find several of his old friends and bandmates were members, too. Bruce (B.C.) Miller from the Benno-era Nightcrawlers was now his sponsor. Former Chessman Phil Campbell was there, as was Glenda Maples, his old teenage sweetheart. It reminded him that he needed to get back in contact with his Oak Cliff roots again, and he re-established many old acquaintances, one of them being Christian Brooks. They had a lot of catching up to do.

Nineteen eighty-six had been a hell of a year for Stevie Ray Vaughan. He had run with the devil, fallen into the snake pit, and managed to pull himself out just in time to avert death. He had been resurrected, so to speak, and after he saw the light, he wanted nothing more than to help others find it, too. He made it his mission in life to make the most out of every day, to share his love with every soul he met, and show them that there was life after drugs.

Stevie's intro to "Life Without You" took on a whole new dimension that night. Just seconds before midnight, Stevie addressed the audience with words of rebirth and hope for the new year: "You know, it's almost that time for us to be able to say we've lived through one more year of our lives. And that means it's more important by one year that we all take care of our lives, put them in the right perspective. It's time to have fun, but it's time to have time to have fun. It's time for us to remember love! You see, we won't bring in the new if we take with us the old. Let's everybody start this new year and the rest of

to stand and gawk, their mouths open wide.

A sober, happy Stevie clowns for the camera. Courtesy of Christian Brooks.

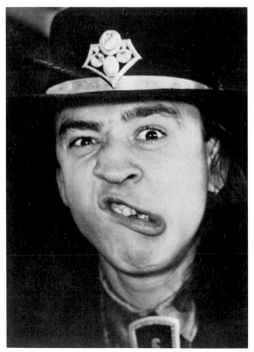

Brooks could relate to what Stevie had been through in their years apart, and they shared similar stories of failure, strength, and survival. "I cannot count all the times he told me 'I'm living on borrowed time' in the later years," Christian said. "I really admired his dedication to himself later in his life—how much care he put into everything, to make every single minute count."

Christian liked to make presents for Stevie at his leather shop; he gave SRV a beautiful custom guitar strap that he wore proudly on his Number One guitar. He says it was "just a way of saying 'Keep up the good work. People do love you for what you are, and whether you believe it or not, you've saved a few lives out there, Stevie.' I know, because he helped save mine. I wanted to give it back to him."

In January '87, Stevie played the State Fair Coliseum, with Lonnie Mack and Omar and the Howlers opening. It was the first time he'd played Dallas sober since he was nine and picking at local talent shows. SRV did a signing party for *Live Alive* at a Sound Warehouse record store earlier that afternoon before heading over to Q-102 for an interview. He was supposed to talk to Redbeard, the reigning AOR jock in the Dallas-Fort Worth area, but opted to talk to Jill Savage, who was still on the air when he arrived at the station. "He just burst in the door, breezed right by everybody, walked in on me, and kissed me on the air!" Savage recalls.

That night at the show, Stevie blew minds and stole hearts. He proved to everybody in Dallas that he was a new, improved SRV. "It sure is good to be back home, live *and* alive!" Vaughan said. During his rap on "Life Without You," instead of his usual lectures on world crises, he turned the subject around to a much more personal dilemma, telling the crowd, "We've got to quit tearing our bodies up and give ourselves a chance."

Now that Stevie was living in Dallas, his friendship with Jill grew stronger than ever, and because she'd done her own dance with the bottle she began accompanying Martha and Janna to Al-Anon meetings (a support group for AA members' wives and families). "Stevie Ray introduced me to the 12 steps," she says, "which saved my emotional life. He became my right arm of inspiration, and brought God back into my life….

"I think God worked things out with a lot of different people through Stevie, if you know what I mean. Once Stevie was sober, he really went out of his way to help and counsel others that needed it." She pauses, takes a deep, grounding breath and adds, "It's beyond the gold records, beyond the world premiers, beyond the scoops… He was good for me, and cared enough about me to

Onstage at the Holiday Star Theatre in Merryville, Indiana, in March 1987. Photo by and courtesy of W.A. Williams/The Image Works.

swoop down and say, 'let me help you, little girl.'"

Stevie Ray's music, songs he had written as well as old blues numbers he'd been performing for years, was beginning to take on a whole new meaning to him. He had spent most of his young life emulating blues masters like Howlin' Wolf, Albert King, and Buddy Guy. Even though he embraced rock and roll, he considered himself true to the blues. But Stevie wasn't as concerned with purism anymore. He told the *Dallas Times Herald* in January 1987, "The blues was a new music once itself. It didn't have so many boundaries then. The boundaries come when you forget the soul it's supposed to have. When you forget the emotion, it seems to lose something—it turns into something else. Instead of music, it turns into notes. It's the emotion that the music's played for in the first place. That's all I've had to keep in mind—keep the heart in the music."

Stevie Ray Vaughan and Double Trouble didn't do much touring in the first half of '87, opting instead to fly in for one-nighters, like a victorious concert at New York's Radio City Music Hall in February. During spring break (mid-March), Stevie played on the beach in Corpus Christi/Padre Island, Texas, and did a huge MTV-sponsored concert at Daytona Beach, Florida. Stevie looked tired. His face was still quite pale and sunken, showing the mileage he'd been putting on since the world last saw him. He was a little shaky in front of the cameras, sober for the first time, but he played well, if still a bit unsure of what was going on around him, afraid to really let go.

In April, Stevie was a special guest on the "B.B. King and Friends" special for the Cinemax cable network. The "friends" included Albert King, Paul Butterfield, Etta James, Chaka Kahn, Billy Ocean, Gladys Knight, Eric Clapton, Phil

On the Riverboat President at the New Orleans Jazz and Heritage Festival, 1987. *Left to right:* B.B. King, SRV, Albert Collins, Reese Wynans, and Katie Webster. Photo by and courtesy of Dale Allen/Killer Cases.

Collins, and Dr. John. Stevie played "The Sky Is Crying" with Albert, B.B., and Butterfield, and also backed the trio of Etta James, Chaka Kahn, and Gladys Knight on the old spiritual "Take My Hand, Precious Lord."

One of Stevie's childhood fantasies came true when he had the opportunity to record a duet of "Pipeline" with Dick Dale (of the Del-Tones) for the Frankie Avalon/Annette Funicello reunion flick, *Back to the Beach*. Vaughan and Dale appeared together in the movie and produced a music video of the song. In it Dick Dale, who plays a custom Surfboard Strat and sports a wild foot-high pompadour, is still a mean mother on the guitar. He's the star of the show, making his guitar scream and playing louder than life. Stevie seems happy to let him have center stage, and plays a docile second fiddle to the Mighty Dick Dale.

Stevie took on another challenging studio project, contributing tracks to a Leonard Cohen tribute album (*Famous Blue Raincoat: The Songs Of Leonard Cohen*) that Jennifer Warnes was doing. The album's tranquil beauty, and Stevie's additions to it, are stunning. He played stark, watery lead lines on "First We Take Manhattan (Then We

Take Berlin)," and appeared in the music video with Warnes and Cohen.

On Memorial Day, he traveled to Austin to appear as a special guest at the annual T-Birds Riverfest on Auditorium Shores. He joined in on an all-star jam at the show's end that included Bonnie Raitt, Joe Walsh, Carlos Santana, Robert Cray, and the Fabulous Thunderbirds. Stevie was elated to be among the ranks of the world's top guitarists, and unlike previous jams, most of them were now clean and sober.

On August 7, 1987, Stevie granted an interview to John T. Davis of the *Austin American-Statesman* in which he talked about taking life on and off the road at a more relaxed pace, doing "normal people stuff." "Mostly I've been trying to ease up and settle some things," Vaughan said. Most of his downtime was spent listening to his substantial record collection, scouring for new licks, new material. "They're like my books, like my school," Stevie noted. "You put it on and it hits you. It's always been that way. I can take just about any one of my records and if something about the way they play or sing gets a hold of me, I'll try to find what they did. I'll wrestle with myself playing their stuff for a while and I'll absorb it into my own sound."

He sounded excited about the upcoming tour, his first extended road trip since his collapse. "It's scheduled at a decent pace. There's even some days off! It's going to be fun to see a little of the places that we're in, instead of going straight to the soundcheck or dying in some hotel room for two hours before a show."

SRV lamented about missing the club days in Austin, saying that he tended to "be a lot freer and take more chances there. I don't know if my pipes

Jammin' with the best of them (*left to right*): Joe Walsh, SRV, Bonnie Raitt, Jimmie, Kim Wilson, Fran Christina, and Carlos Santana (in shadows). Courtesy of Studio D.

could take three hours of singing now. But I'd love to try." When Davis asked him what he'd like to do next, Stevie replied, "Just play one more day."

On August 30, Double Trouble was in Des Moines, Iowa, playing for a small crowd in what looked like a high school gym. But those on hand were treated to a rare, intimate performance from Double Trouble. The band was bursting out of the unstable rut it had been stuck in for months; for Stevie and Tommy, it was almost like learning how to play all over again—clear-headed, sober, and scared as hell. But not scared for long. This little tour was a perfect confidence builder for the band; they had the opportunity to play small midwestern venues in front of appreciative music-starved crowds. In this small, up-close-and-personal setting, Stevie came alive.

"Say What!" was unbelievable, SRV was working two wah-wah's at once, rocking back on both feet and screaming through an Octavia box. He strutted through "Lookin' Out The Window," turning in a wildly fluid solo—clean and inspired, the way he felt. Hitting the mid-section of "Mary Had A Little Lamb," spirit burst out of him like water breaking through a dam, and "The Sky Is Crying" was an imaginative, sultry, and thoughtful voyage deep into the Albert King bag. He closed the show with "Life Without You," which he played with a bittersweet touch, lowering his head and praying to the Lord above, thanking him for the gift that he was sharing with this rowdy midwestern crowd and the opportunity to be here. He'd made it another day, and touched a thousand new souls tonight.

Stevie admitted that it was tough staying sober on the road. If not for his mutual support society, he may have slipped. "In our band and crew right now there's six of us who get together and hold our little meetings and work with each other. There are people in the crew—they're not alcoholics, they're not addicts—but I ain't go nothin' against them havin' a beer or nothin'. If they got a problem and they wanna come for help to one of us that's dealin' with it, they're welcome. We'll give 'em all the help we can give 'em. But it's not 'You drink a beer, you're fired'; it's not that kind of deal."

Stevie avoided going to nightclubs as much as possible; any reformed alcoholic can tell you how hard it is to say no when the stuff is around. He went bowling on off nights with the band and

The Champaign Jam, Urbana, Illinois—summer 1987. Photo by Randy Jennings/Captured Live.

crew, and even read children's books to try and reclaim the childhood he never had.

While touring in Canada, Stevie explained to the TV program "Much Music" that "music is a good reason to care. It's just a vehicle, though. It's a way to try and give somebody something that you feel. Music is the most important thing I can do—except learn." He paused and added, "Learn. Learn to give more. If tryin' the best I can isn't good enough, I'll just have to try harder next time…it's all I can do. If I do the best I can, then at least I did the best I could in this life."

"You know, there's a big lie in this business," Stevie told *Guitar World*. "The lie is that it's okay to go out in flames. But that doesn't do anybody much good. I may be wrong, but I think Hendrix was trying to come around. I think he had gotten a glimpse of what he needed to change, and that he really wanted to change. And I found myself in a similar position. Some of us can be examples about going ahead and growing. And some of us, unfortunately, don't make it there, and end up being examples because they had to die. I hit rock bottom, but thank God my bottom wasn't death."

Life By the Drop

WHEN ON the road, it is customary for a band to pay special attention to the name they sign on the hotel register. It's one way to avoid hundreds of fans swarming the lobby, which generally makes going anywhere a real problem. Pseudonyms are required for big names to avoid unnecessary phone calls and visitors. In the past, Stevie Ray Vaughan always registered as Mr. Tone (sometimes Lee Melone), but now the fake names reflected SRV's new attitude: I.B. Clean, or Iza Newman.

Things changed backstage, too; the dressing room contract riders were rewritten—alcohol was out. Fruit juice, bottled water, and hot decaffeinated tea with lemon were now Stevie's refreshments of choice. He requested more fruit and banished red meat from his meals. (Of course, Stevie always had two fresh pizzas waiting after the show; his passion for pizza was insatiable.) Now the tour itinerary books included the nearest spa/exercise room, and gave directions to AA Meetings. Members of the crew who did wish to partake in drink or smoke had their own tour buses, for the Double Trouble bus was a traveling dry county.

The Stevie Ray who once preferred sleeping all day was now seen shooting basketball hoops or playing touch football with the crew. He'd ride his motorized skateboard contraption around the parking lot before shows. He became obsessive about his health, though he still couldn't seem to drop the cigarette habit, even after several vigorous tries.

When Stevie was at home for a rare few days off, his favorite hobby was still coursing through his record collection, playing disc jockey around the house, spinning one disc after another on his old turntable (Stevie didn't even own a CD player). "I'll just thumb through them and I don't even have to put them on at first," Stevie explained. "Just *looking* at the covers I can remember all the feelings. It's like, 'Okay, I'm home, here's my books. And here's my roots.' And then I'll put something on and it's like being rejuvenated."

On October 12, 1987, Stevie Ray Vaughan and Double Trouble played a stellar concert at Philadelphia's Mann Music Center. The improvement in Stevie's playing and singing was recognizable from the first note; his voice was deep and robust, and his guitar spoke volumes during "Lookin' Out The Window" and "Texas Flood." The latter song found him reaching deep inside himself to unearth hidden treasures he may not have even known were in his grasp. He sang "Cold Shot" like never before, opening up and improvising freely toward the end; "Couldn't Stand The Weather" was moving, but it is "Life Without You" which had grown into SRV's personal testimonial. His speech actually reduced some audience members to tears.

"Right now, the most important thing in my life is to make sure you understand what I'm about to tell you," he began. "First, I thank God that I'm alive today, and I mean that. You see, I spent too many years of my life thinking that, uh, the big party was the whole thing. It took me quite a while to find out that the real deal is to be enough of a person on your own to know when somebody loves you and cares about you. We are here—as far as I can tell—to help each other—our brothers, our sisters, our friends, our enemies. That's to help each other, not hurt each other. Are you listening? [The crowd roars] Thank you.... You see, it's a big

world out there. There's enough pain and misery in it without me going out there and helping it out by hurtin' myself, and consequently, those who care about me. What I'm tryin' to get across to you is—please take care of yourself and those that you love. Because that's what we're here for, that's all that we've got. *Love, people!*" he belted out, thoughtfully adding, "and that is what we can take with us."

In the middle of a worldwide tour to support *The Joshua Tree* album, U2 played the Frank Erwin Center in Austin in November to a sellout crowd. But what the Irish rockers really wanted to do in town was soak up some Texas blues—so they headed to Antone's. Both Stevie Ray and Jimmie Vaughan were on hand that night along with Dr. John and T-Bone Burnett, to help celebrate Lou Ann Barton's birthday.

Stevie had come with Janna, and had a ball seeing all his old Austin cohorts. He made a point of mentioning that he and Janna were going to be married. He showed her off to all his dazzled pals like a new guitar. And they were impressed; Janna was a far cry from the conquests Stevie had shacked up with in his Austin years—those little Texas cuties didn't exactly exude the intrigue or allure of a European fashion model. Heads turned as SRV waltzed through the club with this beautiful girl on his arm.

Jimmie played his lap steel on "Love Struck Baby," trading licks with Dr. John. Bono and The Edge joined in for a long, tired slow blues piece, with Bono composing on-the-spot lyrics about

Top: Bidding goodnight at the Norwich Arts Center, Norwich, Connecticut, 1987. Photo by Dale Allen/Killer Kases.

Bottom: Photo by and courtesy of Randy Jennings/Captured Live.

Stevie with his sweetheart, New Zealand beauty Janna Lapidus. Photo by and courtesy of W.A. Williams/The Image Works.

Miss Lou Ann's luscious legs. U2 became so carried away in the home of the blues that they were pulling girls onstage to dance for them, happily oblivious to their own lack of blues knowledge, or the amused musicians snickering behind their backs. Even with an all-star band like that, the jams were just too loose, often bordering on the absurd. U2 even had an entire film crew document the evening for the still-in-production *Rattle And Hum* movie, but for obvious reasons, the Antone's scenes were canned.

In late 1987, Alligator Records released an album called *I'm In The Wrong Business!* by Chicago blues veteran A.C. Reed. Reed had played sax with the Rolling Stones, Eric Clapton, Albert Collins, Muddy Waters, Buddy Guy, and Bonnie Raitt, among many others. During a 1984 visit to Austin, he had asked Stevie to come play on his record. They went into Riverside Sound together and recorded two songs: "Miami Strut" and "I Can't Go On This Way." At the time, Reed was without a record deal and would cut songs as he got the bread together. Stevie happened to have the time open, and had been thrilled to play for free.

Stevie and Jimmie were having serious talks about recording an album together as early as 1987, but the Vaughans' busy schedules kept conflicting, and it remained just talk. They told Austin scribe Ed Ward that the old animosity was finally gone, and that they now had learned mutual respect for one another. "I'll put it this way," Stevie said, "he's still big brother to me....I'm amazed every time I hear him. Tone, touch, ideas, maturity....His knowledge is incredible to me,"

Stevie continued. "I don't play any better than him. I play *different* than him."

Jimmie interrupted, "He can do all that stuff I can't, man....I'll try and pull off something that I've heard him do, and nine times outta ten, I won't get it."

After all these years, Jimmie Vaughan had finally tipped his hat to Little Stevie in print, and it made SRV feel like a million bucks. All his life was spent trying to impress Jimmie. He didn't give a shit if he impressed anybody else; it was his big brother's respect he always wanted. Now he was getting it. He began to acknowledge what big brother had taught him, and also revealed some truths about their not-so-friendly brotherhood as kids: "He taught me how to play, then he taught me how to teach myself," Stevie told UKTV in a back-seat limo interview. "Some ways were a little more subtle than others," he chortled, diverting his eyes from the camera to stare out the window. He paused. "Once, I didn't get the message, and he said, 'If you ask me to show you anything else, I'm gonna kick your butt!'—and he did!" He laughed. "This was somewhere down the line; he didn't go crazy on me or nothin'. But the rivalry between us was almost always friendly; I'd see him do something better than me and I'd tell myself, 'I'd better get off my can and catch up, you know?'"

In February, 1988, Stevie and Janna filmed a TV commercial for the Europa Oil Company in New Zealand, portraying Stevie as a motorcycle-riding, guitar-playing, Indiana Jones-type tough guy who would do anything to get the girl (played by Janna), including riding on the nose of a locomotive.

Speaking of how difficult it was to keep the same old tunes fresh night after night, year after year, Stevie revealed, "Some nights are a challenge, and it's always fun, but some shows are effortless—that's when the chillbumps come. Your toes curl up, your hair kinda stands up on end and you feel magical. Nothing you do is wrong."

One such night occurred on March 6, 1988, in Akron, playing a show to a wild Ohio crowd. He could be heard loudly warming up behind the curtains minutes before the show began, drawing deafening screams from the anxious crowd. Starting off with "Scuttle Buttin'," his playing was absolutely fluid, loose, and red-hot. During "Lookin' Out The Window," he really came out, reeling back into that famous solo with all his might, squeezing and bending his way through the Hank Ballard shuffle from hell, "Look At Little Sister."

Stevie glided through the first half of "Mary Had A Little Lamb" on the edge of just nearly cutting loose, then he stepped on the gas, pushing Double Trouble into maximum overdrive. Stevie prompted a keyboard solo with "Get It, Reese!" and Wynans obliged, but was soon overshadowed by Stevie, who was on a roll. Although he was only playing rhythm guitar through this section, his legs began to shake, and he began jumping about like a puppet on a string; he appeared taken by a joyous spirit, and caused the band and the entire audience to go wild. This is one of Vaughan's best performances ever of "Mary." Stevie reached the height of perfection during "Ain't Gone 'N' Give Up On Love," playing the song perfectly. At one point in this explosive guitar solo, the audience's screams were actually louder than the music itself, transforming this echo barn into one eternal, rumbling roar.

The echo in the place was so out-of-hand that Stevie's "Life Without You" speech was nearly impossible to decipher. Only one word comes through loud and clear, over and over again— love. He ripped into the final, gut-wrenching solo as if it might be his last, jumping up and down with the spirit, dancing gracefully about the stage, wandering out to the edge to play the final, soul-seeking notes. The lights dimmed. The night ended.

After playing the Kentucky State Fair in Louisville, Stevie met W.A. "Bill" Williams, another former alcoholic and user who had found God and now devoted his life to spreading the word at youth seminars around the country in addition to his hobby as a freelance rock photographer. He took to Vaughan in a heartbeat, and the two talked for a long time about spiritual matters, strength, addiction, and music. Stevie invited Bill to come out and shoot anytime he pleased, with Stevie often picking up the tab.

In late spring, Stevie and Classic Management ended their legal battle, agreeing on a cash settlement of around fifty thousand bucks. SRV also settled suits against him from Richard Mullen, Doyle Bramhall, and Bill Carter (all over unpaid royalties). The fog was clearing.

Stevie and Lenny Vaughan finalized their divorce on June 1, 1988. It had been a hellish affair; filed by Stevie on the shaky legal leg of "personality conflicts" only to have Lenny counter with an adultery charge. She took it to court, and the attorneys battled it out to the tune of $125,000.

In addition, Lenny got a $50,000 settlement and would receive one quarter of Double Trouble's royalties on the albums recorded during the course of their marriage.

Connie Trent had been watching the unstable relationship since day one, advising Stevie when he needed it along the way. "Stevie was good to her," she says. "Right up to the end, he tried to be very fair in the divorce; because in some way I think he felt responsible for what she had become. Understand, she was still a fairly wholesome girl when they met, but hanging around the music scene, the drugs, the money, can turn you into a monster. And Stevie was becoming that monster at the same time. They were both taken in by it, and it changed them as people for a while. Ultimately, I think it tore them apart."

Connie was used to having her phone calls and letters blocked by Lenny, who was insanely jealous of her rapport with Stevie. Getting in touch with Stevie was always a hassle, but things weren't getting any easier. Management often tried to shield him from outside forces, even certain family members. Somehow, Connie found her name crossed off the list. It broke her heart. "For the last two years of his life, it was getting harder and harder for me to get in touch with Stevie," Trent said. "My letters didn't get to him, I didn't know where to call him—he was never home anyway, and I began to have nightmares that something terrible was going to happen to him. Several times the phone would ring in the middle of the night, and I believed it to be him, because he was the only one who would call that late. By the time I woke up and answered it, they had hung up." Stevie was shocked and confused when he later found out her letters had not gotten through. She says, "He thought that *I* was trying to distance myself from *him*! Truth was, the powers that be just never got my messages through to him."

Stevie was busy preaching a message of his own—playing the blues and spreading the news, preaching the private gospel of sobriety and even Christianity. "God" began to creep into his vocabulary more and more; he took to wearing an Egyptian Coptic cross around his neck as a good luck charm, a spiritual connection. Praying became a big part of his life, and he attended church on occasion. But he was still fascinated with the supernatural, the unexplainable—the afterlife, ghosts, ESP, psychic healing, and other phenomena. He had a soft spot for blues voodoo lore, and still collected mojos and crystals, and he kept a

prized Maori fishhook.

To anyone who asked him about these trinkets of power, Stevie said they symbolized his quest for knowledge and spirituality. "And that's where I'm goin' right now," he would say. "I'm startin' to find out that that's what really matters in the first place. For me, anyway. Growing spiritually—at this point, that's what I'm drawn to more than anything."

He stayed busier than ever. He did a month on the road opening for Robert Plant across America in May and June, then spent the rest of the summer playing festivals overseas in Germany, Italy, Holland, The Netherlands, and seven other European countries. "Voodoo Chile" was licensed for the soundtrack of Sam Shepard's *Far North* film, and "Rude Mood" showed up in *Midnight Run*, an action film starring Robert DeNiro and Charles Grodin. He was even approached by actor Mickey Rourke to act in a film called *The Ride*; Stevie was to be cast as a half-Indian biker dude with Charlie Sexton in the role of his younger brother. Stevie turned down the role.

In August, SRV taped an MTV special with Stevie Wonder that celebrated the release of *Characters*. He played on "Superstition," sharing vocals with Wonder and Jody Watley, and contributed guitar on "Come Let Me Make Your Love Come Down." As the only white face in the band, Stevie was a little humbled, but he felt very comfortable even in the presence of Wonder's awesome talent.

One of the cornerstones of Stevie Ray's new

life were all the people who approached him after shows, sent letters, saw him on the street, and let him know how much he indirectly helped *them* attain sobriety. "That was one of the very most important things in Stevie's life," Tommy Shannon told *Guitar Player*.

At a show at Fort Lauderdale's Sunrise Music Theater, Stevie's throat was extremely hoarse, and he relaxed before the performance with a certified massage therapist who performed shiatsu on his neck to relax his muscles and alleviate strain on his vocal folds. "I've got an acupuncturist who does wonders for me," he explained between groans of sweet pain, his face pressed flat against the massage table. "But he's back in New York and he won't travel, so I gotta do what I can on the road."

The massage didn't help the roughness of Stevie's already ragged throat, but his guitar made up for what he lacked vocally. He threw Freddie King's "Hideaway" into the set just for fun before launching into "Scuttle Buttin'," his tribute to Lonnie Mack. He also performed a credible blues version of the Beatles' "Taxman," which Double Trouble had just recorded for the *Strawberry Fields* Beatles tribute album, the brainchild of Michael Jackson, who owned almost the entire Lennon/McCartney catalog. Stevie brought the great Otis Rush onstage, introducing the bluesman to the large crowd. They jammed on "Stormy Monday" and "Got My Mojo Working." Although Rush didn't get to sing any of his songs, the next morning scores of new blues fans would hit the record stores in search of an Otis Rush record. It might be a little late in coming for Rush, but at least the kids were putting his records back in demand again. And for that, Stevie Ray deserved praise.

Stevie's original record contract with Epic Associated expired with *Live Alive*, and before a new one could be renegotiated, the entire CBS/Columbia/Epic conglomerate was bought by the Japanese Sony Corporation, leaving Double Trouble in the lurch. Alex Hodges began pitching Stevie again to the new label executives, pointing to four million records sold, two Grammy Awards and six nominations, four W.C. Handy Blues Awards, Stevie's ever-powerful concert draw around the world, and even his recent clean-up as enticements to renew the band's contract. The record company wasn't thoroughly convinced that the investment would pay off. Stevie Ray Vaughan was a steady seller, but he'd never pulled the multimillions that other Columbia acts like the Rolling Stones and Michael Jackson did. But thanks to label allies like Jack Chase (Regional Epic Manager in Dallas) strongly suggesting that Sony keep Double Trouble, the label finally took heed.

Stevie celebrated his thirty-third birthday at his favorite Mexican restaurant, Dallas' La Suprema organic cafe, where the SRV spinach enchiladas (his favorite dish) were renamed after him. On October 13, he received his one-year chip from Alcoholics Anonymous, marking his first year as a sober man. Stevie Ray couldn't have been more proud.

In late 1988, Vaughan started working on his first studio album in three years. When he first started writing by himself, he was fearful that his creative juices were running dry. He was devising some terrific riffs, but the words simply wouldn't come. He called Doyle, who was now ready to hang out with Stevie and write until the whole

Photo by and courtesy of W.A. Williams/The Image Works.

Photo by and courtesy of Randy Jennings/Captured Live.

record was finished if need be. It was much easier now that Stevie had cleaned up his lifestyle and the lawsuit between them was resolved. When the two had discussed a partnership in 1985, Doyle was clean and Stevie was a mess. Today, they were two friends traveling through the various phases of recovery—and their writing reached a higher level, as did their friendship.

"We knew that every time we got together, something good was going to happen," Bramhall told *The Austin Chronicle*. "Everything started feeling good, and it felt like therapy for us...I'd go home at night feeling so good, so filled up."

A phrase kept sticking in Stevie's mind that he wanted to put into song: "We're never safe from the truth, but in the truth we can survive." Doyle came up with the opening lyrics to "Wall Of Denial" while driving on a Dallas tollway—he raced over to Stevie's house on Travis Street to share the words before he forgot them. He busted in the door only to find Stevie wrapped up in a long-winded phone conversation with Alex Hodges. "All of a sudden Doyle goes, '*A wall of deniyalllll...*'" Stevie recalled, "and I went, 'I'll see you later,' hung the phone up, turned around and said, '*What?!*' And we went from there, started the very first part of the song and I pulled it out and said 'Here's the first verse—you got the chords.'

"The musical part of it started off with me just trying to find a new way to play a 6/8 kind of feel," Stevie remembered. "The more I played with it the more I started looking for something I could use lyrically that really meant something, instead of just...'got a new car,' or 'got a lot of money in the bank'—who cares? Doyle and I would work on it at our get-togethers, which was basically he and I would sit down and talk about what was going on in our lives for a few hours and boil it down to the real and what we could use—we would write it down. I pulled out these pieces and parts of songs that I'd had, or ideas that we had just written and not tied together, and a lot of the things we came up with were things that were just really helping us."

Doyle had been fooling around with a song called "Life By The Drop." He had written it with his girlfriend Barbara Logan about their own trials in overcoming abuse, making amends, and rediscovering the joy in living. Stevie had heard it before, but it never really clicked for him in his heavy-abuser days. While he was in rehab (the very first day, as a matter of fact), he wrote a letter to Doyle begging him to finish the song and deliver a new demo. Stevie wanted to record

Art by and courtesy of Christian Brooks.

it—the song had just grabbed a hold of his heart and wouldn't let go. Stevie kept telling him that he'd like to use it on *In Step*, which was the title of the new album and a reference to the AA program.

The band chose Jim Gaines to produce this effort, and recorded between L.A.'s Sound Castle and Summa Studios and Kiva Studios in Memphis. Gaines had a strong rep for getting killer guitar sounds, and had worked extensively with Carlos Santana. Coincidentally, he had also produced a record twenty years ago for Southern Feeling, which featured Austin friends Angela Strehli, W.C. Clark, and Denny Freeman.

Backstage with fans. *Left to right:* Maxwell Schauf (drummer for Lonnie Mack), SRV, and Dave Gleekman (Epic Records' local promotion manager). Photo by and courtesy of Randy Jennings/Captured Live.

Stevie's vocals on *In Step* were much crisper and controlled than past efforts, and

In the studio, working on *In Step*. Left to right: Reese Wynans, Producer Jim Gaines, Stevie Ray, Chris Layton, and Dale Allen. Photo courtesy of Dale Allen/Killer Cases.

he directed the credit towards Gaines and Doyle Bramhall. "I'm trying, man," he said, almost apologetically. "Taking the time in the studio helped, and hopefully I'm learning to sing a little bit, but I'd imagine it has a whole lot do to with working with a producer, Jim Gaines. He was real concerned that we took the time and we worked at it...there was a lot of patience and a lot of directions. And when we were writing the songs, while I was working out the guitar parts, Doyle would sing at first. So I learned a lot of what I know about singing—which isn't much—but what I do know [I learned] from him."

Even with the record company wavering a bit in terms of support, Stevie wasn't going to bend to all their demands, especially when it came to songs. He still wanted to play the blues—and did, choosing songs like Willie Dixon's "Let Me Love You, Baby," Buddy Guy's "Leave My Little Girl Alone," and Howlin' Wolf's "Love Me Darlin'." Publishers were constantly trying to feed him "hit" songs by popular songwriters like Jerry Lynn Williams and Frankie Miller, but Stevie had faith in the material he was writing with Doyle. He wanted to make a great album, not a collection of radio-friendly singles. "The radio I listen to has more to do with soul stations that don't necessarily play the new stuff," Vaughan told *The Victoria Advocate*. "I don't really care to get into any formula of: 'If you play the game our way, we'll play your stuff.'"

This was the first record Stevie had ever made sober from start to finish, and the process of recording was a little intimidating at first—trying to capture inspiration on tape without an audience or artificial stimulants.

As to be expected, several great songs were recorded and never used, like "Boot Hill" (canned because Stevie felt the murder topic was too harsh), Little Willie John's "Take My Love," a Dyke and The Blazers number called "Let A Woman Be A Woman, Let A Man Be A Man," and the soulful, autobiographical "Life By The Drop." The story on the last one has it that Stevie was hanging out at Kiva Studios when he grabbed his twelve-string and said, "I've got one I want to record." The band rose out of their seats to join him, but he motioned for them to stay behind. "It's something I gotta do alone," he told them, "something personal."

Photo by and courtesy of W.A. Williams/The Image Works.

In the middle of the sessions, Stevie got word that John Hammond had passed away at his New York City home. Vaughan knew that Hammond's health problems had slowed him down considerably, and although the loss hurt him, he felt assured that John Hammond was now in a much more comfortable place, no longer feeling any pain. Just six months ago, Stevie had learned of Hammond's lifelong charity work with drug and alcohol rehabilitation centers for musicians, and he made a point to tell John before he died that he had come clean. Hammond was overjoyed for him, and wished Stevie the best of luck with the new record, as he was too ill to attend the sessions. The man with the golden ears was gone—"they forgot to mention his heart," Stevie told a reporter.

In Step was dedicated to his memory, and shortly after his death, Stevie recorded a long, peaceful instrumental he'd been working on as a way of sending out a message of truth, apology, healing, and love. He called it "Riviera Paradise." The masterpiece was cut in one take.

"To me the song was a much-needed chance to...I don't know any other way to put it, *pray through my guitar*," Stevie recalled. "And be able to express some of the things to some of the people that I don't know how to talk to right now about what I need to talk to them about, say the things that I wish I could say, to become *willing*. Okay? And that's what I was doing. And it's funny, everybody else was in a separate room. I was in an isolation booth so I could be with my amps. They were all in the big studio with a window. And I just turned off the lights in my room. They couldn't see me. The drummer was tuning his drums while we were playing! I had my back to the engineer and the producer, Jim Gaines. They were in the control room going completely nuts because the tape was about to run out (eight seconds later it did, the song clocking in at over ten minutes)."

Upon finishing, Stevie grabbed a yellow legal pad and scribbled a few notes. After thinking for a moment, he slid it across the control panel during playback. It said: "This was/is a prayer for willingness to make right with all those people I've hurt in the past. That's what I was doing when we cut this song."

Stevie must have had some indication in his mind that he was growing into a leader, maybe even a healer. As he told writer Dan Forte at L.A.'s Sound Castle Studios during the making of *In Step*: "'Riviera Paradise' is really soothing to me. I've seen that kind of sound heal me and heal other people. I'm not saying that I'm a healer, I'm saying music is a healer. And I really believe that music carried me through a lot. It was the only thing I felt I could lean on. If I hadn't had the music to play, I probably would've been dead a long time ago."

Good Texan

SRV

ON JANUARY 23, 1989, Stevie Ray Vaughan and Double Trouble played the inaugural blues bash for incoming President George Bush. The gala event was assembled by the late Lee Atwater, a man who used his power and influence to help promote the blues, soul, and R&B music he loved so much, giving the participating artists a great deal of exposure and a nice chunk of change to come and perform for the President of the United States. The event attempted to embrace and perpetuate the ongoing blues revival, and perhaps answer the musical question stated so eloquently by *Rolling Stone*'s Gerri Hirshey: "Can Republicans clap on the backbeat?"

The Washington D.C. Convention Center was transformed into a southern-style ballroom for this four-hour rhythm and blues revue. The stage was graced by Bo Diddley, Percy Sledge, Sam "The Supervoice" Moore (of Sam and Dave), Eddie Floyd, Steve Cropper, Donald "Duck" Dunn, Dr. John, Delbert McClinton, Koko Taylor, Willie Dixon, William Bell, Joe Cocker, Billy Preston, Chuck Jackson, and Carla Thomas. Organizer/GOP Chairman Lee Atwater announced, "These are some of the best artists this country has ever produced. People just had to hear them."

Delbert McClinton introduced the all-star blues band of Double Trouble, Stevie and Jimmie Vaughan, and Albert Collins ("The Master of the Telecaster") for a rousing ten-minute jam on Collins' "Frosty." Stevie let the Iceman steal the

Stevie pauses for a moment at the Third Annual Oak Cliff Reunion. Courtesy of Christian Brooks.

show; he kept his volume down purposely, letting Albert's monster tone outshine him. Jimmie stood off to the right, decked out in his outrageous gold lamé Elvis jacket, plucking a tasty rhythm part and taking his place in line as the three guitarists marched across the stage together. Forgetting himself and the musicians around him, Albert Collins erroneously introduced Stevie as "Steve Cropper." Stevie just shrugged. *What cooler guitar player to be mistaken for?*

Back in Dallas, Christian Brooks was organizing the Third Annual Oak Cliff Reunion at the Longhorn Ballroom, off Industrial Boulevard. Stevie Ray Vaughan was, of course, Oak Cliff's favorite son in a town that didn't boast too many heroes. He was pleased to attend the party, it was a celebration of his musical roots, a chance to see and play with lots of old friends and bandmates from the Oak Cliff blues tribe. He ran into Marc Benno, and the two jammed together on "Further On Up The Road," along with long-lost pals Phil Campbell on drums, Robert Ware on bass, Mike Warner on organ, and David Brown on guitar. Stevie was playing on a pink paisley Strat loaned to him at the last minute by Zak Berry (who had also designed Tommy Shannon's custom bass). Stevie called out, "Let's do 'Pride And Joy'!" The musicians nodded their heads. They knew it well, even though in the old days they all knew Stevie as the smart-ass kid with a flat nose who played a pretty decent guitar. These musicians certainly never thought that someday they'd be playing his music.

On "Texas Flood," Stevie was joined by Smokin' Joe Kubek on guitar. A superior player in his own right, and a Dallas AA buddy to Stevie, the two could have gotten down to some mighty serious six-string combat, but were soon ambushed by two more guitarists strapping up their axes. With four smoking

guitars on stage, the scene began to turn into a bit of a catfight; loud, wailing, screeching guitars yowling out blues licks. Twelve minutes later, Stevie brought the number to a close. All the guitarists played so hard that everyone had knocked themselves agonizingly out of tune. Backstage, Stevie talked for a long while with Marc Benno, sharing warm hugs and weird memories of the crazy L.A. days some sixteen years previous. A cameraman approached them, breaking into the conversation:

"You're not from Oak Cliff, are you?" he asked Stevie.

"Oh, yeah," Stevie responded.

"Oak Cliff sure makes some ugly motherfuckers, dunnit?" the cameraman asked, nearly doubling over with laughter. Stevie shut him up with one question: "You from Oak Cliff, ain't ya?"

He didn't have to prove a whole lot to these people. They had always believed in him. Even as kids, they weren't laughing *at* him—they laughed with him. He came home to Oak Cliff and kicked ass in front of this small crowd (about 600) to prove a point; after fame, fortune, and a fifteen-year hiatus from Dallas, Stevie Ray Vaughan hadn't forgotten where he came from.

Stevie was still rehearsing some *In Step* material at a facility in New York, and was going through the painstaking process of trying to develop a completely new guitar sound for this record. He finally had the chance to start building his massive wall of amps. Vaughan took his plight to Cesar Diaz, his part-time amp tech. "Stevie was being extra particular about everything," Diaz

Photo by and courtesy of Randy Jennings/Captured Live.

136

told journalist Dave Rubin for *Guitar Player*, "to the point where it kind of got on the nerves of some of the other participants. He had a tough time making up his mind about things, so we took thirty-two amplifiers with us. It got to be like the Crusades, a pilgrimage of amplifiers. Stevie would hit a note and the walls would rattle... The whole studio was taken over with amps—upstairs, downstairs, every room was filled with amps.

"There were thirty-two amps running into the board, and Stevie would put his headphones down in the middle of recording and come over to me and say, 'The little Gibson amp upstairs is fucking up!' I'd give him a look like, 'What, are you kidding me?' But then I would go check and sure enough, there was a problem with the amp. Stevie could really hear every little thing. It was amazing."

Born in Puerto Rico, Diaz (known as "the ultimate guitar tech") had been on the road with Stevie before, and learned how to deal with Vaughan's perfectionism through trial and error. When traveling, Stevie would knock on Diaz's door, wanting to ask loads of questions about ways to improve his amp-rig. Around the crew, Diaz was jokingly referred to as "Stevie's pacifier."

Diaz had worked with Clapton, Keith Richards, and Bob Dylan in the past, but had never met anyone who could fry an amp quicker than Stevie Ray Vaughan. "I saw *plenty* of smoke coming out of his amps," Diaz laughed.

Stevie was superstitious about exactly where his amp controls were set. (He wanted his amps' volume set at 6, treble at 5½, and bass at 4.) When Stevie wasn't looking, Diaz would unscrew the knobs and cut the level back to save the amps. Stevie would never know the difference.

After fiddling with various configurations of

Top: Stevie in his "cage" while making *In Step* at Kiva Studios in Memphis. Photo by and courtesy of Dale Allen/Killer Cases.

Bottom: Photo by and courtesy of W.A. Williams/The Image Works.

thirty-two amps, Stevie knew the sound could not be complete without yet another Fender Bassman, so he had to go buy a new one. To make matters even more complex, his four Dumble heads were constantly being shipped back to California because Stevie kept blowing them up. In the main recording room, Stevie kept his four Dumbles, two Marshall 4x12 cabinets, then two tall "bath tub" Marshall cabinets (one with four 12's, the other with four 15" speakers.) Add two more Dumble Steel-String Singers, two Fender Super Reverbs, a MESA/Boogie Simulclass running his Fender Vibratone, and very high voltage, and you've got Stevie's gargantuan main amp set-up for *In Step*.

Maybe it was because Stevie insisted on sitting in the same room with his amps (which can cause weird feedback problems), maybe it was a freak of electricity, but as soon as SRV was ready to cut guitar tracks in Memphis, everybody noticed that something was definitely wrong. An eerie, electronic hum was somehow being transferred to tape through no means known to modern technology. The engineers tried and tried, but could not seem to locate the source of this hum. They obtained permission from the city engineer to completely cut off the whole block's power, but the hum was still there. The crew even toted the gear to an outlet across the street (which was on another circuit), and it worked fine. They then proceeded to drag it all back to the studio, using about 300 feet of extension cord. But when they turned on the machines, the dastardly hum was back again.

Finally, they devised a

plan that would surely work. Since this thing appeared to follow Stevie and his guitar, the crew built a sound baffle that looked like a baseball diamond backstop or an oversized bird cage that Stevie would have to stand in while he recorded. It sounded a little crazy, but it worked, and the album was done.

Stevie finished *In Step* with the realization that although he had approached recording from a completely different angle this time, the experiments had worked. "This record, we took more time to work," he summarized. "We went ahead and kicked out the idea that if you play it more than three times, you're wanking. We would play it a couple or three times, and if it wasn't clicking, we'd stop and figure out why—whether it was one person's or the whole band's approach, or if we couldn't hear each other right, or hadn't eaten yet, or whatever it was, no telling. We would take the time to find out how to make a great record. And if it was obvious that it wasn't going to happen that day, we'd just do something else and come back to it."

During the mastering sessions, Stevie spent some time in New York City talking to Bob Eschenbrenner, a reporter for the Manhattan-based *Music Paper*, and opened his heart about the messages inside the songs.

Eschenbrenner asked him about the dangerous aspects of the limelight.

"What I'm talking about is being completely empty but having all this popularity. Not feeling good inside, but having this mask on," Stevie answered. "...I'm up on the stage to entertain and play music, but that's not all there is to life. If I get stuck in this image deal, where I have been plenty of times before, I'm in trouble. 'Cause I forget who I am...It's part of the deal, but it's a strange predicament to be in."

BE: Why is that unnatural adulation part of the deal?

SRV: It's part of the deal 'cause it kind of goes along with it when you ask for it. You ask for popularity and you get it...It's kind of like auto-

graphs while you eat. I have had photographers follow me into the bathroom and that's not part of the deal.

BE: How does music cleanse your soul?

SRV: You empty it out. Empty it out and let the bare wires hang out there sometimes. And let the wind do it. The wind and the rain.

In May, Stevie Ray Vaughan and Double Trouble hit the road again, this time visiting smaller, far-removed cities like Everett, Washington; Bozeman and Missoula, Montana; and even Boise, Idaho. Stevie always liked to deliver his music to towns off the beaten path that were starved for a great concert. The major tours passed these die-hard fans by, so when Stevie wanted to test his wings on *In Step* material, he took it to the faithful.

Dates on that quickie tour included the Arlington Theater in Santa Barbara, San Diego's Starlight Bowl, and the Redwood Amphitheatre in Santa Clara, California. The band hit Salem, Oregon, and George, Washington, before winding up in Texas at the Mountain Shadows Lake Park in Horizon City, near El Paso. The boys took ten days off at home, then started gearing up for the onslaught of press interviews and promotional appearances that always accompany the release of a new album. That tour took them to the East Coast, through New York, Vermont, Connecticut, Massachusetts, and Pennsylvania, before heading up to Ottawa, Ontario, Toronto, and Montreal.

Jimmie spent a good deal of time in Memphis that summer filming the movie *Great Balls of Fire* (based on the life of Jerry Lee Lewis). In it, he played a guitarist in Lewis's band, along with John Doe (from the band X), and Dennis Quaid as The Killer himself. Unfortunately, the script was weak and the movie flopped, even though the augmenting cast and evocative settings of Louisiana, Mississippi, and Memphis certainly made it very watchable.

Promotional piece for *In Step*, which was distributed at a release party in Dallas. Courtesy of Christian Brooks.

138

In Step was released while Stevie was on the road in June, and although the album was long-awaited, well-publicized, and sold briskly, it only climbed to #33 on the *Billboard* Pop Albums Chart. Stevie was pictured on the cover dressed in a multi-colored serape that he'd bought at a Mexican restaurant in Dallas, kneeling with his old '28 National Steel guitar. The stance was a humble one, with SRV's head bowed as if he were praying—for forgiveness, for strength.

(L to R): CHRIS LAYTON, TOMMY SHANNON, STEVIE RAY VAUGHAN & REESE WYNANS

STEVIE RAY VAUGHAN AND DOUBLE TROUBLE

On the Fourth of July, Stevie was in the Dallas Q-102 FM studios to take phone calls nationwide on the Global Satellite Network's "Rockline" radio program. Stevie sounded happy and alert as he and Chris Layton fielded questions from all over the planet. At one point, Stevie stopped to play a song alone on his guitar. It was a little number he'd been fiddling with, a slow, autobiographical blues piece that recalled Hendrix's "Hear My Train A-Comin'." Its improvised lyrics went: *"When I left home, I was a young boy / Just a young man of seventeen / I set out to chase my dream / I was the wildest thing you ever seen / Summer in Dallas, Texas - 1972 / I got my guitar and my girlfriend / I just knew my time was through..."*

Stevie also played a sizzling "Travis Walk," accompanied by Whipper banging out a rhythm on the Dallas telephone book. He explained to host Bob Coburn that his style evolved out of the eclectic mix of blues and rock and roll he'd heard as a teen in Dallas. "I was exposed to everything at once, so I don't know what a purist is," he boldly stated. "It's all music to me."

While in the Q-102 studios for "Rockline," he spent time chatting with pal Jill Savage. "New lockers for the deejays had just been installed in the offices," Savage remembers, and I said, 'Come over here and autograph it!' He said, 'Well, don't you think we'll get in trouble?' I was like, 'Who cares?' and he just went nuts drawing all over it. And the folks at the station didn't believe it was him the next day. They couldn't believe that he was humble enough to sign a locker door." When Savage finally left the station in 1990, the management let her take the treasured locker door with her. It read: To Jill, God Bless Your Big, Beautiful Heart.

In a special issue of *Guitar Player* completely devoted to the music of Jimi Hendrix, Stevie talked extensively about his love for Hendrix's music and its relation to contemporary blues. "Some people don't see that Jimi Hendrix was a blues player," he stated. "To me, he's like a Bo Diddley of a different generation. If you were a kid and heard Bo Diddley for the first time back when all that was going on, wouldn't you think that was the wildest thing you ever heard?"

Stevie pointed out Hendrix was not the first to use a whammy bar in blues, because of a record he had heard by Sly Williams ("Boot Hill"). The original version by Williams appeared on a compilation album called *Blues In D Natural* (Red Lightnin', 005). "Go get you a copy," said Stevie, "and listen to it, and you'll go, '*Shit!*' I've never heard anybody other than Hendrix get this intensity and play as wild as this guy. And he uses a wang bar real radical. It's like this guy's teeth are sticking out of the record. It's *unbelievable*. Every

Publicity photos for *In Step*. The serape was bought at a Mexican restaurant in Dallas. Photos by Alan Messer. Courtesy of Epic Records.

He was a pro amp technician, and knew exactly what was wrong. He and Martinez got along well, and Stevie liked him, too. Steve and SRV talked for half an hour, and Vaughan was happy to sign all of Wilson's albums and posters. Steve Wilson was well-known for his knowledge of tricky old vintage amps. Stevie took his number; he needed a full-time amp tech on the road, and told Wilson he might call him for the next tour.

Stevie's guitar entourage was streamlined for the *In Step* tour; he brought only his two "Butterscotch" beauties ('61 and '62 Strats), "Charley" (the white E-flat model), "Red" (his '65), and his old faithful Number One. He still used a Vox Wah pedal, the Octavia, and his Ibanez Tube Screamer, but added effects like an HFX (noise gate) and an old Fuzzface unit built by Roger Meyer, Hendrix's gadget man. The amps he traveled with included two Fender Super Reverbs and twin Fender Vibroverbs (the mutant Leslie-type contraption), as well as his Dumbles and some pesky old Marshall Majors that were always frying after being subjected to Stevie's brute force night after night.

In Ohio he saw Randy Jennings, who was now achieving sobriety. For the

time I hear it, it seems impossible that Hendrix didn't hear this guy. And some people think that it might be Jimi playing the guitar.

Concert dates that summer included traveling from L.A. to Philadelphia in less than ten days, with a show each night. Double Trouble played Cincinnati River Bend on July 23, Portland, Maine, on August 6, and East Troy, Wisconsin (yes, Alpine Valley), on August 19, Denver, Colorado, on the 21st, and Albuquerque, New Mexico, on the 30th. Stevie also put in two triumphant nights at the Greek Theater in Los Angeles on August 26 and 27. In September, he returned to Texas to open dates for the Who's much-ballyhooed reunion tour in Dallas and Houston, along with The Fabulous Thunderbirds. After the show, Stevie found Jimmie and told him that there was no need to put off this collaboration album any longer. Jimmie still wasn't ready to commit; his pride wouldn't let him.

At a stop in Indianapolis, Stevie was having trouble with one of his amps. His guitar tech, Rene Martinez, was tearing his hair trying to figure out what was wrong with it. A stocky stranger with sandy blonde hair approached and started checking the back of the amplifier. Before Rene could ask him to leave, Steve Wilson introduced himself.

A soulful moment. Photo by and courtesy of Randy Jennings/Captured Live.

last two years, Randy had dropped out of sight, feeling like he had to hide his abuse from Stevie, who was already clean. He proudly informed Stevie that he had seen the light, and they talked about how good it felt to finally be fully aware of the world around them—it wasn't such a bad place, after all.

Stevie was snoozing soundly in his bed well after ten A.M. on the morning of his thirty-fifth birthday. He was off the road for a few days, and planned to sleep in, but forgot to turn the ringer off on the phone, which rang several times before he finally woke up and answered it. A woman's voice was on the other end. "Mr. Vaughan?" he was asked.

"Yeah."

The woman caller said she was calling from his dentist's office, and wanted to postpone his root-canal. Stevie hung up on her and pushed the phone away. As he nestled back under the blankets, something told him it wasn't a wrong number—she knew his name. What the hell was going on here?

The phone rang again. This time Janna picked it up. "Hello?"

"Janna, Janna, it's me—Jill! Don't hang up!"

"Oh, hi..." Janna yawned.

"Shhhhhh!" Savage pleaded. "I'm playing a little birthday joke on Stevie." She had the whole thing going out over the radio airwaves live, all over Dallas. They both cracked up laughing.

Stevie, now thoroughly puzzled, grabbed the phone from Janna.

"Who is this?" he demanded to know. "What is this?"

"Stevie Ray, this is Jill Savage calling to wish you a very Happy Birthday from all of us here at Q-102 in Dallas!"

Stevie laughed. "Well, thank you, Jill...I...I..." he stuttered, still a little groggy. Jill put on some music, and took him off the air so they could talk privately. Stevie got a good laugh out of

Photo by and courtesy of W.A. Williams/The Image Works.

it, and complimented Jill on her well-planned, sneaky birthday gag.

"Well," she replied, "I can't take all the credit. Your Uncle Joe put me up to it...bye!"

Jill and Stevie loved to play practical jokes on each other, and their friendship began to attract the attention of Q-102's management, which wasn't exactly sure what to make of the stunts. Savage recalls, "I mean, the guy was so *normal*! But he was such a little rascal. We were just a couple of mischievous little kids, and that's what people need to know." Stevie even used to call her on the air to yak for long periods and request songs.

"He really wanted to hear the radio playing 'Scratch And Sniff,'" Jill recalls, "and the label wouldn't release it. It meant a lot to him because it was written about the love he had for Janna, which was a very under-the-surface thing, and he wanted to let people know he had found love. So, I would always play that one when he wanted to hear it, which no other radio stations would play... "Love Struck Baby" was my favorite song. He used to call me up and say "I dare you to play it!" I would get in trouble all the time for playing that song. I wasn't supposed to do it," she shrugs. "It wasn't on our playlist."

"You know, he never liked 'Willie The Wimp,'" she insists. "That song became very popular on the radio, and he hated it because it was glorifying a pimp and mafia guy. He wasn't sober when he chose that song to be included on the record.... He used to call me on the air and ask me why we were playing it, and I just had to tell him that this was the one the label wanted to push. He just didn't understand this. This business really frustrated him, and that's how I could help him—to explain the politics of rock and roll to him—from the radio side, anyway."

While in Dallas, Stevie was informed that he had been inducted into *Guitar Player*'s "Gallery of the Greats," and in addition, had been chosen to become the official spokesman for Fender Guitars that year. Soon after, Stevie was visited at his Travis Street home by Fender's John Maher and an entire camera crew. Arriving early in the morning, Maher found Stevie alone with a T-Bone Walker record on the turntable and a fresh pot of coffee on the stove. "When he grabbed my hand," Maher recalled, "it was both a motion of shaking it and pulling me into the living room at the same time. He had this big ol' grin on his face as he took me on a Texas-sized guided tour of the most incredible collection of blues records I have ever seen…he pulled out his '59 Stratocaster and explained, in minute detail, the history of every little ding and scratch.

"All he wanted to talk about was the listening to, and playing of, that bittersweet mother of rock and roll called the blues. He was so unassuming, so real and so into it, I completely forgot why I was there!" Maher says that Stevie gave a great poolside interview, but sadly reports that something weird happened to the film, and no footage could be salvaged. The two planned to reschedule the endorsement film, but it never came to be. Stevie was flattered by all the attention bestowed upon him by Fender, *Guitar Player*, the Grammys, the Handys, and the music media this year, but he was still a bit perplexed as to why everyone thought he was so damn special.

Epic Records brainstormed a great promotional tour that would put two of their hottest guitar slingers together while providing an additional boost to both instrumentalists' record sales in the process. They dubbed it "The Fire Meets The Fury," starring Stevie Ray Vaughan and Jeff Beck. Beck hadn't toured in almost a decade, but his mercurial legend cast a long shadow, even on a now-established top gun like Vaughan. Managers haggled for months over who would get top billing; how to publicize it properly so that

no one would come out smelling sweeter than the other—it had to be a fair fight.

They rehearsed at Prince's Paisley Park Studios before beginning the tour at the Northrop Memorial Auditorium in Minneapolis on October 25. The two respected guitarists decided to toss a coin to determine the headliner, just a few hours before going on. They would reverse the order night to night, alternating as the tour moved down the road. Everything was done diplomatically, even the backstage passes—one side read "Stevie Ray Vaughan and Double Trouble" followed by "Jeff Beck With Terry Bozzio and Tony Hymas"; flip them over and the order was reversed.

Stevie and Jeff arrived a day early to the Chicago gig so that they could squeeze in a visit to Buddy Guy's new club, Legends. Stevie had helped Buddy open the bar and provided a promotional shot in the arm by trumping it up to everybody he knew. The building, at 708 Wabash, had once housed the legendary 708 Club in the fifties that was a regular haunt for Muddy Waters, Howlin' Wolf, and Otis Rush. It was also the first stage Buddy every played upon in the Windy City in 1959, back in the days when he was just another country bumpkin in overalls fresh up from Louisiana. While he was onstage, someone at the bar reportedly called Muddy at home, and held up the phone to let the King of the Blues hear this amazing new guitarist. Within ten minutes, Muddy was there to pick Buddy up in his car. Guy was bowled over when Waters offered to make him a sandwich, asking, "Boy, are you hungry?" Guy didn't know what to say—he was starving, but he was too proud to ask this great man for anything. When Guy said no, Waters slapped the hell out of him and said, "Get in the

Jeff Beck cowers jokingly from Stevie Ray in Cincinnati, Ohio. Photo by and courtesy of W.A. Williams/The Image Works.

goddamn car!" "He made me eat that sandwich, too!" Guy remembers today.

In that same spirit, Stevie had wanted to give Guy his support without Buddy having to ask for it. Before long, Eric Clapton was dropping by Legends to jam with Guy, as were Ron Wood and Keith Richards. So when Stevie showed up with none other than Jeff Beck at his side, Buddy was ready for action. Beck was hesitant to jam when summoned, apologizing sincerely, "No, really...really, I can't." Stevie dragged Beck up to the stage despite his protests, and the three guitarists went head to head. Stevie and Beck came back humbled. Guy was the King.

The next night Beck headlined the Chicago performance, and local newspapers ruled Jeff the winner of the six-string showdown the following day. Stevie's own show was very strong, but apparently not strong enough to impress the hardened Chicago critics who knew the blues first-hand from the black masters who had invented the art form. However, on November 8, Stevie was the headliner at The Centrum in Worcester, Massachusetts, and local critics said that Vaughan clearly upstaged Beck! Even Beck himself had to agree. Jeff raved to *The Boston Globe* after the show, "Stevie is just amazing. He's a tough act to follow—and his guitar is ten times louder than mine!"

At a stop in Cleveland, Stevie and Beck talked with writers Matt Resnicoff and Joe Gore about the tour and recording techniques, shared guitar tricks, and let their mutual admiration shine through.

Here are some excerpts from that interview:

You both have a very strong sense of the placement of the right hand on the guitar. Do you think about that?

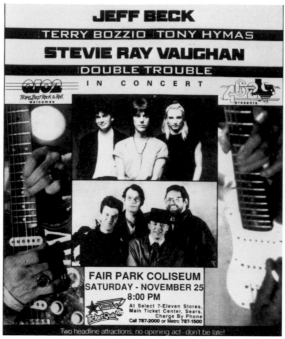

Official promotional poster for The Fire and the Fury Tour, 1989. Courtesy of Thomas Kreason/ Rockabilia.

JB: Not me. I'm just thinking about getting through the song without fucking up! (laughs)

SRV: I'm just trying to find the most tone I can get. Sometimes I can find it; sometimes I want to choke my amp. But then there are the nights when it doesn't seem like I've got anything to do with it. That's the one you always play for. There have been nights when I started playing chord solos, and I don't know any of the chords! (laughs) There have been nights when I completely lost it, and by the time it struck me, I wouldn't even know what song I was playing anymore.

Is the tour working out?

JB: I think it is. I'm not too happy with our set. Stevie, you've been much more constant with yours.

SRV: That's what's funny, that we're looking at ya'll and saying, '*Oh man, this is happening!*' (laughs) ...The better they're doin' the better it makes me feel. Of course, it'll kick you in the butt (laughs), but that's okay.

What physical price do you play (for playing hard)?

SRV: We're both missing part of our fingers.

JB: I broke my thumb.

SRV: (to Jeff) A lot of your tones are really tones of meat and fingers. It's a lot warmer, and a lot more personal...Getting to know this guy is one of the coolest things about the tour for me...it's been a lifelong thing to me, listening to you, man, and for me it's an honor to be

Backstage in Dallas with friends Pamela Mount and Christian Brooks. Photo by Harold Dozier.

**Stevie and Martha Vaughan.
Photo by Harold Dozier.**

out here with you now. And I'm not just being a parrot talking shit. This is the real deal.

JB: I think Stevie's playing state-of-the-art blues at the moment. There's no one who has that tone, and the *venom* that goes with it.

Moving up into Canada, the tour arrived at Toronto's Skydome, a mammoth baseball arena and the site of the 1992 World Series, where Beck and Vaughan slugged it out in their respective sets; Jeff, Tony Hymas and Terry Bozzio tore it up for 90 minutes, followed immediately by Double Trouble. Stevie had been immensely popular in Canada since the release of his first album, and this was his turf. He played like liquid fire on "Tightrope," "The House Is Rockin'," and "Crossfire," and threw in an especially rousing "Texas Flood" for the capacity crowd. Beck joined him onstage for an astounding encore of "Goin' Down'," the song's Texas roots updated by Beck's hyped-up British attack.

The high point of the Vaughan/Beck tour was the triumphant sold-out gig at Madison Square Garden. Stevie had spent almost an hour fiddling with his amp at soundcheck that afternoon—the tone just wasn't right. While warming up with the band on "Crossfire," he finally got it right, and left the stage apparently satisfied, relaxed, and ready to play one of the biggest shows of his career. After the show, Stevie rushed over to the Beacon Theater just in time to play the last encore with the Fabulous Thunderbirds.

Jeff Beck and Stevie Ray Vaughan brought their "Fire And The Fury" tour to Dallas' Fair Park Coliseum on Saturday,

November 25, 1989. Not surprisingly, Vaughan was the headliner in Dallas. Backstage was old home week for Stevie; he chatted with old high school friends like Pamela Mount and Christian Brooks (who wore big stars on their backstage passes indicating they were "family"), and posed for pictures with Martha, Uncle Joe, and John Crouch. Mitch Mullins hadn't seen his old buddy in years, since way before Vaughan became a superstar. He couldn't even get tickets to the sold-out concert, so he resorted to parking his truck outside the backstage door to at least listen, one more time, to Steve Vaughan play those blues. In the middle of the show, a roadie lifted up the roll-up door, and Mitch could see Double Trouble onstage. Stevie turned around, recognized Mitch, and waved at him. "He then proceeded to turn up the volume, lowered his head, and played harder than I'd ever seen him before," Mullins remembers. "It was almost like going back in time twenty years."

After an Austin performance a few days later, Stevie reunited with another old pal from the old

Onstage in Dallas, November 23, 1989. Photo by Harold Dozier.

A new high—Stevie cruises the parking lot on his motor scooter. Photo by and courtesy of W.A. Williams/The Image Works.

days—Shirley Beeman. They had not seen each other since 1982, when Stevie first started climbing the staircase of fame. Now Shirley was sober, too. "I just had to tell him," she says, an intense smile upon her face. "Me and David Murray went to see him backstage at the Frank Erwin Center, and he was so happy for me that I had gotten my faculties together; he hugged me real tight and he had that sparkle in his eyes that said, 'Hey, we really got through all of it alive!' That was the last time I ever saw him."

The tour was winding down on the West Coast by the end of the month, and at a stop in Albuquerque's Tingley Coliseum (to record for a Westwood One's "In Concert" Radio Series), Stevie and Jeff both grew a little sentimental, not really wanting the tour to end. They exchanged warm hugs and compliments before the show, but as soon as Jeff started playing, Stevie excused himself from the backstage bunch and planted himself by the side of the stage to watch Beck. Jeff played a shimmering, sonic version of "People Get Ready," and there was Stevie, leaning over the railing like a teenager, shouting his appreciation.

Long after the show, Double Trouble was relaxing on their tour bus during the all-night drive to Denver. Stevie spent over an hour talking with Steve Pond from *Rolling Stone*, who was traveling with them for a few days. Vaughan had been extremely accommodating, for the band was intent on changing the magazine's negative perception of them since *Texas Flood*. But Stevie simply couldn't stay awake any longer, and stood up to head for bed. "I only got to see

one or two of Jeff's songs tonight. At the beginning of this tour, I watched his whole set almost every night. He always amazes me. And he intimidates me, too."

"Intimidates you in a good way, right?" Janna asked him.

"Welllll..." Stevie hesitated. "Sometimes."

Beck did his best to pump Stevie up in *Rolling Stone*, handing out the highest compliments possible: "He's one of the finest components of blues guitar. He's dirty and very simple—deceptively simple, you can't emulate him—and very attractive. And we haven't heard the best of him yet. I think this is the tour that's really going to plant his roots."

Near the end of the year Stevie was featured on an edition of *Timothy White's Rockstars*, a nationally syndicated radio program. He and White sat in a studio "in the hard heart of New York City," as White put it, and talked for hours about the blues, rock and roll, and the distance in between. Stevie described the Texas rhythm as "the sound of a freight train coming down the tracks," and pointed out that "Texas and Chicago were linked by a train line, so the music from those two places is a lot closer than you think." Before he could even finish his thought, he was off into a solo rendition of "Dirty Pool," his warm, breathy vocal making love to the mike. Again, Stevie cited Albert King for teaching him an important lesson about the blues. "Blues is to soothe. It makes people who were feelin' bad feel good again. That's the true feeling of the blues. It's not a depressing music, as some folks have been led to believe," he sum-

Oops! Stevie consults Rene after falling and scraping his arm. Photo by and courtesy of W.A. Williams/The Image Works.

marized, adding, "My goal is to still be playin' Albert King's music in the year 2010!"

In December, Stevie returned to Austin for a hometown performance on *Austin City Limits*. But this wasn't just an opportunity to plug his new album—the show was a tribute to W.C. Clark, whose contributions to Austin's rich blues heritage were tenfold. It was a reunion of old friends like Angela Strehli, Lou Ann Barton, Kim Wilson, Denny Freeman, and Jimmie Vaughan, who all came together to rally their support for W.C. Stevie was pleased to be involved, and Double Trouble took the bull by the horns from the git-go, storming the stage with "The House Is Rockin'."

Stevie's eyes scanned the crowd for familiar faces, and saw plenty: old booking agents, club owners, musicians, ex-girlfriends, pals, and the faithful fans who supported him through his lean years, all here tonight to witness the return of "Little Stevie" Vaughan.

He stepped back onto sacred blues ground with "Leave My Little Girl Alone," confident that the Austin audience would respond in kind to his blues. The way he sang that song, the way he hit the solo—gnawing away at the strings like a shark in a feeding frenzy—proved that Stevie Rave On meant business. His face was scrunched up in anguish. He could hear Austin screaming for him the way it used to do, and this spurred him on to even greater heights. When the solo finally ended, the place went bananas. He plowed through the rest of the set, "Cold Shot," "Crossfire," and "Riviera Paradise," with ease and grace, telling his old friends, "I sure am glad to be alive so that I can be with you here today." Stevie also performed "Couldn't Stand The Weather" and "Tightrope," but both were edited out due to TV time constraints.

SRV reunited with former bandmate W.C. Clark for an informal, funky jam, a throwback to the Triple Threat days. The audience was hoping for a Triple Threat reunion, but this was as close as it got, since Lou Ann couldn't participate, because she was having her own reunion with a bottle of gin backstage. W.C. was joined by Kim and Jimmie on "Make My Guitar Talk To You,"

Photo by and courtesy of Randy Jennings/Captured Live.

and Angela Strehli and Denny Freeman joined the fun for a swinging version of Eddie Taylor's "Big Town Playboy." Lou Ann finally showed up for the last number, a big family-style jam on Al Green's "Take Me To The River" that was, as always, soul-stirring. Lou Ann did manage to contribute background vocals, but Stevie looked over sadly as she had to be helped off the stage. W.C. closed the show with a tear-jerking "Ain't It Funny How Time Slips Away," leaving everyone with a sweet feeling about the good old days. But, as Stevie realized that night—the good old days were over. The new days, it seemed, had just begun.

One afternoon Stevie was having lunch at Good Eats Cafe in Dallas, keeping his head low as he sat in the corner, and for a few precious minutes, everything was quiet. Then the waiter ambled over and asked for his autograph. Easily done. The waiter started babbling rather loudly to the couple at the next table about how much he loved SRV: "I've seen this guy about twenty times; my girlfriend really likes him, too, and we make love to his music all the time. It has a real sensual quality to it, sort of real powerful, you know?"

Stevie sank down in his chair and tipped his hat to the bemused couple, who could clearly see his red-faced embarrassment. The jig was up now, and everybody in the place knew that Stevie Ray Vaughan was there. First came a couple more employees, asking him to sign the walls, followed by a girl wanting her picture snapped with him, and before you knew it, a line had formed. Stevie dutifully signed each and every last autograph and listened to their compliments and stories. When everybody had gone, he looked down at the cold lunch he'd never even touched. Minutes later he left a tip and a guitar pick on the table, grabbed his doggiebag, and slipped quietly out the door.

On the drive home, Stevie was tickled as he remembered himself at thirteen, sneaking into the Losers Club and trying to work up the nerve to ask B.B. King for his autograph. *What a long, strange trip it's been....*

Tick
Tock

SRV

I

N THE LAST FOUR YEARS
of his life, Stevie Ray would tell his audiences that
he was living on borrowed time. It was as if he
knew his time wasn't long—he figured he should
have died years ago after one too many nights of
drug-addled debauchery. Each day was a bonus,
he said. Every new moment a gift. In his thirty-
fifth and final year, Stevie's mind seemed obsessed
with preparing for the next life, making up karmic
debts to friends and associates, so that when he
finally left this planet, his slate would be clean and
people would know that he had loved them.

"Stevie talked about death a lot," says Jill
Savage, who had many intimate conversations
with Vaughan on the subject. "I think he knew
that his own death was coming; he always used to
say that he was living on 'borrowed time.' We
would often argue the theory after concerts. He'd
get off on some trip about 'I don't deserve to be
here, everybody. I don't deserve all this money and
success.' And sometimes, he'd get really out there,
you know? And it scared me. And we would just
tangle asshole over elbow about this subject for
many hours."

In February, *In Step* won a Grammy Award
for Best Contemporary Blues Album. Stevie was
elated as he picked up the statue, said a quick
thank you, flashed a determined smile, and added,
"Now let's get Buddy Guy one of these!"

Stevie appeared on MTV's new *Unplugged*
series a few days later, showing the world at large
his astonishing mastery of the acoustic guitar.

Starting off with "Rude Mood" (on a 12-string), he watched jaws drop all around the studio as he blistered up and down the neck. Host Jules Shear ambled up to Stevie, thrust a microphone in his face, and asked him what he was going to play next. "Pride And Joy," Stevie said softly, his eyes cast downward. The audience clapped along in time, and Stevie's "acoustic apprehension" fell away when he realized that he had this intimate group under his thumb. "Life Without You" was cut from the broadcast for no apparent reason, as were several other songs, including some amazing slide work on a dobro. He closed with "Testify," during which an overwhelmed Joe Satriani (the show's other special guest) can be seen drooling in the wings. Jules ushered Stevie off to wild applause, feebly explaining "Stevie's gotta catch a plane—he's outta here!"

Stevie was spending more time than ever on airplanes; flying was the only way to make the necessary quickie trips to L.A. or New York for talk show appearances, studio work, award shows, and interviews between gigs with Double Trouble. A running joke about his increased use of private chartered flights was what Stevie called "Flying the Otis Express," alluding to the death of Otis Redding, another former client of Alex Hodges.

The offers kept rolling in, more of them than ever. Stevie Ray Vaughan had spent seven years in the spotlight—long enough to confirm his staying power, long enough to grow. He did the rounds of all the hip TV programs, including "The Arsenio Hall Show," "The Tonight Show," "Late Night with David Letterman" (appearing twice within six months), and "The Today Show," where Vaughan was grilled about his drug use by a hard-nosed Jane Pauley, who confirmed her squareness by calling Vaughan "loud" and covering her ears as he played.

Stevie Ray was making the scene on his own, often making appearances without Double Trouble at his side. After ten years with the group, Stevie was longing for at least a temporary change of scenery. He was ready to make music with some other musicians, ready to try a new sound. Jimmie was in the same position; he had spent fifteen years with the Fabulous Thunderbirds, but the music just didn't thrill his soul like it used to. Kim Wilson was moving in a blues and soul direction, and Jimmie was growing away from his blues purist roots, wanting to explore new ideas of his own. But first, he had to change the rut his personal life was in. Finally, in late 1989 Jimmie followed

Stevie's lead and entered a rehab program. Upon completing it, Jimmie had a new lease on life, too. He told Stevie he was finally ready to make the brothers album.

"I felt this real need to go home and be with my family," Jimmie said. "Me and Stevie got together a whole lot, and something told me I needed to make an album with him right then. It was almost like a premonition that I was supposed to go home."

Stevie and Jimmie started hanging out together, getting to know each other all over again for the first time since they were kids, without hesitation, jealousy, or facades. They holed up in the garage of Jimmie's South Austin home, enjoying the sensation of playing guitar together and being able to write together for the first time in their careers. They recorded demos in Dallas and Austin, with the brothers playing all the parts themselves, then booked some studio time around their frantic touring schedules, making plans to record in Memphis, New York, and Dallas between concert dates.

In March, Stevie attended the Eighth Annual Austin Music Awards ceremonies to pick up his clean sweep of honors including Record of the Year (*In Step*), Single of the Year ("Crossfire"), Record of the Decade (*Texas Flood*), Musician of the Year, and Musician of the Decade. He thanked the people who "loved me back to life," and thanked God for being alive. Stevie held the stack of framed certificates lovingly in his hands, looked up in the air, smiled, and put them away. Backstage, he visited with old friends W.C. Clark, Clifford Antone, Paul Ray, and Margaret Moser, who had organized the awards show.

On April 9, Stevie Ray Vaughan and Double Trouble were at the Fox Theater in St. Louis (the site of Chuck Berry's infamous *Hail, Hail, Rock and Roll!* concert film). He added an old favorite to the set list—"The Things (That) I Used To Do"—sounding better than ever, notes crashing against the back wall of the old theater. From the balcony, Stevie looked like a tiny red-and-black Texas fireant playing with a twig, his red kimono flying behind him. It was a sit-down crowd (the hardest to please), and the applause was polite, but the house wasn't rocking. Stevie adjusted to the docile setting by easing up and talking more to the crowd, telling stories about the songs; before "Wall Of Denial," he announced that "this is something we all gotta do before can talk to each other—we gotta tear down these walls between us." He followed with a gushing "Riviera Para-

dise," wishing that "anyone out there who is suffering might find some peace."

"Superstition" started them off to the races, the entire band rushing tempo so much, the complex rhythms became impossible to play. Feeling adventurous, Stevie added another unannounced number to the show, explaining, "We haven't played this since last December. We didn't like it then—let's see if we like it now!" and blasted into an absolutely screaming version of "Goin' Down." He delivered the words to "Voodoo Chile'" with murderous intent, his silver cross catching the lights and radiating a white aura around his head: "I won't see you again in this world..." True enough—it was the last time SRV would have the St. Louis Blues.

Stevie spent the next two weeks in Memphis with Jimmie, recording the album (tentatively title *Very Vaughan*) at Ardent Studios. As producer they hired Nile Rodgers, whom Stevie had worked with before on Bowie's *Let's Dance* album. The two hadn't seen much of each other since Stevie had found stardom, but Rodgers had noticed some big changes in the kid he'd met in 1982. "Stevie really grew up, he became a different guy," Nile told *Musician Magazine* later. "Stevie was always a loving guy; that part of him was no different. But he was much more gentle now, and very focused. You could tell he found a different life when he gave up drugs. And his spirit was stronger than ever. There's a soulful, simple song called 'Tick Tock' on the new album, and when Stevie sang it in the studio, I just sat there with tears in my eyes thinking, 'He doesn't even understand his power.' "

"Tick Tock," a plea for world peace and the album's single, had actually been written nearly twenty years ago. "I was sitting out on my front porch one day playing my guitar," Jimmie re-

called, "and I came up with the main musical part of that. It was always there, and I tried throwing it into a couple of songs, and it never worked. Most of the songs I contributed to the record are like that—the song that wouldn't go away over the years, the one nobody else liked, but I had a feeling for it." Final lyrical and musical assistance for "Tick Tock" were provided by Rodgers and songwriter Jerry Lynn Williams.

The album was, as Jimmie envisioned it, "a short history of who we listen to," a tip of the hat to their heroes—Albert King, B.B. King, Johnny "Guitar" Watson, and T-Bone Walker. For "Brothers" (the only blues track on the record), it was decided that the song should reflect and maybe even mock the brotherly rivalry, and that they should try stealing the guitar from each other for the solos.

The album was therapeutic for both Vaughan brothers; they were cutting loose of tried-and-true formulas, writing songs that carried uplifting messages, and finding that after so many years of ambitious, often heated competition, Jimmie and Stevie Vaughan really did love each other. "We've

probably gotten closer making *Family Style* then we have been since we were little kids at home," Stevie shared in the promotional Video Buyways trailer for the album. "And I can honestly say I needed it. Jimmie's still my favorite guitar player in the world."

Jimmie and Stevie enjoyed working together so much on the project that a tour was being discussed. The brothers agreed that they would not use Double Trouble or the Thunderbirds as backing players: "Stevie and I had discussed getting our own band together and touring behind the album," Jimmie revealed to *Rolling Stone*. "We were moving in a new direction together, we were bustin' out. I don't know where the next one would have gone. I can't tell you how excited we were at the possibilities. We wanted to do all this stuff—it was kinda like Lightnin' Hopkins goes surfing."

In late April, Stevie Ray Vaughan and Double Trouble hit the road to do a brief series of dates in the mid-South, moving from the New Orleans Jazz and Heritage Festival to the three-day Memphis in May event on May 1, and Oklahoma City the next day, where Stevie spent hours backstage talking with fans and visiting with blues society members. These die-hard blues groupies remembered when Little Stevie used to take round trips to the city with Blackbird, Triple Threat, and early Double Trouble. When Stevie left that night, he carried a proclamation naming him the Oklahoma Blues Society's Honorary Chairman of the Board, an award he accepted with pride.

The next afternoon, Stevie was due for a noon press conference in Abilene, Texas. He had hardly slept on the bus, blinking at the clock, staring out the window at the rain-soaked night, and reviewing last night's show in his racing mind.

Photo by and courtesy of Randy Jennings.

Praying through the guitar, Oklahoma City. May 2, 1990. Photo by and courtesy of Paula Mickelson.

He thought about the unfinished album with his brother, and the fast pace that was working him like a dog. The weariness showed in his face as he fielded lamebrain questions like "How do you write a song, Stevie Ray?" and "Why did you come to Abilene?" To which he replied, "There's people here!"

"What's your favorite album, Stevie?"

"I like *In Step* a lot—I like 'em all, to some degree. Maybe my next album will be my favorite," he answered, forcing a weary smile. Stevie was worn out, and wanted nothing more but to check into a hotel so he could get some sleep before the show. An annoying electronic feedback permeated the room. He rambled on about the five inches of rain in Oklahoma City the night before, calling the thunderstorms on the bus trip down "intense."

"Of course," Reese Wayans interceded, "Stevie only heard about the storms. He was dead asleep."

"Yeah, right!" Stevie laughed.

"What's your touring schedule like, Stevie?"

"Well, it's relaxing a bit this time around," he said. "When it's too relaxed, though, the band get edgy. When it's too fast-paced, I get cranky." The band nodded agreement.

Stevie Ray in the light (Abilene, Texas). Photo by and courtesy of Priscilla Gwilt.

"When is the next album due out?"

"We go into the studio late this year to start a new album," he responded. "We have had to postpone a lot of things, and shuffle schedules because of tour dates. We still haven't gone to Europe for *In Step*. I want to play places we haven't played yet, like South Africa, Brazil...there's all kinds of things that I still want to do."

"What can the Abilene audience expect tonight from Stevie Ray Vaughan and Double Trouble?"

"The very best that we can give." The reporters were silent. "It's the truth," he said, standing up to make his exit. After a shower and little time backstage spent with his Uncle Jerrell Cook, who lived in town, Stevie walked onstage at the Taylor County Expo Center to give it the best he had to give, as promised.

The next stop was Austin on Friday, May 4, for the "Rites Of Spring" concert on Auditorium Shores. Stevie wowed his adopted hometown with "The House Is Rockin'," "Let Me Love You, Baby," and "Voodoo Chile," and sang of his Austin misadventures in "Tightrope." After the performance, Stevie got the chance to talk with an old friend from the Lubbock days, C.B. ("Stubbs") Stubblefield. Stubbs was thrilled to see that Little Stevie had gotten his act together, and offered to deliver a hot plate of his famous barbecue anytime, anywhere Stevie wanted it.

Soon afterwards, Ronny Sterling was in Austin, playing Antone's with Smokin' Joe Kubek, and decided to drop in on Jimmie. "We called him about ten in the morning, and he told us to come on over," Sterling remembers. "We didn't know that Stevie was there, but when we walked in, they were both at the kitchen table, drinking coffee, smoking cigarettes, and playing their guitars. They were trying to work up some stuff for that *Family Style* album. We heard some of the earliest versions of the songs that day, and I remember them fighting over who was going to sing the lead vocal on 'White Boots.' Stevie said he wouldn't touch it with a ten-foot pole, and Jimmie was trying to tell Stevie that he didn't want to sing anything. The bickering was really kinda cute; it was just like they were kids again."

On a warm spring day, Stevie and Jimmie ventured out to the little town of Elgin for a photo shoot that would produce the *Family Style* album cover. (Elgin lies about fifteen miles east of town on Highway 290, just beyond Bert's Dirt Shop and the This Is It Club.) While in town, the brothers feasted on a plate of Elgin's world-famous barbecued sausage, then walked around the corner of Central and Avenue C to the location of a boarded-up old record shop. The white paint had chipped away long ago, exposing the faded red brick wall, but the large black letters that advertised the shop's bill of fare were still legible: "*Record Shop—Bop, Rhythm and Blues, Spirituals...*" There they stood

Poster for what became Stevie's last concert in Austin. Art by Jagmo. Courtesy of Sam Schott Collection.

for about an hour, guitars in hand, while the winos across the street watched in amazement.

The brothers went back to Dallas for three weeks to do some more work on *Family Style*. Stevie and Doyle Bramhall had come up with three excellent compositions—"Hard to Be," "Telephone Song," and "Long Ways From Home." These did not carry the heavy, life-altering messages that *In Step* did; instead, they dealt with the simple human emotion of missing the one you love. Doyle told writer Brad Buchholz how the songs were constructed:

"While Stevie was laying down vocal parts and guitar tracks. I'd go into one of the small rooms in the recording complex and start working. Then Stevie would take a break after a couple of hours, stick his head in and

A collection of rare backstage passes. Courtesy Thomas Kreason/ Rockabilia.

say, 'You got anything?'…or, 'I've got five minutes, what do you got?' So I'd hit him with something, then he'd immediately come back with another idea, and I'd work with that. It worked out just fine."

Doyle's fondest memory of the sessions was getting to play drums on "Brothers," the dueling guitar blues track. It seemed only natural; Doyle had played with Jimmie in Storm, and with Stevie in the Nightcrawlers. Now they were having a gas recreating the past and forging the future. He laughed as he watched Jimmie and Stevie try to pass one guitar back and forth while the tape was rolling, the brothers getting tangled up in cords, getting the guitar strap caught behind Stevie's kneecaps, busting strings like crazy. Stevie and Jimmie were laughing together, genuinely enjoying the experience. This gave Doyle a different view of the Vaughan siblings he knew as teenagers; Jimmie didn't want to ignore Little Stevie anymore—he finally wanted to be his buddy, his friend, his…brother.

Jimmie and Stevie—together again for *Family Style* in Elgin, Texas. Photo by Lee Crum. Courtesy of Epic Records.

Jimmie accepted Grammys for himself and Stevie for *Family Style* at the 1992 awards. Photo by Arlene Richie/Media Sources.

On May 15, 1990, Mitch Mullins was driving past the Vaughan family home in Oak Cliff, and decided to stop in on a whim. He was amazed when he walked in the found Jimmie and Stevie sitting there together, under the same roof once again. Mullins recalls, "I gave Stevie a song list from Cast of Thousands and a tape of one of his early performances that someone had recently bootlegged, and was selling for money. Stevie got up, paced around the room, and said 'Mitch, that sucks!' I saw him look over at Jimmie, who just shrugged his shoulders and smiled." That was the last time Mitch Mullins would ever see Steve Vaughan.

Stevie had become infatuated with the physical and psychological healing powers of music, and developed a working relationship with a clinical social worker named Michelle Sugg, who worked for the Yale Psychiatric Institute at The Yale University School of Medicine. He wrote her several letters describing the effect his music had on young people, and how his messages inspired them to drop drugs and alcohol in favor of staying in school, and even picking up the guitar. Several of Sugg's patients had reacted very favorably to Stevie Ray's music, and he finally began to realize the power he had to help people through his songs. He and Janna made plans to visit the institute in late August of 1990 to work with Sugg on a music therapy project.

Although Stevie had embraced Christianity in recent years, his interest and belief in the supernatural, especially the afterlife, only grew. When Stevie embarked on the 1990 Benson and Hedges Blues Festival Tour in early June, he spent as much time conferring with Dr. John on hoodoo spirituality as he did learning guitar licks from B.B. King backstage. "I remember there was some little thing that he had gotten, some kind of little Mexican talisman or something," Dr. John remembered. "He put this thing in my hand and said, 'What do you feel about this?' I held it for a minute, you know, and said, 'Well, it feels cool to me, I don't feel anything bad coming from it.' And he says, 'Well, I been keeping it and I *knows* it feels good!'

"The same day, I was onstage playing my show and here he comes standing off the side of the stage. He just stared real deep at me, gave me this strange look, and he had that thing in his hand again. Before he split, he flashed it to me in the sunlight, and smiled and then he was gone. That was the last time I actually saw him alive."

For the remaining months of his life, Stevie would send messages to Dr. John through other people around the coun-

Stevie shared the stage with B.B. King night after night on The 1990 Benson and Hedges Blues Tour. Photo by Ralph Hulett.

job for the roadies to strike the stage in the very short time allotted on festival packages, and SRV decided he needed more help. Sure enough, Steve Wilson's phone rang at his home in Louisville, Kentucky. Mark Rutledge, Double Trouble's production manager, asked Wilson if he could be in Mountain View, California, to begin rehearsals in early June. The first few dates took them through their paces in Costa Mesa and San Diego before hitting "The Tonight Show" on Thursday, June 7, 1990.

Backstage, Stevie met with representatives of Fender Guitars, who had brought with them two new amps to try, along with the original prototype for the Stevie Ray Vaughan Signature Series guitar. Stevie wanted to play the guitar on television, but it didn't have his trademark initials on the pickguard. Steve Wilson ran down to *The Tonight Show's* art department and had them whip out some custom white Letraset letters which he installed before showtime. Stevie had to give the guitar back to Fender, but he liked the letters so much he picked up a few extras, and rubbed them off onto Number One, replacing the old faithful truck-stop metallic letters. When Fender finally released the SRV Model after his death, the outline of the SRV Letraset initials remained.

Onstage with Joe Cocker for The Passion Tour in 1990. Photo by and courtesy of W.A. Williams/The Image Works.

try, usually dealing with spiritual matters; he would ask questions of Dr. John, as though he were Stevie's personal psychic advisor, and Rebennack would send back answers. "He sent me a message through his brother Jimmie about six months before he died that was scary shit," Dr. John admitted, his voice shaking. "I really don't want to say what it was—Jimmie is the only other person who knows, and if he wants to talk about it someday, that would be okay. It wasn't necessarily an 'I know I'm going to die' thing, but it was something spiritual that, me being the superstitious coonass that I am, it was a shock and a half."

Stevie spent most of June and July on tour with Joe Cocker. Dubbed the Power And Passion tour, it was a full-scale operation that played large stadiums and amphitheaters across the U.S. On some dates, they were hooked up with the Benson and Hedges Blues Festival. It was a big

Stevie's last Houston appearance was on June 13 at the Cynthia Woods Mitchell Pavilion, with Joe Cocker. His last song, most appropriately, was "Texas Flood," the old Larry Davis number that he grew up with and that was cut right there at Houston's Duke Records building in 1958.

On Sunday, June 17, Stevie played his last Dallas date at the Starplex Amphitheatre, a Benson and Hedges show with Cocker,

Photo by and courtesy of W.A. Williams/ The Image Works.

Dr. John, Irma Thomas, and B.B. King. Vaughan was supposed to open the bill, but this was Dallas, and he was unanimously elected to headline. During sound check, Stevie began to play "Texas Flood." Suddenly, the clear blue sky turned black. Lightning flashed and thunder roared, and a heavy downpour quickly turned the Starplex into a swamp. The power cables that led to the stage became soaked, a potentially deadly situation. Fearing electrocution, the crew killed the power in mid-song and ushered Stevie Ray off the stage. Stevie nonchalantly laughed it off later.

The Power and Passion tour took Double Trouble through Alabama, Tennessee, Ohio, Michigan, Indiana, and Pennsylvania in June. Bill Williams had been accompanying Stevie on several shows taking pictures and providing spiritual support. Stevie and Bill were talking late one night, and Williams asked him how the death of his father had affected him. Stevie just looked at the floor and didn't say anything. Finally, he shifted his hat, cocked his head, looked over at Bill, and said, "Man, I thought I hated him." He explained that because he'd been taking drugs, he had lost touch with his feelings; it was hard to find love in his heart for the old man who had given him so much tough love as a kid. After cleaning up and screwing his head back on straight, Stevie confessed that he felt ashamed of having those feelings toward Big Jim—he found he really did love him, after all.

Stevie loved Williams' work so much, he collected as many of his photographs as he could in a portfolio that he carried with him everywhere he went. It was his "inspiration book," containing photos of Hendrix, Howlin' Wolf, and Muddy Waters, along with friends and his favorite shots of himself. The official T-shirt for Stevie's last American tour featured one of Bill's photos plastered across the front.

After a show in Nashville on June 20, Williams was off to shoot Lonnie Mack and Eric Johnson, who were also touring in the area. Bill pulled out his portable tape recorder, and asked Stevie to record personal messages to the guys. Upon delivery, Williams had Lonnie and Eric record short messages that he would take back to Stevie. "That required a tremendous amount of trust," Williams insists. "All those musicians knew that I wasn't going to go sell the tape or anything, they knew it was all between friends."

On July 1, Double Trouble played Veterans Park in Manchester, New Hampshire, a show *Boston Herald* rock critic Dean Johnson called "a

triumph." He saw old friend Ronnie Earl (now leading a band called the Broadcasters) backstage, and the two prayed together. Stevie had been Earl's sponsor in Narcotics Anonymous, and they supported each other through sobriety with messages of strength and faith.

On Saturday, July 7, Stevie was playing The Garden State Arts Center in Holmdel, New Jersey, a lavish outdoor amphitheatre that usually featured orchestral performances. Large fifteen-foot flat sound baffles, used for symphonic concerts, had been stacked against the wall, but someone made the mistake of tying off the curtain to one of the flats. As Stevie was coming off stage after the last encore, the curtains closed, and the heavy scenery came crashing down. It narrowly missed Stevie, who was heading for the stairs, but crushed six or seven of his guitars and could have cold-cocked Rene Martinez but good if he hadn't (by a stroke of dumb luck) knelt down at that very moment.

"I was standing there watching from across the stage, and this thing came down," Steve Wilson remembers. "I couldn't even speak, it happened so fast. It crushed or seriously damaged every single guitar on the stands, and I thought it had gotten Rene. Luckily, he had just bent down to change a battery in a floor effect pedal; he always took the batteries out every night and threw them away. When he bent down, that shell-piece wedged itself, or made a roof, if you will, across the lighting dimmer rack and Stevie Ray's guitars, and Rene was boxed in under that thing. If he would have been standing up, it definitely would have hit him. And I was speechless. Stevie came running out, and he didn't say anything but ask Rene if he was okay. He didn't look at his guitars. He didn't say a word about them.

"Y'know, he was in the [12-step] program, and he tried to deal with things, not let things get him upset. But he was obviously hurt—I mean, you could tell it just shattered the neck on Number One. That's the only guitar that it really shattered. But he said, 'Those are just guitars, they can be replaced,' although I could see that he just wanted to cry. He was just glad that Rene wasn't hurt, I think."

Word about the incident traveled quickly in Vaughan's inner circle. He had barely averted another brush with death, yet the fact that his favorite guitars were crushed gave those who knew him an ominous feeling. "When that scaffolding fell, just missing him in July, everybody got nervous," Jill Savage remembers. "Something told

Photo by and courtesy of W.A. Williams/The Image Works.

The next night Stevie was at Jones Beach in Wantagh, New York, and he was upset. Not only were his guitars in bad shape, but now his old Marshall Major amp was driving him crazy, and he wanted Steve Wilson to fix it immediately. "At least every other night it would go down," Wilson recalls, "Short a tube socket, or a tube, or a fuse...it was *always* something. He would look over his shoulder and watch the pilot light on that every night, then he'd play "Voodoo Chile," and he'd click on every pedal he had, and he'd hit the guitar harder than anybody I've seen before. I always thought it was some kind of cat-and-mouse game he played with me; like '*Hey! I can blow this up!*,' and I'd have to fix it.

"The Marshall company even stopped making that particular amp because it did blow up regularly; there was a design problem with it. I told him that, and he didn't want to hear it. When it finally went down for good, he was really mad, looking at me like 'Can't you do *something?*' I had to order Marshall to ship custom tubes and transformers that had long ago been phased-out overseas from England.... At first, I don't think he really wanted to believe me about the problem, because he took it to another technician, and he was told the same thing I had been saying all along. But he walked straight up to me at the next show and said, 'Steve, I owe you an apology.' And I said, 'No you don't.' And he just grabbed me and hugged me so hard, and he said, 'I hope you can help me stop being such a shithead.' Stevie was obsessive about his equipment, especially the old

stuff. It was almost mystical to him. He didn't need a bunch of reasons why things wouldn't work—he just knew it felt good, and that somehow it would work for him."

On July 21, Stevie was playing the Champs Music Theater outside of Seattle, when he was spooked by another bizarre incident. A fan had given him a white envelope filled with small pieces of Jimi Hendrix's grave marker. There was a note inside, too—it read, "James Marshall Hendrix—Forever In Our Hearts." A cold chill ran through his body, and he ordered that the envelope be destroyed immediately.

Family Style was completed at Manhattan's Skyline Studios in late July. The twenty-ninth was press day for Rodgers, Jimmie, and Stevie. They taped the promotional video for the album, and met with photographer Stephanie Chernikowski, a former Austinite who was now working for *Details*, a men's fashion magazine. Stevie chomped on choco-

Fielding questions from reporters in Houston, July 1990. Photo by Arlene Richie/Media Sources.

late bars and Jimmie constantly smoked cigarettes while they rapped on and on about the album they had always dreamed of making. Stevie revealed that the brothers did not play together on all the tracks; their hectic schedules forced them to send tapes back and forth for overdubs. SRV reminded Stephanie that she was the first to hear the raw mixes, kidding her with, "you looked at my painting before I finished."

It felt good for Jimmie. So good, in fact, that he bid the Fabulous Thunderbirds—his band—adieu once the Vaughan Brothers' album was complete. To Jimmie, in recent years, the band had become a caricature of its former self, still trying to come up with another "Tuff Enough." The butt-rockin' days were over. It was Kim Wilson's show now, and Jimmie had plans...big plans with his little brother.

There was a record preview party at Dallas Sound Labs for *Family Style* on August 22, while Stevie and Janna were on vacation in Hawaii. Some sources say that this last vacation was a management set-up to get Stevie out of town, as Sony conveniently overlooked inviting Stevie's family to the party. Others say that Stevie and Janna were considering eloping and tying the knot while in the islands, but for some reason didn't go through with it. They had been talking about doing it for months, and were starting to make plans. Janna had just done a photo shoot for a Dallas bridal magazine in a white wedding dress, but her dream of becoming Mrs. Stevie Ray Vaughan was not to be. It was the last she would see of SRV.

Stevie came back revitalized and ready to finish up the tour, to which an extra series of make-up dates had been added. The next day, he left Dallas at 2:35 P.M. on a plane to Chicago. He checked into room 4007 of The Four Seasons Hotel on Delaware Place, where he would remain, commuting to dates via van, through August 27. On that Monday, Vaughan was due to catch American Airlines Flight 501 bound for Dallas.

Photo by and courtesy of W.A. Williams.

That was one plane Stevie Ray Vaughan would miss.

On Friday, August 24, Stevie played the Kalamazoo County Fair in Michigan to a wildly appreciative crowd, then made the 120-mile drive back to Chicago after the show. The next day, the band drove into East Troy, Wisconsin, for a big two-night stand with Eric Clapton and special guests at the Alpine Valley Music Theatre.

The next afternoon, while Stevie was doing his sound check on the Alpine Valley stage, he noticed Steve Wilson walking around wearing an Andrew Dice Clay T-shirt, and stopped him, asking, "Dice— Isn't he that comedian that tells *nigger* jokes and thinks they're funny?"

Wilson felt bad. He didn't know what to say, but offered to take the shirt off immediately. "Naw, you don't have to take it off," Stevie said, somewhat defiantly. He shook his head and walked away. Perplexed, Wilson ran and changed shirts quick. "Boy, it really offended him," Steve Wilson remembers, "and I felt bad about that, but that's just the way he was, man. You didn't talk bad about anybody around Stevie Ray."

Although Stevie was supposed to ride to the Saturday show in the van, he had the opportunity to take a helicopter into the festival grounds. Stevie was digging the view down below; all the people, spread out like ants, waving up at him from below. Production Manager Mark Rutledge's wife Nancy was sitting next to him, and he asked her to take a picture out the window. She managed to catch Stevie, his arm hanging out the window, looking down upon Alpine Valley and smiling. Stevie liked the helicopter ride—he especially dug skipping over the heavy traffic jam from Chicago. He made it clear that if possible, he would like to travel by helicopter all weekend.

After that night's show, Stevie was walking down the hotel hallway with Steve Wilson, whose suite was right next to his at the end of the hall.

"The electricity from the concert was still in the air," Wilson recalls. "I mean, this was a really big night for Stevie. I said, 'Hey, boss, I've got a stack of stuff that I'd like to get autographed for some friends at home, if you've got time tomorrow night.' And he said, 'We'd better do it tonight.' He signed some 8x10 photos and album covers for the guys in the Kentucky Head-hunters [who Wilson is currently touring with]. We sat and talked for about fifteen minutes about some changes we were going to make to his stage set-up, and then I left his room. If I had waited until the next day, it would have been too late. It's almost as if he might have known something. I don't know."

That night, Stevie tossed and turned in his bed, sweating his way through a horrible dream. In it, Stevie Ray visited his own funeral. He was looking down upon the crowd of thousands gathered by the graveside, and he saw all the familiar faces he knew and loved so vividly; it terrified him beyond words. Yet, there was something almost…peaceful about the whole scenario. The next day, Stevie took the band and some trusted crew members aside and told them of his dream.

Stevie Ray Vaughan and Double Trouble's Alpine Valley set list

"In The Open"
Unreleased jump instrumental
"The House Is Rockin'"
"Tightrope"
"The Things (That) I Used To Do"
"Let Me Love You, Baby"
"Leave My Little Girl Alone"
"Pride And Joy"
"Wall Of Denial"
"Riviera Paradise"
"Superstition"
"Couldn't Stand The Weather"
"Goin' Down"
"Crossfire"
"Voodoo Chile (Slight Return)"
"Sweet Home Chicago"

They all shared a big hug, and tried to reassure him that it was only a dream.

The sold-out dates at Alpine Valley August 25 and 26 also featured an all-star lineup of Bonnie Raitt, Jeff Healey, Robert Cray, Buddy Guy, and brother Jimmie Vaughan. The elaborate stage plan included two large video screens for the audience. Four or five cameras circled the stage on booms and dollies, but no video recordings were made. This was by design; in fact, Clapton's people meticulously combed the venue both nights, making sure that no tape was rolling. The only bootleg that exists is a low-quality audience audiotape. The world would never see these famous last shows.

A few months earlier, Stevie had been asked if he played differently at shows that he knew were being recorded, and his reply was startling, but very Vaughan. "Well, I'm playing it for that day," Stevie answered. "The way I like to look at it is if that's the last time I ever got to play, I'd better give it everything I've got. Because it sure would be a drag to look back and go, 'Well, blew that one…'"

The Sky Is Crying

ERIC CLAPTON WAS awakened the morning of August 27 by the telephone's incessant ringing. He looked at the clock impatiently. It was seven o'clock. It had been well past four when he got to bed. Who could it be? He pulled the covers up over his head and tried to ignore it, but it just kept on yelling at him. He reached over and fumbled with it, looking for a ringer switch or a volume knob to silence it. There were none. Annoyed, he finally grabbed the receiver.

"Umm...hello?"

"Eric?" A thick British accent inquired. It was Roger Forrester, his manager for the last twenty years, and Eric knew that he wouldn't be calling at this ungodly hour unless it were earthshattering.

"Roger? What's going on, man?"

"One of our choppers didn't make it back last night. There was an accident," Roger replied quietly.

"Oh no—was anybody hurt badly?"

"They all perished."

Eric sat up. "Who?"

Roger spilled the bad news. "Bobby [Brooks], Colin [Smythe], Nigel [Browne], the pilot, and...Stevie Ray was with them, too."

Eric's heart sank fast. He had just lost his booking agent, his assistant tour manager, his personal bodyguard, and one of his closest friends in one fell swoop—it just couldn't be true. But it was.

More names to add to the list. He remembered Duane Allman, Jimi Hendrix, Keith Relf,

Carl Radle, Nicky Hopkins, Rick Gretch, Freddie King, and many others over the years. So much death around him. Drugs and suicides, unhappiness and talents wasted. But this was different. Something totally unforeseen had claimed their lives. These were five bright, young, together people who had a lot to look forward to—taken in the prime of life. Eric felt a pain he had known before and fell silent. Moments passed slowly. He had completely forgotten the phone.

"Eric? Are you all right?" Roger asked.

"No, I'm not bloody all right! All right?" The anger was back, the cruelty of losing every person he got close to. It was a curse that seemed to follow him all of his life, and he hated it. "Oh…hell. I'm sorry, Roger. I didn't mean that at you," he apologized.

"They need you to come identify the bodies, man."

"Does Jimmie Vaughan know yet?" Eric asked softly.

"Yes…Yes, I'm quite sure he does."

"Tell him I'll see him in a few minutes—and that I'm terribly sorry," Eric said, dropping the phone.

The first flash came over the AP newswire at 7:32 A.M., reporting five fatalities, including "a musician." AP updated with details every half hour. The mysterious "musician" then became "a member of Eric Clapton's entourage," and then "a guitarist." By 9:30 rumor began to spread that Stevie Ray Vaughan, Austin's favorite son, was aboard the doomed craft.

Martha Vaughan sat with her morning coffee and the "Today" show in her Dallas living room. Hearing news of a copter crash after a concert that featured both of her sons put her in a worried frenzy. She immediately called her brother, Joe Cook, and said, "Please come over right now—something's happened to the boys."

The news spread like wildfire. Jimmie's father-in-law, John Crouch, called Jill Savage at 7:30 A.M., and told her, "You don't wanna hear this on the radio. Stevie's gone." Jill became hysterical. "I didn't want to believe it," Savage

Eric Clapton shared the stage with Stevie at Alpine Valley. Photo by Lisa M. Hill.

remembers. "I called Mama V right then. I said, 'Please tell me this isn't true.' She said, 'Jill, if there's anyone who believes in being a survivor it's you, and it can't be my son! He can't be dead. Until the Coast Guard gets on the ground and finds his body, I will not believe it.' She had the church on the other line."

The family awaited news from television reports at Martha's house in Oak Cliff. "Martha and I kept watching," Joe Cook recalled. "She said, 'It hasn't been confirmed. I just know he has a guardian angel…he's gonna be O.K.'… Then they said there were no survivors."

At 11:30, Clapton's manager confirmed the worst. Stevie Ray Vaughan was an official fatality. He had played his last show with Clapton, Robert Cray, his brother Jimmie, and Buddy Guy before 35,000 people.

By noon, a shock wave was reverberating through Texas' capital. Students walked the streets near the university in a quiet daze. It wasn't unusual to pass somebody with tears in their eyes that afternoon—the whole town was disoriented and numb. Friends called friends who called friends. "I found myself calling people I hadn't talked to in fifteen years," Natalie Zoe says. "Everyone was reaching out and trying to connect with people who knew how important Stevie was to them. I mean, he was our homeboy."

By five o'clock, everybody knew; businessmen and women came home from work and discovered the tragedy on TV, shops posted signs and banners proclaiming "We Love You, SRV," "Goodbye, Hurricane," and "So Long, Stevie." Even the City Coliseum replaced its Welcome, Texas Dog and Cat Show billboard with a somber SRV R.I.P. At six, fans began converging on the Zilker Park riverside for the first candlelight vigil since John Lennon's murder in 1980. The sunny sky suddenly grew very dark; heavy black clouds rolled in over Auditorium Shores, looking like a horrible thunderstorm could come crashing down, but it never did rain.

By 7:30, more than 3,000 mourners had

gathered around its caves, all clutching candles, praying, and listening to his music pumped through several loudspeakers and transistor radios. Austin's faithful were all here together, trying to find an acceptable way to deal with the shock and confusion. KLBJ-FM aired a rough recording of Stevie's "Tin Pan Alley," cut live at Steamboat in 1980, and it sliced right through the heart. It was long before he was Stevie Ray Superstar—back then, he was just Little Stevie "Hurricane" Vaughan. This was the town that knew him when; who made fun of his wild threads, scolded him when he swiped one too many Albert King licks, patted him on the back when he got his first break at Montreux, bought outrageously priced tickets to his Dallas shows opening for the Rolling Stones in 1982, and cheered him through all his gold and platinum records. Now, here they were, rallying together one more time for the greasy little kid who played the blues.

Everywhere you looked, there were people hugging people, joining hands with total strangers, and making new friends—all with one common bond—Stevie Ray Vaughan had touched them when they were low, and he made them feel better.

As the cloudy sky gave way to night, the crowd kept growing as more and more people heard about the vigil. Unfortunately, a large number of people came only for beer and disrupted the silence with cries of "Fuckin' A!" By nine, nearly 5,000 had congregated on Zilker's grassy hillside. It was just one huge, glowing mass of people.

But across the river at Antone's, the close friends, the musicians, and the old-time Austin scenesters came together to play the blues one more time for Stevie. Fans drove from as far south as Galveston and as far north as Oklahoma just to be there. Driving to the club, you could switch your radio dial back and forth between tributes on KLBJ, Z-102, and KUT, where Paul Ray was holding court.

Ray held back the tears, remaining professional and keeping his composure over the airwaves that night, only occasionally letting the grief get to him. That's when he'd reach over and slap a killer record on the turntable. "Here's one little Stevie cut with the Cobras in 1977. A lot of you will remember...a little thing called 'Texas Clover.'"

Meanwhile, the local and national press were swarming Clifford's club with cameras, tape recorders, and notepads at the ready, all waiting for just five minutes with the elusive Mr. Antone,

the one man most responsible for giving Stevie and countless others a stage in Austin during the years when the town was experimenting with cosmic cowboy consciousness, and nobody gave a hoot about the blues.

Clifford tried to duck and dodge the reporters for as long as he could. He knew he was in no emotional state to make any kind of coherent comment. Realizing the futility of escape, he settled down with KXAN-TV, a local NBC affiliate, with W.C. Clark by his side for support. But Clifford broke wide open as soon as the lights went on.

"I met Stevie when I was twenty-two and he was seventeen," he sobbed. "The kid could always play. I mean, he was as good then as he is now...or, was. People like that...it's just born in 'em, you know? He was Little Stevie back then, just a kid. He'd hang out and play when he got the chance and make you laugh. It was a very simple thing. It had nothing to do with the record business or movies or TV or any of that shit. Him, me, Jimmie, Denny Freeman, Doyle Bramhall...we were just a bunch of kids drawn together by our love of the blues, you know?

"We all came up through really, really hard times, and nobody ever gave us anything. And even in recent years when I'd see him, I'd say, 'how ya doin', kid?' I mean, he was my friend, just this little guy who played a mean guitar. The rest is the world's trip, you know?" Antone said softly, rubbing his forehead, "It's gonna take a long time to even comprehend it. I mean, I'm sitting right here talking to you, and I still don't believe it. I...you know...no one that alive could be gone!" He turned his red face from the harsh bright light of the camera and covered his eyes.

"I'm dumbfounded," said Clark. "I felt like a benefactor to him. I kinda raised him... We were really close, and I...hell, I don't know what else to say about it. It just hurts too much." W.C. departed for the stage—his only sanctuary from the media hounds—and began his second set.

The audience was full of familiar faces: Doug Sahm, Marcia Ball, Lou Ann Barton, David Grissom, David Murray, Derek O'Brien, Van Wilks, Kim Wilson, and Paul Ray, all hugging and wiping away the tears. TV cameras zoomed around the room, closing in on a few unsuspecting local celebrities. A teary-eyed Lou Ann Barton told a reporter, "This is just too close to home—this is family. He and Jimmie couldn't be any closer to me than my own brothers. We've lived together for about twenty years, lived in the same neighborhood and actually raised each other. We came up from the depths when we were getting fifty cents per night per head to play R&B that nobody liked, and being white kids as well. He really worked hard to make his success possible. He was just so damned talented. There's nobody like Stevie Vaughan, nobody has fingers like Stevie. When I lived with him, that boy ate, lived and breathed that guitar. That boy came from nowhere, and he went everywhere. I'm just in shock, it's a total tragedy. We loved each other, and I'm just devastated."

"I think Stevie's message was to love everybody you meet," said Ruth Ellsworth, co-writer of some of SRV's most popular songs. "He was a very tender-hearted person, who felt that love was the number one reason that we're all here. Like the song 'Crossfire'—I think that song really touched Stevie because he realized how hard it is to be a tender-hearted person and how you can get caught in the Crossfire being that way."

Jody Denberg, Austin's most popular deejay and author of the liner notes for *In The Beginning*, came down to the club as soon as he finished his airshift at KLBJ. Jody had followed Vaughan's career since Steamboat and was the only Austin deejay to play Double Trouble on the air as early as 1980. "I think Stevie came straight from the heart, like his album said—Soul to Soul," Denberg affirmed.

But it was Marcia Ball, who, with her soft-spoken disbelief for the loss of a friend and an Austin icon, summed it all up in just a few words. "He's Austin's pride and joy," she said, bowing her head. "It's just terrible."

For as long as Austin can remember, W.C. Clark has finished his show every night with a rousing rave-up of the Reverend Al Green's "Take Me To The River." Tonight, as on hundreds of nights before, special guests flooded the stage. Some of the biggest names in Texas music found their way to the microphone, but nobody really felt like singing. Somewhere in the course of the song, something miraculous happened—W.C.'s powerful tenor went soaring over the lines: *Take me to the river / wash me on down / Soothe my soul / put my feet on the ground…*"

A certain brief moment of joy swept the entire place. The crowd stood up and joined in the chorus, couples flooded the dance floor, and the entire house just wailed. For the first time that day, it seemed as though nothing had changed and folks were still boogeying at the Armadillo. Life went on, and Austin still knew how to have a good time.

Jimmie Vaughan sat silently on a private jet somewhere over middle America, shaken and shocked. He was heading home to Dallas with Stevie's remains. It had been the worst day of Jimmie's life, and he was ready for the whole thing to end. It would be so nice to just fade back into sleep, to call it just a dream, to forget that it ever really happened. But he couldn't sleep. His thoughts were driving him crazy. His mind raced like the twin jet engines below him—the phone calls and the news and then seeing his brother's lifeless body…

He fought back the tears; the whole day had been one constant cry. Reaching into his breast pocket, he produced a necklace. It was Stevie's Coptic cross, which investigators had found on a nearby hill. It had never left his neck. It was a reminder of spirituality, said Stevie, letting him know that every action he put out today would be marked for or against him in some great file cabinet in the sky. He cherished it and would often hold it when he'd speak about something special, or just grab it when he was deep in thought.

Jimmie's mind wandered back to last night. Just twenty-four short hours ago, he was standing by Stevie's side, having so much fun, laughing wildly—nothing too terribly special, it just felt like another great show. He smiled as he thought of standing backstage next to Eric Clapton, Buddy Guy, and Robert Cray. Heroes and disciples. Friends. Seeing Stevie that happy, and knowing that Stevie wanted him there, meant so much more to him now. He'd been by his brother's side for his last night on earth—as if it were supposed to be that way.

After the show they were all packing their things to leave the hall when Chas Comer came and asked Stevie how he'd like to travel. Stevie had planned to drive back to Chicago with Jimmie and his wife Connie until Comer informed him that traffic was backed up as much as five hours along the tiny two-lane blacktop that led to and from the theater. Stevie asked him to check on the availability of seats on a helicopter. Charles returned five minutes later and said there were seats for the three of them.

They jumped in the van and drove through the thick fog to the copter pad, where four Bell 206B Jet Ranger whirlybirds were running and checking controls, as this was certainly not a night to fly by sight alone. Getting out of the van, they were told that there was actually only one seat left.

Stevie looked Jimmie in the eye and said, "Do you mind if I take it? I really need to get back."

Jimmie didn't like it. "Well, yes, I kinda do, since I came all this way to see you."

Stevie pleaded. "No, you don't understand. I have to go. Please, Jimmie."

"Alright, then—go!" Jimmie said, forcing a smile.

"Thanks, man." Stevie pulled an overnight bag over his shoulder. "I hope you understand."

"Sure, I do," Jimmie assured him.

Stevie hugged him one last time. "I love you."

Jimmie stood by the van, watching Stevie climb on board the copter. He took the right front seat. Stevie poked his head out the door and yelled back, "See you in Chicago!"

Stevie waved farewell, beaming that goofy toothy grin of his, which would become etched in Jimmie's mind forever.

The plane jolted down on the runway and taxied to a stop. The day had been so chaotic that Jimmie'd hardly stopped to notice the date—it was August 27. Their father had passed away four years ago to the day. Jimmie breathed deep and went down to meet his mother. He wiped his eyes, gently reached for Martha's hand, and squeezed it tight. He touched her cheek and looked into her eyes—and saw the Vaughan family spirit looking back at him. He was the last living male of the family, and now, at thirty-nine, truly the man of the house. He must have felt a sense of responsibility like he had never known before. As he began to lead his disoriented mother to the car, he stopped for a moment and told her: "Mama, I've always been Little Jim. That's what you always called me. I guess I'm Big Jim now." Martha tried to soothe her only boy's aching mind. "It's okay, Jim. I'll be okay." Jimmie just stared at her, not knowing how to believe it.

Then it was off to Laurel Land Memorial Park in Oak Cliff to leave the body and arrange a funeral. Jimmie knew it was all over as he stared out the tinted windows at the dark night sky. It was eleven P.M. on the longest day of his life, but at least he was home now, watching a full moon shine over his familiar Dallas.

The morning brought news of pilot Jeff Brown's prior flight record. The FAA confirmed that Brown, forty-two, had been involved in two crashes and one minor violation concerning aircraft identification markings. Official records described the crashes as "an uncontrolled collision with the ground" in 1977 and a 1989 mishap blamed on an engine malfunction.

Rumor had it that Clapton and Vaughan had switched helicopters at the last minute. When questioned by local authorities, Roger Forrester adamantly denied the reports, insisting that was "the Hollywood version, trying to rewrite *The Buddy Holly Story*." However, Stevie's press agent, Charles Comer, later confirmed the switch; he had been the one to tell Stevie about it. If this is true, Eric Clapton might have been the victim instead of Stevie Ray. Any way you look at it, it was someone's turn, and it was Vaughan's name that was called.

According to Federal Aviation Agency records, the helicopter took off in heavy fog at 12:45 A.M., bound for Chicago's Midway Airport. Sweet Home Chicago would never be reached. Moments later, the chopper smashed into the side of a man-made ski hill. Several witnesses leaving the concert saw the choppers lifting off, and all noticed that the one carrying Stevie banked sharply to the right, and the headlights went out just moments before it fell from the sky. They heard a thud—most didn't think anything of it; others called authorities. No action was taken at that time. Upon impact, Stevie was thrown fifty feet and died instantly. All on board were killed most likely before they knew what hit them. From the way the wreckage was scattered, it was obviously one hell of a crack-up. Chunks of wreckage and human bodies were spread out in a 250-foot circle.

The chopper had lifted off from the southeast end of the ski resort, and was supposed to circle all the way around the mountain and take off for Chicago. For some reason, the copter took off in a different direction than the other three, and turned smack dab into the mountain, about 100 feet from the top of the summit. When the helicopter was later found, its built-in clock read exactly five seconds past one a.m.

At 1:30 A.M., the third of Clapton's four helicopters was reported missing when the craft's black box emergency transmitter went off. A search for the lost copter wasn't begun until 5 A.M., although the Civil Air Patrol acknowledged the helicopter's distress signal at 1:30 A.M., and had notified the Walworth County Sheriff's office immediately. Why it took four hours to assemble rescue teams is anybody's guess. At 6:50 A.M., a sheriff's deputy discovered the tragedy in a very quiet field. The stench of gasoline was everywhere, and all the remains were wet with gas and morning dew. He checked for signs of life among the victims, but all were long gone. Oddly, a considerable sum of dry paper money was also found at the site, blowing around in the breeze.

Stevie was officially pronounced dead by the Walworth County Coroner at 7:55 A.M. The primary cause of death was listed as exsanguination (loss of blood) due to a transverse laceration of the aorta. In plain English, Stevie Ray Vaughan died of a broken heart.

All the bodies were immediately taken to Lakeland Medical Center in Elkhorn, a tiny town ten miles from Alpine Valley. "As soon as I came to work, my office was flooded with calls asking if it was true that Stevie Ray Vaughan was dead," recalls Jim Wincek, marketing director for the hospital and an SRV admirer. "I got phone calls from Sweden, Belgium, The Philippines, Malaysia, even Russia, begging to know what was going on. The hospital was full of media people from everywhere, and we managed to keep them contained in a small room right across from the morgue—but that was the coup; they didn't know how close they really were to their story! It was bizarrely chaotic.

"I was responsible for escorting Eric Clapton and Jimmie Vaughan to the morgue to identify the bodies; they were both visibly shaken, and although I am what you would call a fan, none of that mattered when I met them," Wincek says. "I knew I had a hard job to do; to show them the bodies of their friends that they had just seen alive last night. It was very traumatic for them, and we had a counselor in the morgue, helping them deal with what they saw in there. Luckily, the bodies were not burned or dismembered, and they were then transported back to Chicago by hearse to be put on a plane that took the bodies home." Routine autopsies and toxicology exams were performed, and Stevie Ray came out clean; the only drug in his system was nicotine.

It would take a year of investigations conducted by the National Transportation Safety Board, the FAA, and local authorities to rule out mechanical failure as having any role in the crash. It would take another year for the final report to be completed. Authorities blamed the crash on "pilot error," meaning that pilot Jeff Brown had attempted to fly by sight rather than by his controls. The fog also played a big role, masking the oncoming mountain in a blur of white that probably just looked like a big cloud.

"I'm still trying to find out who gave the authority for the goddamned helicopter to fly in the fog, in the dark, at that hour with visibility

being as bad as it was," Charles Comer would tell a reporter a few days after the crash, his cool Irish exterior melting. "Buddy Guy made a statement that he couldn't see ten feet off the ground after his own helicopter took off."

On TV, Buddy Guy broke down in front of some news team's camera, crying about how much he still couldn't believe it. "It's the most hurtinest thing that's ever happened to me. Stevie is the best friend I've ever had, the best guitarist I've heard, and the best person anyone will ever want to know," a choked-up Guy said. "That guy did for us what Muddy Waters did. He put the blues over, and then he came back and got us. We'll all miss him...I...I really can't say anymore...goodbye." Stevie had been his best friend for the last five years, and now that he was gone, and Buddy was left to try and pay it all back, to keep his blues, his message alive.

Eric Clapton had some hard decisions to make in the wake of some very trying times. He met with the entire crew and they made the decision to carry on with the tour. Clapton told *Rolling Stone*, "it was the best tribute I thought we could make—to go on and let everybody who was coming to see us know that it was in honor of their memory," he said.

Clapton played the Sandstone Amphitheatre that night in Bonner Springs, Kansas, to 15,000 fans, many of them wearing black armbands in memory of those killed. Eric dedicated three numbers to Stevie and his friends who had died in the helicopter crash the night before.

Meanwhile, the Vaughan family and Double Trouble dropped out of sight to mourn in private. Joe Cook was the only one that could be reached for comment, and he simply stated that Martha was "devastated by the crash. I know Stevie was in a hurry to get back home the night of the concert. He was in a hurry to get back with Janna. He had a few days before the European tour. He caught one of the first copters out. It just happened to be the death seat."

Thursday night, a crowd of about 300 got together in Dallas' Kiest Park for another candlelight vigil, only this one drew Stevie's oldest acquaintances and fans. The mood here, unlike Austin, was peaceful and respectful. Christian Brooks organized the vigil and gave a touching testimonial. There were a lot of unbridled tears and uneasiness, as everybody knew that tomorrow was the day Stevie would be laid to rest.

On Friday, August 31—the end of the hottest week of the year, and perhaps the most cathartic four days in Texas since the Kennedy assassination—3,000 people converged in the sweltering 102-degree heat upon Laurel Land Cemetery in Oak Cliff, Stevie Ray's final stop.

Inside the chapel, a private ceremony was being held for the family and close friends. Dr. John played a New Orleans funeral drag as the casket was ushered down the aisle, and Stevie Wonder opened the service with a shattering a capella shout of "The Lord's Prayer." The casket was placed inside a white hearse that drove slowly to the site, the mourners following behind on foot. Martha Vaughan wore a purple dress; purple was the color that Stevie felt had healing powers, and the color he was wearing when he died. Jimmie and Uncle Joe were in black, and Janna turned out in a white dress. Celebrity faces dotted the crowd: Kim Wilson, Charlie Sexton, Jeff Healey, Dr. John, ZZ Top, Clarence "Gatemouth" Brown, Ringo Starr, and Colin James. Buddy Guy, overcome with grief, slipped out of the chapel and into a waiting car.

The mourners listened quietly as Bonnie Raitt, Jackson Browne, and Stevie Wonder sang "Amazing Grace." Bonnie carried the melody as the other two harmonized. Stevie Wonder took the second verse. His magnificent voice swirled around the notes with awesome power, causing many in the audience to break into tears. Tears kept flowing as he sang:

Amazing Grace, how sweet the sound
that saved a wretch like me
I once was lost, but now I'm found
was blind, but now I see.

While Connie was watching the service, she felt a hand on her shoulder and turned around to find Lenny. Lenny threw her arms around Connie. "I was crying to the point where I couldn't even speak," Connie recalls. "She held me and told me to just let it all out. She apologized to me for all the times she kept me and Stevie apart through the years—now she understood how I felt."

The Reverend Barry Bailey of the First United Methodist Church of Fort Worth opened the public service with some personal thoughts, and recited The Serenity Prayer, the 23rd Psalm, and The Prayer Of St. Francis, a copy of which was found in Stevie's jacket pocket the night he died.

Ex-Nightcrawler Bruce (B.C.) Miller stepped to the podium and read two sections from the book AA members receive upon entering the program. One is called "How it Works," which includes the 12-step program for cleansing the system, and the second, "A Vision for You," is a promise of what the successful AA enrollee can look forward to. As he finished, he placed the book on Stevie's casket. Jackson Browne shyly approached the mike to say a few words: "I don't have much to say here, because words don't really describe the loss. He was an extremely gifted musician, and he will continue to be an inspiration to me. I saw genius standing there."

When Nile Rodgers took the stand, he was shaking. "I brought a tape with me today of the last song I produced for him—nobody's heard this yet, but it's called 'Tick Tock,' and in it, he sings the refrain 'Remember' over and over. And now I know—what Stevie was trying to tell me, and I guess all of us…he was trying to say, 'Nile, remember my music. Remember how important music is to all of us. And just remember that it's a gift.' Stevie was truly touched by the hand of God. He had a powerful gift. And through his music, he made us all remember things that are very, very important, like love and family.

"Stevie taught me about love…about universal love. And I feel very, very sorry that I wasn't able to say to his face, 'Thank you, Stevie. Thank you for making me remember music, thank you for sharing your music with me. Thank you for sharing your love with me. Thank you for making me a part of your family. Thank you for making me your brother. I'll always love you,'" he exclaimed, bursting out in tears. "I'll always cherish the moments we spent together—and believe me, Stevie—I'll always remember."

After the service, the crowd was invited to walk by the casket. As people moved by, many asked the attendants to place objects somewhere near the burial ground. A young boy with his parents handed over a simple purple ribbon. Others left friendship bracelets, books, guitar picks, pictures, poems, and single roses.

The last man to pass by was Doug Castor, a sweat-drenched thirty-three-year-old from Pittsburgh, who slowly struggled to guide his wheelchair along the pebbly path. "Every once in your life someone touches you in an important way," he whispered as he began to sob softly. "I had to be here. I really can't afford it, but I just had to come."

As the body was being lowered into the ground (space 4, lot 194, section 25), people sat on their haunches, stood under umbrellas, or lined up for water or ice. The relatives and friends talked in the front rows, trying to appear strong. Jill Savage and Martha Vaughan retreated under a big shade tree, trying to put the last four dizzying days in perspective. "The shock was wearing off, and exhaustion was weighing in," Savage recalled, "and she just seemed so—at peace somehow, I don't know how to explain it. And I was losing it, crying and all, and she held me and said, 'Honey, everything happens for a reason.' Just then Janna grabbed me and said, 'Remember what he taught us. Just remember.'"

The pallbearers were Alex Hodges, Chris Layton, Reese Wynans, Tommy Shannon, Rene Martinez, tour manager Skip Rickert, production manager Mark Rutledge, and stage manager Bill Mounsey. When their job was done, they gathered in a small circle under a shade tree, whispering in low tones and embracing.

About two P.M., the long white limousines began to drive the family away through the winding roads of the cemetery. As Jimmie Vaughan was preparing to climb inside his limo, something made him turn back one more time. He shook his head, tightened his jaw, and gave Stevie one final thumbs up, holding back his sorrow. Security officers and Dallas police steered the few remaining mourners away.

Long after everyone else had left, Doug Castor was reluctant to push his wheelchair away from the grave, despite the oppressive heat and the urgings of caretakers who were shoveling dirt down onto the casket. He broke into hysterics, and was wheeled away by security guards as he cried out, "It's not fair! Dammit! It's not fair! He had so much left to give everybody…He can't be gone! Oh, why? Why?"

❖❖❖

Buddy Guy was finally ready to play his guitar again. He had only played once since Vaughan's death, at a pre-arranged jam with Carlos Santana that he didn't have the heart to cancel. Then Clifford Antone called him up a few days after the crash. Buddy was obviously distraught, and Clifford told him he needed to get out of Chicago and take some time to make peace with Stevie's passing. Antone invited him down to Austin to stay for a week, see some familiar faces, and most important, to play the blues for a bunch of hungry Austin kids who missed Stevie. Buddy said yes, it sounded like the thing to do.

Buddy pulled out all the stops at Antone's,

The final resting place. Photo by and courtesy of Dale Allen/ Killer Cases.

performing two nights to over-capacity, call-the-fire-marshal crowds. Friday night, Guy's throat was raw and he might have had one too many; he stumbled over even the most familiar lyrics, cursed a lot at his amplifier, and yelled at the waitress to bring five or six Crown and Cokes to the stage. "You'll have to excuse me, people, because I really don't drink anymore, but tonight…well, tonight's different, ya'll."

But when he'd just shut up and cut loose on the guitar, it was easy to see how a little whiskey couldn't hurt. Buddy was on fire; his tone screeching out through one of Clifford's favorite tweed Fender bassman amps, burning eardrums from the front to the back of the club. He played "Mary Had A Little Lamb" for Stevie, John Lee Hooker's "In The Mood," T-Bone's "Stormy Monday," Guitar Slim's "The Things That I Used To Do," and turned in his rousing rendition of Little Walter's "Everything's Gonna Be Allright." As Buddy belted and cooed out those well-worn lyrics over the Antones' (the house band) rumbling, descending rhythmic lines, it was pure soothing magic:

"Hey, baby!
Let me hold your worried head
I said—everything's gonna be allright
(yes it will, everybody)
Everything, everything, everything
Is gonna be allright…"

Saturday night, Buddy felt much stronger and was in better voice to pull himself through another marathon concert. Again, the joint was packed to the rafters with college-age kids, all professed blues experts. Where do kids this age get that firm a grip on blues classics? The answer is plain—Stevie Ray had spread the word.

Halfway through his set, Buddy lost it. He began to play a slow, mournful blues. He stood there, crouched over his guitar, bending low and hiding his face. When he looked up again, his tears were flowing, silencing the crowd. He soloed for close to four minutes before he stepped up to the microphone, wiped his eyes, and began to sing:

We miss you, Stevie.
Yes, the pain just
grows and grows
And the way I feel
tonight
Oooh well, I guess you'll never know.

Buddy choked on the words. He began to sob harder and louder, until he just had to turn his back to the audience. This was what he had feared all week—getting out there in front of nearly a thousand people and breaking down under the lights. He felt like such a fool. As he tried to collect himself enough to play, his guitar wouldn't sound. He looked at the amp. It was on, volume up—but wouldn't say a thing for him. Soundmen and musicians flocked to the amp to see what was the matter, while Buddy stood there, bewildered. They fiddled with the knobs, the cord, the connection; but nothing could make it work.

The hushed crowd began to feel uneasy, as

Two weeks after the accident, Buddy Guy traveled to Austin "to play for Stevie's people." Photo by Keri Leigh.

if a presence had entered the room. Then Buddy got it. *It was Stevie pulling the plug on him.* It *had* to be. Stevie didn't want anybody crying for him and found a way to distract the sorrow. Buddy got the message. 'O.K., Stevie…I'll leave it alone," he laughed over the mike, and signaled the band to stop the song. Sure enough; no sooner had he called the ending—his guitar came back on full force. He just shook his head, fired off into an uptempo shuffle, and his smile returned—Stevie would have wanted it that way.

Of all the hundreds of written tributes to Stevie Ray Vaughan, perhaps Michael Corcoran's, in the *Austin Chronicle*, was the most comforting and poignant: "Though this was a tragic *loss* of life, it wasn't a *waste* of life. He turned a lot of white suburban kids on to the blues and its pioneers and away from drugs. His work will continue on with us although he is no longer with us in body. He made his mark.

"It's somewhat soothing to realize that Stevie Ray Vaughan died soon after jamming alongside his brother and his childhood idols, with the echo of applause still ringing in his ears."

Coda

ON SEPTEMBER 25, 1990, Epic Records hastily released *Family Style*, the long-awaited Vaughan brothers' album. It was more than just a last word; it was a lifelong dream come true for Jimmie and Stevie. At the next Grammy Awards, Jimmie collected Grammys for Stevie and himself for *Family Style* as Best Contemporary Blues Recording and also for Stevie's "D/FW," which won Best Rock Instrumental.

❖

Jimmie went into seclusion after Stevie's death, making nary a public appearance for several months. He made a cameo appearance at Eric Clapton's annual Royal Albert Hall concert in February 1991, along with Robert Cray and Buddy Guy. He was seen around Austin infrequently, sitting in with Lazy Lester, Charlie Sexton, Doyle Bramhall Jr., and Bob Dylan (Jimmie and Stevie had played on Dylan's *Under A Red Sky* album, released in September 1990) at local clubs and concerts.

Jimmie took on a variety of studio projects, working on a Muddy Waters tribute album, contributing guitar to John Lee Hooker's *Boom Boom* record, and cut some songs with Les Paul. He plunged deeper into his classic car hobby and took his custom '51 Violet Vision Chevy, among others in his vast collection, to car shows around the country, often walking away with first place.

Recently, Jimmie reunited with Lou Ann Barton and Denny Freeman to form a new band, which made its debut at the Royal Albert Hall with Eric Clapton in February 1993. He is currently working on a solo project that will be released in late 1993.

❖

On November 29, 1990, Tommy Shannon and Chris Layton boldly left behind the ashes of Double Trouble and created a new band with Charlie Sexton and Doyle Bramhall Jr. They dubbed themselves the ARC Angels (named after Wayne Nagel's popular Austin Rehearsal Complex), and quickly became the rage of Austin. The band was immediately snatched up by Geffen Records and went into intensive rehearsals to come up with some original material—a missing link in their early shows. Their self-titled debut CD was released in April 1992.

❖

In February 1992, Fender Musical Instruments unveiled the long-awaited Stevie Ray Vaughan Signature Series Stratocaster. Model 010-9200 was commissioned by Stevie himself shortly before his death, and included all the features that made his sound so unique. The SRV Commemorative Strat had a suggested retail price of $1299.99. Stevie would surely have gotten a good laugh at that—all that money for a guitar fashioned after an old "piece of shit" that he didn't have to pay a cent for. Stevie often said he was offered up to half a million dollars for that "piece of shit" in later years, but his answer was always the same—"Not for sale."

❖

On August 27, 1991, the one-year anniversary of Stevie's death, the Vaughan family issued a statement asking the media and fans not to plan any special remembrances around the sad anniversary. They asked people to celebrate Vaughan's life by observing his birthday instead. Buddy Guy released an album that day (*Damn Right I've Got The Blues*) that closed with a blues instrumental called "Rememberin' Stevie." On October 3, 1991, Governor Ann Richards proclaimed his birthday Stevie Ray Vaughan Day in Texas, and celebrations were low-key and respectful. Benefit concerts were held in his name in Dallas and Austin, and the proceeds were donated to the Stevie Ray Vaughan Memorial Fund.

❖

Not every fan paid Stevie Ray the respect he was due after his death. In the beginning, his grave at Laurel Land Cemetery became a gathering place for fans who would leave gifts, personal notes, and flowers. However, letters eventually began to disappear from the grave marker—stolen by overzealous fans. The entire headstone was even stolen, not once but twice. To this day, the grave is continuously defaced and the family is considering moving Stevie and his father (whose grave is next to SRV's) to an undisclosed location if the vandalism doesn't stop.

❖

The SRV Memorial Fund, which is overseen by the Communities Foundation of Texas, has collected a great deal of money in past years. Donations have ranged from the $10,000 given by Bruce Springsteen to an anonymous gift of two crumpled one-dollar bills. Every day fifteen or twenty new letters and individual contributions are received by the fund, often accompanied by a heartfelt testimonial or greeting card, which all get forwarded to the Vaughan family. More than $72,000 has been granted in Stevie's name to the Dallas Area Parkinsonism Society (the disease that took Big Jim's life) and the Ethel Daniels Foundation, a drug and alcohol rehab facility.

❖

Rocky Athas, David Brown, Mike McCullough, and Robert Ware can still be found in Dallas, leading their own blues and rock bands. Christian Brooks owns Blues Suede Shoe, a leather shop in Deep Ellum, and plays guitar and drums in blues bands at night. Marc Benno can still be found playing around the region, as can Mike Kindred, Kathy and David Murray, Lou Ann Barton, Natalie Zoe, and W.C. Clark. Mary Beth Greenwood, Bill Williams, and Randy Jennings are successful photographers, and Clifford Antone's mid-town juke joint still plays the blues.

Connie Trent recently married, and Martha Vaughan moved to Duncanville, Texas, where she volunteers a great amount of time to the church. Lenny Vaughan remarried and moved to Fort Worth, Texas, and Lindi Bethel remained in Austin. Janna Lapidus returned to her modeling career just two weeks after Stevie was laid to rest. A little more than a year later, she moved to Tokyo.

❖

In February 1993, Jimmie accepted two more posthumous Grammys for his late brother; "Little Wing" won Best Blues Instrumental, and *The Sky Is Crying* took top honors for Best Contemporary Blues Recording. This brought the total to seven Grammys, three of which Stevie won before turning thirty-five—a tremendous accomplishment for a man who'd only been in the national spotlight for seven years.

None of Stevie's albums went platinum in his lifetime. Five did so after his death. Record sales doubled from gold (500,000 copies) to platinum (one million copies) almost immediately after the tragedy occurred; some turned platinum in less than a month. *The Sky Is Crying* shot up to #10 on the *Billboard* Pop Albums chart (higher than any of Stevie's previous albums), and sold a record 1.5 million copies within weeks of its release. The market for bootleg Stevie Ray tapes remains stronger than ever; despite poor quality, the material continues to sell for exorbitant amounts.

❖

In *Blade Runner*—SRV's favorite film—Rutger Hauer knows he is going to die and goes to meet his maker to beg for more time. He thinks of every possible escape from death, but there is none. Finally, the man who made him explains, "the light that burns twice as bright only burns half as long. And you have burned extremely bright. You have done extraordinary things. Revel in your time."

Stevie Ray Vaughan took this advice to heart; his last four years were a triumph. He may have never found the ideal love or religious experience that he searched for all his life; perhaps he never fully unravelled the musical mysteries that perplexed him so. But rest assured that in the presence of heaven and the company of angels, Stevie Ray Vaughan finally found what he was looking for.

Bibliography

Interviewees

Al Sterling
B.B. King
Bruce Iglauer
Buddy Guy
Christian Brooks
Christian Plicque
Clifford Antone
Connie Trent
Dale Allen
Danny Thorpe
David Brown
David Murray
Doug Castor
Dr. John
Jill Savage
Jim Wincek
John Griebel
Fabulous Thunderbirds, The
Kathy Murray

Kim Wilson
Koko Taylor
Lew Stokes
Manuel Ruiz
Margaret Moser
Mary Beth Greenwood
Michael Ventura
Mike McCollough
Mitch Mullins
Natalie Zoe
Priscilla Dickenson
Randy Jennings
Robert Ware
Rocky Athas
Ronnie Sterling
Shirley Beeman
Steve Wilson
Stevie Ray Vaughan
Tim Duckworth
Vicki Virnelson
W.A. "Bill" Williams

Articles

Adair, Sue. "Vaughan: Hot Licks." *Anchorage Daily News*, July 26, 1990.

Aledort, Andy. "Chris Layton Remembers Stevie Ray." *Guitar*, March 1992.

Aledort, Andy. Interview. *Guitar*, May 1991.

Aledort, Andy. "So Real." *Guitar for the Practicing Musician*, December 1990.

American Federation of Musicians' Engagement Contracts: The T-Birds at the Armadillo, February 21, 1976; Cobras at the Armadillo, December 1, 1976.

"America's Hottest Men." *Playgirl*, November 1985.

Arsenault, Tim. "Virtuoso Vaughan's Career Cut Short." *Halifax Mail-Star*, August 28, 1990.

Austin, Beth, Steve Dougherty, and Barbara Sandler. "A Wisconsin Helicopter Crash Claims a Legend-in-the-Making." *People*, September 1, 1990.

"Austin's Top Bands," Reader's Poll. *Austin Sun* 1976.

Australian Tour Program, SRV & Double Trouble, 1984.

Ayers, Keith A. "Merchandising a Legend: Stevie Ray Vaughan." *Texas Beat*, September 1992.

Ayers, Keith A. "Tribute." *Texas Beat*, September 1990.

Bentley, Bill. "The Vaughan Brothers—Mainline Blues." *Austin Sun*, April 28, 1978.

Bishop, Nancy. "Vaughan Brothers Dazzle Nick's Uptown Crowd." *Dallas Morning News*, November 1986.

"Blues Legend on Special Mission." *The News*, Adelaide, Australia, March 24, 1986.

Brumley, Al. "400 Hold Candlelight Vigil for Guitarist Vaughan." *Dallas Morning News*, August 31, 1990.

Buchholz, Brad. "Antone's—Austin's Home of the Blues." *Dallas Morning News*, July 15, 1990.

Buchholz, Brad. "Doyle Bramhall: Living Life by the Drop." *Austin Chronicle*, January 31, 1992.

Campbell, Bob. "Audience 'Hypnotized' by Stevie Vaughan." *Lubbock Avalanche-Journal*, summer 1978.

Campbell, Bob. "Lou Ann Barton & Stevie Vaughan: Double Trouble." *Lubbock Avalanche-Journal*, February 18, 1979.

Clark, Mike, Turrentine, Jeff. "Austin's Greatest Blues Guitarist Dies at 35." *Daily Texan*, August 28, 1990.

Claypool, Bob. "Audition with Jagger Could Be Ticket to Fame for Stevie Ray Vaughan's Band." *Houston Post*, late 1982.

172

Claypool, Bob. "Stevie Ray Vaughan: Playing It Straight." *Houston Post*, January 25, 1987.

Claypool, Bob. "Texan a Hit at Carnegie Hall." *Houston Post*, October 6, 1984.

Claypool, Bob. "Texan Vaughan Heads for the Big Time, Going Against Techno Trends." *Houston Post*, July 15, 1984.

Cobras Press Releases and Fan Club Information, 1976-1990.

Coleman, Chico. "Austin Blues: Hottest Brand Going." *Daily Texan*, April 12, 1976.

Corcoran, Michael. "The Coldest Shot of All." *Austin Chronicle*, August 31, 1990.

Corcoran, Michael. "Stevie Ray Vaughan: Straight from the Heart." *Austin Chronicle*, January 21, 1987.

Coryell, Larry. "Praying through the Guitar." *Musician Magazine*, December 1989.

Davis, John T. "Guitarists Lost Loved One." Obituary for Big Jim Vaughan. *Austin American-Statesman*, August 29, 1986.

Davis, John T. "Life Without You." *Austin Weekly*, August 29, 1990.

Davis, John T. "Vaughan Pauses for a Breather Between Projects." *Austin American-Statesman*, August 7, 1987.

Drozdowski, Ted. "Blues Power." *Boston Phoenix*, October 6, 1991.

Drozdowski, Ted. "Guitar Slingers Shoot It Out." Beck/Vaughan. Concert Review. *Rolling Stone*, November 30, 1989.

Eschenbrenner, Bob. "Weathering the Storm." *The Music Paper*, December 1989.

The Fabulous Thunderbirds Press Releases and Fan Club Information, 1980-1990.

"Fatal Vaughan Crash Blamed on Helicopter Pilot." Associated Press Report (nationally syndicated), September 16, 1992.

Forte, Dan. "Blues Brother." *Guitar World*, July 1989.

Forte, Dan. "Brothers: Jimmie Remembers Stevie." *Guitar Player*, March 1991.

Forte, Dan. "Jimmie Vaughan: Fabulous Thunderbird." *Guitar Player*, July 1986.

Forte, Dan. "Soul to Soul: Double Trouble Remembers SRV." *Guitar Player*, March 1991.

Forte, Dan. "Stevie Ray Vaughan." *Guitar Player*, October 1984.

Forte, Dan. "Walk Softly, Carry a Big Guitar." *Austin Chronicle*, August 31, 1990.

Frost, Deborah. "Lou Ann Barton's Big Date." Record Review. *Rolling Stone*, early 1982.

Gamino, Denise. "So Long, Stevie Ray." *Austin American-Statesman*, August 28, 1990.

George, Nelson. "Dancing with Nile Rodgers." *Musician Magazine*, July 1983.

Guterman, Jimmy. *Soul to Soul* Record Review. *Rolling Stone*, April 19, 1986.

Hall, Michael. "Clifford Antone: Blues Is All I Understand." *Austin Chronicle*, June 15, 1984.

Hall, Michael. "Hammond on Vaughan." *Austin Chronicle*, July 8, 1983. Hall, Michael. "Texas Flood: Stevie Rising." *Austin Chronicle*, July 8, 1983.

"A Helluva Bluesman: Stevie Ray Is Remembered by his Peers." *Guitar World*, December 1990.

Henke, James. "Eric Clapton's Blues." *Rolling Stone*, October 17, 1991.

Hirshey, Gerri. "Attache' Case Full of Blues: The Bush Bash." *Rolling Stone*, March 9, 1989.

"Jagger: Have Gun, Will Travel." Random Notes. *Rolling Stone*, June 10, 1982.

Jennings, Diane. "Mourning a Blues Master." *Dallas Morning News*, August 28, 1990.

Jennings, Diane. "No More Wild and Crazy Days for this Guitar Guru." *Dallas Morning News*, June 10, 1990.

Joseph, Frank. "Rough and Tumble Blues for the Eighties." *Guitar World*, September 1983.

Kennedy, Helen. "Vaughan Remembered as a Modern Guitar Master." *Boston Herald*, August 28, 1990.

Knight, Robert. "Forever in our Hearts." *Guitar*, May 1991.

Kornbluth, Jesse. "Blues Brothers: Stevie Ray Vaughan and John Hammond." *New York*, April 2, 1984.

Kronke, David. "He Breathed Life Back into the Faded Blues." *Dallas Times Herald*, August 28, 1990.

Kronke, David. "The Way Back: Stevie Ray Vaughan 'Live Alive' and Well." *Dallas Times Herald*, 1986.

Laffoon, Janice. Interview. *Nightflying*, Fall 1990.

Leigh, Keri. "The Buddy Guy Interview." *Austin Chronicle*, September 18, 1990.

Leigh, Keri. "C-Boy Parks, R.I.P." *Austin Chronicle*, January 31, 1991.

Leigh, Keri. "Mean Texas Flood Sweeps the Southwest." *Back Beat*, May 1990.

Leigh, Keri. "Musician of the Decade." *Austin Chronicle*, March 15, 1990.

Leigh, Keri. "SRV's Guitar Heroes." *JAM*, July 1989.

Leigh, Keri. "Stevie Ray Skips the Part about Dying Young." *Daily Oklahoman*, August 22, 1987.

Leigh, Keri. "Stevie's Back—And Better than Ever!" *Oklahoma Gazette*, July 12, 1989.

Leigh, Keri. "Vaughan Combo Rocks the Zoo." *Daily Oklahoman*, July 1986.

"Letters to the Dead." *Austin Chronicle*, November 1, 1991.

Loder, Kurt. "Couldn't Stand the Weather." Record Review. *Rolling Stone*, September 24, 1984.

MacCambridge, Michael. "Blazing New Trails." *Austin American-Statesman*, November 25, 1989.

MacCambridge, Michael. "Friends Mourn a Great Loss." *Austin American-Statesman*, August 28, 1990.

Maher, John. "Fly On My Friend." *Fender Frontline*, Fall 1990.

Malone, Bill C. "Lone Star Strings and Strummers."

Texas Highways, June 1987.

Marshall, Wolf. "A Tribute to Stevie Ray." *Guitar School*, March 1992.

Marshall, Wolf. "Well-Healed." *Guitar*, 1986.

Mattingly, Rick. "Prescriptions from the Amp Doctor: Steve Wilson." *Musician Magazine*, September 1991.

McBride, James. "You Can Take the Boy out of Texas, but You Can't Take the Texas out of Blues' Golden Boy Stevie Ray Vaughan." *People*, March 25, 1985.

McCullough, L.E. "C-Boy Parks: Just a Blues-Type Person." *Austin Chronicle*, June 15, 1984.

McLeese, Don. "'Beginning' Shows Young Vaughan Lacking Subtlety." *Austin American-Statesman*, October 6, 1992.

McLeese, Don. "Fitting Tribute to Stevie Ray: Brother Jimmie Compiles Powerful Album." *Austin American-Statesman*, October 5, 1991.

"Mechanical Failure Ruled Out in Vaughan Crash." Associated Press Report, August 14, 1991.

Menconi, David. "'With Respect, Blood, and Memories,' the Late Mr. Vaughan Rave On." *Blues Access*, Christmas, 1990.

Milkowski, Bill. "The Good Texan." *Guitar World*, December 1990.

Milkowski, Bill. "Song Sung Blue." *Guitar World*, December 1990.

Milkowski, Bill. "Stevie Comes Clean." *Guitar World*, September 1988.

Millard, Bob. "Soulful Notes: Stirring Words Accompany Donations to Vaughan Fund." *Dallas Times Herald*, October 1990.

Millard, Bob. "Stevie Ray's Last Project: Brotherhood." *Dallas Times Herald*, September 26, 1990.

Miller, Ed. "Rockabilly Past, Present, and Future." *Buddy*, May 1992.

Minutaglio, Bill. "The Man with Blues in his Blood." *Dallas Life Magazine (Dallas Morning News)*, March 17, 1985.

Minutaglio, Bill. "3,000 Say Farewell to Vaughan." *Dallas Morning News*, September 1, 1990.

Monroe, Larry. "Sweet Memories of Stevie in Chicago." *Austin Weekly*, September 12, 1990.

Morse, Steve. "Death of a Blues Star." *Boston Globe*. August 28, 1990.

Moser, Margaret. "Stevie Vaughan & Double Trouble." *Austin Sun*, July 27, 1978.

Moser-Malone, Margaret. "The Early Years of a Voodoo Chile." *Austin Chronicle*, August 31, 1990.

Nixon, Bruce. "Blues to Bowie." *Guitar Player*, August 1983.

Nixon, Bruce. "It's Star Time!" *Guitar World*, November 1985.

Nixon, Bruce. "New Album May Be Vaughan's Best." *Dallas Times Herald*, September 29, 1985.

Obrecht, Jas. Obituary. *Living Blues*, November/December 1990.

Palmer, Robert. "Historic Bookends to Texas Blues."

New York Times, October 7, 1990.

Patoski, Joe Nick. "Play That Funky Music, White Boys." *Texas Monthly*, April 1978.

Patoski, Joe Nick. "Requiem in Blue." *Texas Monthly*, October 1990.

Pellechia, Michael. "R&B Binds Oak Cliff Picker and Legendary Songwriter: Doc Pomus/Fabulous Thunderbirds." *Dallas Times Herald*, 1978.

Perry, Claudia. "Blues Brothers." Album Review. *Houston Post*, September 23, 1990.

Petrek, Melissa. "Austin Radio Station Suggests Stevie Ray Vaughan Memorial." *Daily Texan*, September 28, 1990.

Point, Michael. "City Council Stalls on Vaughan Tribute." *Austin American-Statesman*, October 3, 1990.

Point, Michael. "Fans Felt Music with their Hearts." *Austin American-Statesman*, August 28, 1990.

Point, Michael. "SRV: 1954-1990." *Pulse!*, October 1990.

Point, Michael. "A Tribute for Stevie Ray: Sculptor to Highlight Musician's Contemplative Side." *Austin American-Statesman*, November 20, 1991.

Point, Michael. "Vaughan Anniversary to Pass Quietly." *Austin American-Statesman*, August 23, 1991.

Point, Michael. "Vaughan's LP Relaxed, Fun." Record Review of "Family Style." *Austin American-Statesman*, September 26, 1990.

Pond, Steve. "Alone Together: SRV and Jeff Beck Hit the Road." *Rolling Stone*, January 25, 1990.

Price, Mike H. "Little Stevie: Coming of Age." *Texas Jazz*, August 1982.

Racine, Marty. "Stevie Vaughan and Group: Success Is Strange but Nice." *Houston Chronicle*, June 20, 1983.

Racine, Marty. "Texas Blues Guitarist Leaves Legacy that Will Be Taken Seriously." *Houston Chronicle*, August 28, 1990.

Resnicoff, Matt. "Epitaph." *Musician Magazine*, November 1990.

Resnicoff, Matt, Gore, Joe. "Of Meat & Fingers: Stevie Ray Vaughan and Jeff Beck." *Guitar Player*, February 1990.

Ressner, Jeffrey. "Dense Fog May Have Caused Crash/Vaughan's Pilot Crashed Twice Before." *Rolling Stone*, October 4, 1990.

Rhodes, Joe. "Fame the Next Gig for Blues Guitarist out of Oak Cliff." *Dallas Morning News*, April 17, 1983.

Rhodes, Joe. "Jimmie Vaughan." *Dallas Morning News*, December 28, 1986.

Rhodes, Joe. "Stevie Ray Still Cares." *Dallas Morning News*, December 15, 1984.

Rhodes, Joe. "Stevie Ray Vaughan at Carnegie Hall." *Dallas Times Herald*, November 28, 1984.

Rodriguez, Vincente. "Air Crash Kills Guitarist Stevie Ray Vaughan." *Dallas Morning News*, August 28, 1990.

Rodriguez, Vincente. "Public Funeral for Stevie Ray

Vaughan Set Friday." *Dallas Morning News*, August 29, 1990.

Rubin, Dave. "Cesar Diaz: Guitar Guru." *Guitar Player*, April 1993.

Santelli, Robert. "Stratocasting the Blues with a Touch of Texas." *Music And Sound Output* Magazine, October 1985.

Scherman, Tony. "Lost and Found and Lost Again." *Musician Magazine*, November 1990.

Seal, Mark. "Stevie Ray's Missing Wa-Wa (*sic*)." *Dallas Observer*, December 1986.

Siegel, Jessica, Worthington, Rogers. "Fog's Role Probed in Crash that Killed Rock Star." *Chicago Tribune*, August 28, 1990.

Smith, Russell. "Dallas-Born Rocker Kicks His Addictions." *Dallas Morning News*, January 25, 1987.

Smith, Russell. "A Divine Badness." *Dallas Morning News*, Fall 1985.

Smith, Russell. "Oak Cliff Recalls Favorite Musical Son." *Dallas Morning News*, August 28, 1990.

Smith, Russell. "Vaughan Travels Long Road from Oak Cliff to Fair Park." *Dallas Morning News*, July 12, 1984.

Stern, Chip. "Let's Dance" Record Review. *Musician Magazine*, July 1983.

"Stevie Ray Remembered." *Oak Cliff Tribune*, October 3, 1991.

"Stevie Ray Vaughan—Bound to Be a Star." *Sounds of Austin*, November 1981.

Stolder, Steve. "In Memoriam." *RAM*, September 1990.

Swenson, John. "Picking Up the Pieces: Jimmie Vaughan Carries On." *Rolling Stone*, February 7, 1991.

Swenson, John. "Stevie Ray Vaughan, 1954-1990." *Rolling Stone*, October 4, 1990.

"Texas Tornados: A Guide to the Heaviest Guitarists in the Lone Star State." *Buddy*, August 1978.

Ventura, Michael. "Blues for Stevie." *Austin Chronicle*, September 1, 1990.

Verosky, Eddie. "The Arc Angels." *Austin Music & Entertainment*, January 1992.

Walters, Chris. "Rolling with the T-Bird Rhythm." *Austin Chronicle*, February 28, 1986.

Ward, Ed. "Blues Brothers." *Musician Magazine*, May 1987.

White, Timothy. "Talking with the Master." *Musician Magazine*, June 1991.

Whittington, Jeff. "Austin Blues-Rock Family Tree." *Austin Chronicle*, June 15, 1984.

Wilonsky, Robert. "Caught in the Crossfire." *Austin Chronicle*, August 14, 1992.

Wilonsky, Robert. "Sleaze-Z Top & the Nightcaps." *Dallas Observer*, August 20, 1992.

Wilonsky, Robert. "Sole Brother: Jimmie Vaughan Turns Music Back On Without Stevie Ray." *Dallas Times Herald*, March 1991.

Wilonsky, Robert, Cantu, Hector. "Goodbye to a Bluesman." *Dallas Times-Herald*, August 30, 1990.

Wisby, Gary. "Death in the Fog." *Chicago Sun-Times*, August 28, 1990.

"Wives Reach Settlement in Vaughan Crash." Associated Press, December 2, 1992.

Young, Ron. "Remembering Stevie Ray." *San Antonio Light*, August 28, 1990.

Zahn, Michael. "Vaughan Was Considered One of the Best Guitarists." *Milwaukee Journal*, August 28, 1990.

Zepp, Louise, Waddell, Ray. "Industry Mourns Vaughan and Friends." *Amusement Business Magazine*, September 3, 1990.

Books

Antone, Susan. *Antone's: The First Ten Years*. Austin, TX: Antone's (self-published), 1985.

Antone, Susan. *Picture the Blues*. Port Townsend, WA: Osbourne's, 1990.

Brammer, Billy Lee. *The Gay Place: Being Three Related Novels*. New York: Vintage Books, 1983.

Burroughs, William. *Naked Lunch*. New York: Grove Press, 1966.

Coleman, Ray. *Clapton: An Authorized Biography*. New York: Warner Books, 1985.

Crosby, David and Carl Gottlieb. *Long Time Gone*. New York: Doubleday, 1988.

Dalton, David. *Piece of My Heart: The Life and Times of Janis Joplin*. New York: St. Martin's Press, 1985.

Dance, Helen Oakley. *Stormy Monday: The T-Bone Walker Story*. New York: Da Capo Press, 1989.

Dixon, Willie and Don Snowden. *I Am the Blues: The Willie Dixon Story*. New York: Da Capo Press, 1989.

Friedman, Myra. *Buried Alive: The Biography of Janis Joplin*. New York: William Morrow & Company, 1977.

Govenar, Alan. *Meeting the Blues: The Rise of the Texas Sound*. Dallas: Taylor Publishing Company, 1988.

Guralnick, Peter. *Searching for Robert Johnson*. New York: Penguin Books, 1989.

Guralnick, Peter. *Sweet Soul Music: Rhythm and Blues and the Southern Dream of Freedom*. New York: Harper & Row, 1986.

Hammond, John and Irving Townsend. *John Hammond on Record*. New York: Summit Books, 1977.

Henderson, David. *'Scuse Me While I Kiss the Sky: The Life of Jimi Hendrix*. New York: Bantam/Doubleday, 1978.

Hopkins, Jerry. *Bowie*. New York: Macmillan, 1985.

Minutaglio, Bill. *The Hidden City: Oak Cliff, Texas*. Dallas: Elmwood Press and the Old Oak Cliff Conservation League, 1990.

Murray, Charles Shaar. *Crosstown Traffic: Jimi Hendrix and the Post-War Rock 'n' Roll Revolution*. New York: St. Martin's Press, 1989.

Nelson, Susie. *Heart Worn Memories: A Daughter's Personal Biography of Willie Nelson*. New York: Eakin Press, 1987.

Oliver, Paul. *The Story of the Blues*. Radnoe, PA:

Chilton Book Company, 1982.

Palmer, Robert. *Deep Blues*. New York: Penguin Books, 1982.

Patoski, Joe Nick and Bill Crawford. *Stevie Ray Vaughan: Caught in the Crossfire*. Boston: Little Brown and Company, 1993.

Pittman, Bill. *A.A.: The Way It Began*. Seattle: Glen Abbey Books, 1988.

Reid, Jan. *The Improbable Rise of Redneck Rock*. New York: Da Capo Press, 1974.

Willoughby, Larry. *Texas Rhythm, Texas Rhyme*. Austin, TX: Tonkawa Free Press, 1990.

Wilson, Burton. *Burton's Book of the Blues: A Decade of American Music, 1967-1977*. Austin, TX: Edentata Press, 1977.

Collector's Guide to Stevie Ray Vaughan

Official Releases with Double Trouble

1983—*Texas Flood*, Epic FET/EK 38734

1983—*Blues Explosion*, Atlantic 780149-1 (features Grammy-award winning "Texas Flood" performance from Montreux Jazz 1982.

1984 *Couldn't Stand The Weather*, Epic FET/ EK 39304

1985—*Soul To Soul*, Epic FET/EK 40036

1986—*Live Alive!*, Epic EGT/EGT 40511

1986—*Atlantic Blues Guitar*, Atlantic ATC 81695-1 ("Texas Flood")

1989—*In Step*, Epic OET/EK 45024

1990—*Stevie Ray Vaughan: October 3, 1954—August 27, 1990*, Epic ESK 2221 (limited edition tribute disc released shortly after his death)

1991—*The Sky Is Crying*, Epic ET 47390 (posthumous compilation of unreleased masters and out-takes)

1991—*Interchords—Stevie Ray Vaughan and Double Trouble*, Epic ESK 4418 (promotional CD, interviews with SRV, Jimmie V., and band)

1992—*In The Beginning*, Epic ET 53168 (Live from Steamboat, 1980)

Releases with Other Artists (LPs)

1971—*A New Hi*, (local compilation album of Dallas bands featuring Cast Of Thousands with SRV and Mike McCullough on guitars)

1983—*Let's Dance*, David Bowie, EMI-America SO-17093

1983—*Texas Twister*, Johnny Copeland, Rounder 2040

1983—*Soulful Dress*, Marcia Ball, Rounder 3078

1985—*Strike Like Lightning*, Lonnie Mack, Alligator AL 4739

1985—*Twilight Time*, Benny Wallace, Blue Note BT 85107

1985—*Heartbeat*, Don Johnson, Epic 40366

1985—*Rocky IV* motion picture soundtrack, James Brown, Scotti Bros. 40203 (features "Living In America")

1985—*Living For A Song*, Roy Head, Texas Crude (catalog number unknown)

1986—*Gravity*, James Brown, Scotti Bros. 5212-2-SB

1986—*Emerald City*, Teena Marie, Epic 40318

1987—*Back To The Beach* motion picture soundtrack, Columbia SC40892 (features the "Pipeline" guitar duel with Dick Dale)

1987—*Famous Blue Raincoat; The Songs Of Leonard Cohen*, Jennifer Warnes Cypress 661111

1987—*I'm In The Wrong Business!*, A.C. Reed, Alligator AL 4757

1987—*Characters, Stevie Wonder*, Motown MCD 06248 MD (SRV on CD only)

1988—*Loaded Dice*, Bill Carter, CBS BFZ 44039 (with Jimmie Vaughan)

1988—*Distant Drums*, Brian Slawson, CBS 42666

1988—*Bull Durham* motion picture soundtrack, Bennie Wallace, Capitol 90586

1990—*Family Style*, The Vaughan Brothers, Epic ZT/ZK 46225

1990—*Under The Red Sky*, Bob Dylan, Columbia C46749 (with Jimmie V.)

1991—*The Blues Guitar box*, Lonnie Mack, Sequel TBB 47555

1991—*The Blues Guitar box*, Vol. 2, Lonnie Mack, Sequel NXT 185

1991—*The Alligator Records 20th Anniversary Collection*, Alligator ALC-105/6 (with Lonnie Mack and A.C. Reed)

Singles

1975—"Other Days" b/w "Texas Clover," The Cobras, Viper 30372

1979—"My Song" b/w "Rough Edges," The Cobras featuring W.C. Clark and Stevie Vaughan, Hole HR-1520

1983—"Let's Dance" b/w "Cat People," David Bowie, EMI EA 152 (also available as a 12-inch extended dance mix single)

1983—"Modern Love" b/w "Modern Love," David Bowie, EMI EA 158 also available as a 12-inch extended dance mix single)

1983—"Without You" b/w "Criminal World," David Bowie, EMI B-8190

1983—"Love Struck Baby" b/w "Rude Mood," Epic A 3689

1985—"Look At Little Sister" b/w "Change It," Epic 05731

1985—"Living For A Song," Roy Head, Texas Crude (catalog number unknown)

1985—"Living In America" b/w "How Do You Stop?" James Brown, Scotti Bros. Z58 69117 (from *Rocky IV* motion picture soundtrack—also available as a 12-inch extended dance mix single)

1986—"Heartache Away" b/w "Love Roulette," Don Johnson, Epic 06426

1986—"Superstition" b/w "Pride And Joy" (Live), Epic 06601

1986—"Superstition" b/w "Willie The Wimp" (Live), Epic 06996

1987—"First We Take Manhattan" b/w "Famous Blue Raincoat," Jennifer Warnes, Cypress 661115-7

1987—"Pipeline" (with Dick Dale) b/w "Love Struck Baby," Columbia 07340

1990—"Tick Tock" b/w "Brothers," The Vaughan Brothers, Epic 73576

1991—"The Sky Is Crying" b/w "Chitlins Con Carne," Epic 34-74142

1991—"Wham!" b/w "Empty Arms," Epic 34-74198

Official Promotional Videos

1983—Love Struck Baby

1984—Cold Shot, Couldn't Stand The Weather

1985—Change It

1987—I'm Leavin' You (Commit A Crime) (from New Orleans Jazz and Heritage Festival)

1987—Pipeline (from *Back to the Beach*) with Dick Dale

1989—The House Is Rockin'

1990—Tick Tock, Good Texas (Jimmie Vaughan)

1990—The Vaughan Brothers profile (interview with SRV & Jimmie V.)

1990—Pride And Joy (Compilation of videos by Double Trouble), Sony Music Video, 17V-49069

1991—Live at the El Mocombo, Sony Music Video, 19V-49111

1992—Little Wing (film montage of SRV, bluesmen, Fender factory) (Courtesy of Epic Records)

Selected Audio Bootlegs (CD, Cassette, LP)

Live Storm 1970 (with Jimmie Vaughan, Lewis Cowdrey and Doyle Bramhall) Blackbird demo, Austin, Texas, 1972

Marc Benno and The Nightcrawlers' A&M sessions, Los Angeles, California, 1973 (includes first version of "Dirty Pool")

The Nightcrawlers' demo for Lone Wolf Productions, Houston, Texas, 1974

Cobras' studio recordings, 1975 (includes ("Thunderbird," "Lonely, Lonely Nights," "St. James Infirmary," and "Hambone's Tune")

Stevie Vaughan with Albert King—First Jam, Antone's, Austin, 1975

The Cobras with Albert King, Houston, Texas, 1975

The Electric Graceyland Sessions, 1978 (early Double Trouble demos)

The Triple Threat Revue, Soap Creek Saloon, Austin, Texas, 1978

The Rome Inn, Austin, Texas, 1978

The Austin Blues Festival, May 1979 (Double Trouble with Lou Ann Barton)

Studio 21, San Antonio, Texas, August 30, 1978 (with Lou Ann Barton)

Stubb's Barbeque, Lubbock, Texas, December 1978 (with Lou Ann Barton)

Paul Ray and The Cobras, Live at the Armadillo, Austin, Texas, 1979

Juneteenth Blues Festival, Houston, Texas, June 19, 1979 (with Lou Ann Barton)

Miss Lou Ann Barton and Double Trouble at Fat Fry, Austin, August 20, 1979

Peona's, Austin, Texas October 1979

Jack Clement Sessions, Nashville, Tennessee, November 1979 (with Lou Ann Barton)

Live At Steamboat, April 1, 1980 (same as *In The Beginning* except contains seven unreleased tracks. Unedited version.)

King's Bay Inn, Norfolk, Virginia, July 22, 1980

Fort Worth, Texas, August 30, 1980 (SRV and Double Trouble)

Cheatham Street Warehouse, San Marcos, Texas, 1980 (with Charlie Sexton)

Mother's Day party, Dallas, May 1981

Harling's Upstairs, Kansas City, Missouri, July 4, 1981

Chef's, Baton Rouge, Louisiana, September 9, 1981 (with Tommy Shannon on Bass)

Stevie's Birthday Party, Antone's, Austin, Texas, October 3, 1981

Fitzgerald's, Houston, Texas, October 14-19, 1981

Barton Creek benefit, Antone's, Austin, Texas, March 7, 1982 (with Omar and The Howlers, Kim Wilson)

Antone's, Austin, Texas, 1982 (with Albert King)

Fitzgerald's, Houston, Texas, December 18, 1982 (with Johnny Copeland)

Antone's, Austin, Texas, February 27, 1983

The Continental Club, Austin, Texas, February 28, 1983

The Ritz, Dallas, Texas, March 19, 1983 (with Alan Haynes)

"I Need Love," Alan Haynes single, 1983 (still unreleased—Stevie plays six-string bass)

Serious Moonlight Tour rehearsals, Las Colinas Soundstage, Dallas, Texas, April 27, 1983 (with David Bowie band)

The Bottom Line, New York City, May 9, 1983

Live in Chicago with Buddy Guy, WXRT-FM Broadcast, 1983

Tennis Rock Expo, Pier 84, New York City, May 23, 1983 (with Aerosmith, Clarence Clemmons and John McEnroe)

The Agora Ballroom, Dallas, Texas, June 3, 1983 (with Eric Johnson)

Fitzgerald's, Houston, Texas, June 20, 1983

The El Mocombo, Toronto, Ontario, July 11, 1983 (audio version)

Pier 84, New York City, July 23, 1983 (with Buddy Guy)

Rosa's, Colorado Springs, Colorado, August 15, 1983

Rainbow Music Hall, Denver, Colorado, August 16, 1983

Reading Festival, England, August 27, 1983 (radio broadcast)

Paradiso Theater, Amsterdam, Netherlands, September 9, 1983 (radio broadcast)

The Music Hall, Houston, Texas, October 6, 1983

City Coliseum, Austin, Texas, October 7, 1983

The Spectrum, Philadelphia, Pennsylvania, October 19, 1983 (radio broadcast)

Ripley's Theater, Philadelphia, Pennsylvania, October 20, 1983 (radio broadcast)

Gilly's, Dayton, Ohio, October 1983

McNichols Arena, Denver, Colorado, November 28, 1983

The Beacon Theater, New York City, December 28, 1983

The Wax Museum, Washington, DC, December 29, 1983 (with Bob Margolin)

The Hollywood Palace, Hollywood, California, 1983 (radio broadcast)

Couldn't Stand The Weather recording sessions, Power Station Studios, New York City, January/February, 1984

The Spectrum, Montreal, Ontario, 1984 (radio broadcast)

The Voss Jazz Festival, Norway, March, 1984

Live at the Budokan, Tokyo, Japan, 1984

The Palladium, Los Angeles, California, June 16, 1984

Carnegie Hall, October 4, 1984 (with Dr. John, Jimmie Vaughan, Angela Strehli, Roomful of Blues' horns, George Rains)

Soul To Soul recording sessions, Dallas Sound Labs, March 1985

Red Rocks Blues Festival, Morrison, Colorado, June 19, 1985

Blues Festival, Stockholm, Sweden, July 7, 1985

Montreux Jazz Festival, July 15, 1985 (Double Trouble's entire set, plus jam with Johnny Copeland)

Toronto, Ontario, July 27, 1985 (with Albert

Collins and Jeff Healey)

Dallas, Texas, August 1, 1985 (with Eric Johnson)

Seattle, Washington, September 1, 1985 (with Bonnie Raitt)

Sunday Night Blues program, KZEW-FM, Dallas, September 6, 1985 (with David Johnson)

University Of Colorado, Boulder, Colorado, October 8, 1985

Cowboys for Indians Benefit, Berkeley Community Theater, Berkeley, California, October 14, 1985 (acoustic solo performance plus electric jam with Hank Ballard, Albert Collins)

Veteran's Memorial Coliseum, Phoenix, Arizona, October 29, 1985

Memorial Auditorium, Burlington, Vermont, Halloween night, 1985

Milwaukee, Wisconsin, December 7, 1985

SEVA Benefit, Los Angeles, California, 1985 (solo acoustic set)

Rockefellers', Houston, Texas, January 31, 1986 (with John Lee Hooker, Robert Cray, Roy Rogers)

The Easy Street, Des Moines, Iowa, February 1986

Memorial Hall, Kansas City, February 8, 1986 (with Jimmie Vaughan)

Royal Oak, Michigan, February 22, 1986

T-Bird Festival, Dallas, Texas, March 31, 1986

Rockline 1986 (syndicated radio call-in interview program)

Pier 84, New York City, June 26, 1986 (with Jimmie Vaughan and Steve Winwood)

Austin Opera House, Austin, Texas, July 17 and 18, 1986 (*Live Alive!*)

Starfest, Dallas, Texas, July 19, 1986 (*Live Alive!* recordings)

Red Rocks, Morrison, Colorado, July 24, 1986 (with Taj Mahal)

New Year's Eve/Fox Theater, Atlanta, Georgia, 1986 (with Lonnie Mack)

Redux Club, Dallas, Texas, January 21, 1987 (radio broadcast with Robert Cray)

The Majestic Theater, San Antonio, Texas, February 1, 1987

New Orleans, Louisiana, February 1987 (Jazz and Heritage Festival set)

Texas State Fair, Dallas, 1987 (with David Brown)

Civic Auditorium, La Porte, Indiana, May 10, 1987

Red Rocks, Morrison, Colorado, June 7, 1987

Poplar Creek, Hoffman Estates, Illinois, June 20, 1987

Zoo Amphitheater, Oklahoma City, Oklahoma, August 12, 1987

Mann Music Center, Philadelphia, October 12, 1987

Apollo Theater, Manchester, England, June 1988

The Stone Pony, Ashbury Park, New Jersey, December 29, 1988

Poughkeepsie, New York, June 27, 1989

Rockline, July 4, 1989 (syndicated radio call-in interview program)

Riverfest, St. Paul, Minnesota, July 28, 1989

Legends Club, Chicago, Illinois, July 30, 1989 (Buddy Guy's birthday party)

Red Rocks, Morrison, Colorado, August 21, 1989

Met Center, Minneapolis, Minnesota, October 25, 1989

Timothy White's Rockstars, 1989 (syndicated radio special)

"Fire Meets The Fury" promotional CD, 1989 (half Vaughan, half Beck)

The Pavillion, Chicago, Illinois, October 28, 1989 (with Jeff Beck)

Philadelphia, Pennsylvania, November 7, 1989 (with Jeff Beck)

The Fieldhouse, Troy, New York, November 12, 1989 (with Jeff Beck)

Cincinnati River Bend, Ohio, November 15, 1989 (with Jeff Beck)

The Omni, Atlanta, Georgia, November 19, 1989 (with Jeff Beck)

McNichols Arena, Denver, Colorado, November 29, 1989 (radio broadcast)

Tingley Coliseum, Albuquerque, New Mexico, November 30, 1989 (radio broadcast)

Los Angeles Sports Arena, December 1, 1989 (with Jeff Beck)

Oakland Coliseum, Oakland, California, December 3, 1989 (with Beck & Santana)

The Ritz, New York City, December 31, 1989 (New Year's Eve)

Music Hall, Omaha, Nebraska, April 22, 1990

Auditorium Shores, Austin, Texas, May 4, 1990

Sound on Sound Studios, New York City, May 12, 1990 (interview with acoustic)

Star Lake Amphitheatre, Pittsburgh, Pennsylvania, June 28, 1990

Waterloo Village, Stanhope, New Jersey, July 5, 1990

Columbus, Ohio, July 14, 1990

Starflight Theater, Kansas City, Missouri, July 16, 1990

Fiddler's Green, Denver, Colorado, July 17, 1990

Alpine Valley, East Troy, Wisconsin, August 25, 1990

Alpine Valley, East Troy, Wisconsin, August 26, 1990 (includes final encore of "Sweet Home Chicago" with Guy, Clapton, Jimmie Vaughan, and Robert Cray)

Advance promo-only cassette of *Family Style*, Epic Records, September 1990

Advance promo-only cassette of *The Sky Is Crying*, Epic, September 1991

Advance promo-only CD of *The Sky Is Crying*, Epic, October 1991

A Tribute To Stevie Ray Vaughan,

MediaAmerica Radio Program, August 27, 1991

The 94-Minute Rock 'N' Roll Connection, KLBJ-FM, October 3, 1992

For more information about SRV, send a SASE to:
The Stevie Ray Vaughan Fan Club
c/o Lee Hopkins
P.O. Box 800353
Dallas, Texas 75380

To make a charitable donation in Vaughan's name, write:
The Stevie Ray Vaughan Charitable Fund
c/o The Communities Foundation of Texas
4605 Life Oak
Dallas, Texas 75204

Index

About the Author

Keri Leigh became a journalist at seventeen and has since penned numerous articles on rock stars, including the Rolling Stones, Aerosmith, Robert Plant, John Cougar Mellencamp, Heart, Edie Brickell and The New Bohemians and Van Halen, in addition to her extensive work on Stevie Ray Vaughan. Keri's favorite pieces are those she wrote on blues artists like Buddy Guy, Bo Diddley, James Cotton, Koko Taylor, La Vern Baker, Snooky Pryor, and the late Johnny Shines. In 1988 she founded the Oklahoma Blues Society—her heart is true to the blues.

Leigh also sings the blues with her band, The Blue Devils. She spends most of her time on the road, preaching the blues to faithful congrega-

Photo by and courtesy of Burton Wilson.

tions and following in the footsteps of Vaughan, even playing several of the same concert halls he did during his career. Keri Leigh and The Blue Devils have two albums available on Amazing Records: *Blue Devil Blues*, and *No Beginner*. (Write to Amazing Records at P.O. Box 2164, Austin, Texas, 78768 for a free catalog of Texas blues and jazz by artists such as Cornell Dupree, Ellis Marsalis, David "Fathead" Newman, Denny Freeman, Gary Primich, Carmen Bradfor, Tom "Bones" Malone, The Mannish Boys, The Juke Jumpers, and Omar and The Howlers.)

Her writings regularly appear in *Blues Access* magazine.